Military Regimes and Development

BY THE SAME AUTHOR:

Military Politics in Nigeria: Economic Development and Political Stability (New Brunswick, NJ: Transaction Books, 1978)

Military Regimes and Development

A comparative analysis of African states

T. O. ODETOLA

Senior Lecturer in Sociology, University of Ife

London
GEORGE ALLEN & UNWIN
Boston   Sydney

George Allen & Unwin (Publishers) Ltd,
40 Museum Street, London WC1A 1LU, UK

George Allen & Unwin (Publishers) Ltd,
Park Lane, Hemel Hempstead, Herts HP2 4TE, UK

Allen & Unwin, Inc.,
9 Winchester Terrace, Winchester, Mass. 01890, USA

George Allen & Unwin Australia Pty Ltd,
8 Napier Street, North Sydney, NSW 2060, Australia

First published in 1982

British Library Cataloguing in Publication Data

Odetola, Olatunde
  Military regimes and development
1. Military government
2. Africa—Politics and government
I. Title
306'.27 JF 1820
ISBN 0-04-301154-3

Library of Congress Cataloging in Publication Data

Odetola, Theophilus Olatunde
  Military regimes and development
Bibliography: p.
Includes index.
1. Africa–Armed Forces–Political activity.
2. Military government–Africa.   3. Africa–Politics and
government–1960–   .   4. Africa–Economic policy.   5. Africa–
Social policy.
I. Title.
JQ1875.033   1982   322'.5'096   82–11479
ISBN 0-04-301154-3

Set in 10 on 11 point Times by Gilbert Composing Services, Leighton Buzzard,
and printed in Great Britain
by Richard Clay (The Chaucer Press) Ltd. Bungay, Suffolk.

Contents

Acknowledgements

This book, which has been in preparation for several years, is an attempt to elaborate further on my previous work, *Military Politics in Nigeria: Economic Development and Political Stability,* and owes its inspiration to the continued encouragement of my friend and mentor Irving Louis Horowitz.

I owe a great debt to my friends and colleagues David Aweda, Ade Ademola and Bola Faseun with whom I have shared ideas. My appreciation and thanks also go to Sheilah Ekong and Israel Alo who read and corrected parts of the typescript. I also thank Agboola Ajani and John Rotimi who have spent sleepless nights on the typing of the manuscript.

To Lani, Lola, Fola, Kunle, Yinka and
their mother Yetunde Omolara

Introduction

Interest in writing on the role of the military and their performance in Third World countries started about 1960 and has continued in recent years. This continued interest is in part a result of the unabated activities of military men in Third World countries as well as the interest in building theory generally in political sociology. The trend in more recent years has been towards comparative analysis; and the main methodology employed in this direction is the use of large cross-national aggregate data to compare nations and arrive at general conclusions about the performance of the military. The kind of conclusions that have been made recently have not in general differed from those made earlier. What this means is that the characterisation of military role, military organisation and performance have hardly moved beyond what they were ten years ago. I believe therefore that while comparative analysis is important in building theories, the attention of scholars should be turned more towards in-depth analysis of situations in the countries that have been compared.

One other reason I have undertaken this study is to make progress on the case study which I made on Nigerian military politics published in 1978. My aim in this study is to attempt to expand the scope of theory by selecting some African nations in order to study them in depth and compare them, while at the same time using examples from other African and Latin American societies.

I have in Chapter 1 examined the body of the literature fairly extensively in an attempt to see what scholars have said about the role of the military men in Third World societies in general. I have also attempted to relate these views to particular African situations, because the literature in military sociology has treated the Latin American societies far more extensively than it has done African societies. The scholars have characterised the military as either conservative, progressive, or anti-revolutionary, and evidence has been produced to support each of these characterisations. The use of the concept 'conservative' to describe Third World militaries is a reflection of the liberal-democratic bias of Western social scientists and policy-makers in general. While I agree that the old organisational characteristics of the military may make it conservative, the new roles that it has to perform in the African situation have belied this simple characterisation. Furthermore, those who characterise the military as progressive have been too sanguine and over-enthusiastic in their view of the military. Again, therefore, while the military has proved progressive in some areas it has not been so in a number of others, making highly imperative therefore a careful study of situation by situation, society by society, in the effort to arrive at meaningful conclusions. A description of the military as anti-revolutionary derives from the pro-Latin American orientations of a generation of US scholars who were opposed to the capitalist exploitations of South American societies by the USA. In the language of the more radical social scientists, to be revolutionary is to be leftist. But I have attempted to extend the meaning of revolutionary to include those efforts by the military to restructure their societies. Some of these efforts may indeed not quite qualify as revolutionary in the language of these scholars. I have attempted to compare three societies–Ghana, Ethiopia and Nigeria–at some length.

The Nigerian and Ghanaian situations have been fairly similar. They came under military rule about the same time, had had fairly similar colonial experiences, and the military left politics for the barracks in both countries at about the same time. This affords good opportunities for comparison. However, in neither of these countries did we have a situation that can be characterised as straightforwardly revolutionary in the language of the more radical scholars, except perhaps for the brief rule of Flight Lieutenant Rawlings. The inclusion of Ethiopia is important because of the socialist orientation of its present ruler, Colonel Mengistu Miriam. While facing an internal war, this ruler has also restructured his society in a way that is different from what has been done in either Ghana or Nigeria. The orientation of Mengistu is also similar to what is being practised in some other military-ruled African societies, for example in the Congo-Brazzaville Republic.

The more sanguine supporters of military rule have advanced the argument that the military have certain organisational values which give them a special role to perform in the modernisation of their societies. Included also was the notion that they are the most highly skilled category of modern men in their societies. This view has been critically examined in the second chapter where I have argued that these statements are only partially valid. While the military men have been trained in the values of order and discipline and a number of them have attempted to show these values in their rule in African societies, we have seen examples where the military men have been as corrupt and undisciplined as ordinary civilians. It is also true that it is not always possible for military men to employ their skills in the African societies. In addition, I have argued that some African societies possess skilled men in the civilian sector in numbers as large as those in the military organisation.

What is the relationship between military social origins and social class and the effect of this on the military performance? In Chapter 3 I have taken a fairly close look at the relationship between the military and social class. There has been an effort to examine whether the military have allied with the higher classes to maintain the *status quo* or to increase the opportunities of the exploited classes in the society. To me the significant issue about development is the extent to which the activities of groups have altered the structure and the pattern of the relationships in the society in the effort to make the society grow. In other words, the difference between growth and development is the idea that emphasises the development of institutions which alter the pattern of behaviour, aspirations, orientations and general economic development in that society. Development therefore has much wider ramifications than change or growth. In this sense, therefore, I have attempted in Chapter 3 to look at the changing structures and stratification in the African societies as they relate to the activities of the military men.

In Chapter 4 I have advanced the thesis that before the military has to play the role of arbitrator among competing social and ethnic groups in the African societies and also because of its orientation to nationalism, it has attempted to build state power as a rallying focus for the activity of the competing groups, to which all of them would now owe loyalty. I have also argued that the relationship between military nationalism and the effort to build state power has consequences for the kind of economy and society which the military will in the end be building. The relationship between nationalism and the building of state power may explain a lot of the differences between the African nations. In this exercise we will be examining two different types of societies and economies that the relationship between those two variables has produced. These two types are the state-controlled socialist system and the state-controlled capitalist system.

In Chapter 5 we shall take a look at the similarities and differences in the manner in which the militaries have employed coercion and nationalism to develop the national economy. Chapter 6 examines the ability of the military to foster political integration and to build political institutions. It further explores civil–military relations with reference to political participation and political action. The role of the state in providing social welfare under military rule is critically examined in Chapter 7. Chapter 8 draws together the conclusions made in the text.

1
Military Regimes and Development: Contrasting Viewpoints

There are three major points of view with respect to the role of the armed forces in the modernisation and development of Third World countries. The first view holds that the military is, by definition and tradition, an apolitical, institutionally conservative force, untrained in the tactics and strategies of civilian rule and political management. It further asserts that the military has an inherent institutional desire to serve its corporate interests, and is thus incapable of leading these modernising nations to advancement. The first generation of contemporary scholars in this area of study focused on the role of the military in Latin America.

Lieuwen (1960, 1962, 1964a, 1964b) has said that on balance the military is not a force for change. Huntington (1962, 1967, 1968, 1969) also supports this position. He holds the view that the military is incapable of making real efforts towards building political institutions even though they are modernisers *par excellence*. Huntington's emphasis thus centres around the distinction between modernisation on the one hand and development on the other. Development, according to him, is a phenomenon which involves the building of political institutions that will far outlast military rule. Lieuwen has himself agreed that the younger military officers are reformist in their approach: that is, the young military officers attempt to make some changes which may alter present situations slightly but which changes may not, in the final analysis, be profound or far-reaching. The fact that both scholars emphasise the inability of the military to make fundamental changes underscores the unity of this viewpoint. In a recent castigation of the military role in Latin America, José Nun (1967) has cast very serious doubts on the military as a force for change, national unity or development in any form.

On the African scene, Bienen (1971), Welch (1970), Price (1971b) and Zolberg (1968) have expressed doubts in various forms and in varying degrees on the ability of the military to bring about political stability and to stimulate economic development.

A second view asserts that revolution is the only mechanism by which development and reform can be brought about and that the regular military are the principal obstacles to this process in developing nations. This, it is argued, is because the military (especially in Latin America) have frequently allied with the oligarchy and/or the middle classes to uphold the *status quo*, and have often acted as, or supported, counter-insurgency forces to oppose and thwart real change in their own countries.

This view is, in part, related to the first in its emphasis on military conservatism, although the main thrust differs. Stressing a neo-Marxist viewpoint, it rejects the notion that the Third World military is capable of any real development due to its dependence on the 'big powers' for hardware, training and other procurements. On the Latin American scene, this school of thought is exemplified by the works of Nun (1967), Petras (1970) and Cockcroft *et al.* (1972). One of the few works on Africa in this area (Murray, 1966) believes that the military in Africa is essentially reactionary. In Murray's view only the military of Congo-Brazzaville, because of its Marxist orientation at that time, was truly developmental. The military rulers of Ethiopia would certainly qualify for good marks in Murray's judgement because of their Marxist orientation.

Some other writers have stressed the dependence of Third World military on the First World, but do not subscribe to the general view that the military is incapable of real development. Gutteridge (1969) entertains high hopes that the African military will be more effective than political parties in modernising their societies. Horowitz (1966) has argued that military assistance to the Third World becomes a focal point in maintaining exclusive relations with the former imperial power. He, however, maintains that the military is an important agent of development.

The third view asserts that military values, skills and ideologies are the antithesis of the first two positions–that the military politicians in the Third World make the best, the most thorough-going and perhaps the only reliable managers of social change.

Implicit in the last point of view is the argument that the military in Third World nations is the most effective supervisory agency for directed change. This, it is argued, is because the military is itself, as a rule, the most modernised and most highly disciplined nationwide institution capable of guaranteeing the political stability so necessary for economic development. Halpern (1962, 1963) and Pye (1962) are the most sanguine supporters of military rule in the Third World countries. Other prominent writers in this category are Shils (1962) and Johnson (1964). Some of those who hold this view temper it with some cautious modification. Horowitz (1966) says that it is doubtful whether the military is capable of ruling with democratic norms or even ruling for a long time and emphasises the negative influence of military budget on development projects. This third view is a highly controversial one. It had indeed been responsible for the generation of the second viewpoint which came as a reaction to it. It is my intention in the second part of this chapter (1) to examine the theoretical basis of each position, and to explore systematically the various sub-themes in relation to the actual performance of the military in African societies, and (2) to highlight the theoretical and methodological weaknesses inherent in the analysis made in the body of the literature. But first I will give a general overview of the literature as it helps to illumine the development of the three points of view.

Development of the Major Points of View
and an Overview of the Literature

Western political analysts have, in the traditional literature, displayed a strong normative and prescriptive tone for the political role of the military. Their position has derived from the Western conception of the duties and roles of the professional soldier as subordinate to and subject to civilian control. It has also stemmed from eighteenth-century nationalism together with nineteenth-century positivism which traditionally regarded violence as 'evil and abnormal'.

In a general review of research writings on the role of the Latin American military, McAlister (1966) concluded that the trend of research opinion expressed by Western analysts points in a similar direction of regarding the military as aberrant and abnormal. A characteristic view of this liberal-democratic position is expressed by de Tocqueville (1959) in the question, 'How do you deal with the problem of this unassimilated group in the community, forming a small nation by itself where the mind is less enlarged and habits more rude than in the nation at large?' Echoes of this tradition are evident in the opinions expressed by African civilian politicians on the military.

This approach gave birth to a powerful intellectual bias whereby the analysis of the political experiences of Third World nations were based on the democratic-civil model. Political analysts argued that the military should, because of military professional tradition, be non-political. Political development and modernisation in these nations, they argued, are already moving towards democracy and any deviation from this norm is conceptualised as an intervention. Such intervention, they argued, constitutes a political process which hinders the smooth movement towards this perfect model. The military role is, therefore, inherently evil. This tradition of analysis is not confined to the Latin

American scene. It has spread to the analysis of African societies (Welch, 1970).

Thus, the first view (that is, that the military is a professional, apolitical organisation) has its roots in this tradition. The military, according to this tradition, is not an interest group, and its role is not susceptible to systematic analysis. Even though its role is acknowledged and described, such a role is generally to be deplored (McAlister, 1966). It is my intention in this book to demonstrate that this position is only partly valid. It has systematically derived from and consistently led to a peculiar selectivity about Western historical and political experience (Glick, 1967). More significantly, it has given rise to a biased evaluation of whatever role the military is playing in Third World countries.

The issue here is not to deny that the military can be conservative, nor is it to say that the military is the moderniser *par excellence* (I shall expose the weakness of that position too). However, the good deeds of the military are not often given full credit, thus leading to unbalanced, generalised and poor conclusions. This situation is due to an important theoretical weakness. Perhaps the controversy in the analysis of the military as a moderniser stems from a failure to link theoretically subsequent military rule with the declared purpose for intervening militarily in the first place. This can be rectified by analysing comparative data which is, in fact, the aim of this work.

It has been clearly demonstrated in the Latin American and African cases that the military is indeed an interest group and that its role is amenable to systematic analysis. In Ghana, the military revolted and came to power in 1966 mainly to claim its rights and privileges and proceeded to do so (Price, 1971b). The same can be said of the middle period of military rule in Nigeria and of the first coup in Ethiopia.

Huntington has written that the armed forces will properly be controlled not by maximising some civilian power–for instance, civil versus crown or bourgeois versus aristocracy–but by maximising military professionalism: 'as one approximates to the model of military professionalism, so the problem of civil–military relationship will be solved'. The recognition of an independent sphere of military expertise implies the removal of the military from politics. Objective civilian control can achieve this by making the military the tool of the state. He has argued that the antithesis of objective civilian control is military participation in politics.

Thus, according to Huntington (1969) professionalism makes military officers uninterested in matters not strictly professional–that is, professionalism involves political neutrality. A major objection to this view is that Huntington has made the two terms 'professionalism' and 'objective control' coterminous, inseparable theoretical concepts (Abrahamsson, 1972).

The issue raised by Huntington's position is this: where can we draw the line between policy involvement of the military and real political involvement? The advice of the military leaders is vital to a policy decision as to whether to go to war or not, and indeed as to how to prosecute any war. Pressures of military men can be brought to tilt decisions in one or other direction or even to initiate the idea of war in the first place. In France, the military has posed an ideological challenge to civilian control. Historical evidence also reveals that the German army cannot be said to be free of political involvement over the centuries. What is certainly more difficult is to draw the line between military professionalism and political involvement of the military in Third World nations, particularly those in Africa. The vacuum created in political leadership coupled with the problems of development are such that professionalism, were it present at the desired level, becomes a secondary if not a nearly irrelevant factor. In Australia, evidence has shown that military professionalism has been rated below the wider consciousness of a citizen soldier who is as versatile in his civilian role as in his military role. Military rank is complemented by prominence in various other spheres including public administration, education, politics and business (Encel, 1968, pp. 14–15).

Abrahamsson has pointed out that it becomes empirically impossible to establish the relationship between the degree of professionalism and the degree of political neutrality (1972). Huntington's thesis therefore becomes 'a covert definitional truth' (Hempel, 1968, p. 193): that is, professional officers never intervene because, if they do, they are not true professionals. It is easy, then, to see how Huntington arrived at the wholly inadequate analysis of the Wehrmacht of the Third Reich in Germany and his rather dubious conclusion that those professional soldiers who did not obey civilian authorities 'abandoned professionalism for politics' (Abrahamsson, 1972).

Abrahamsson challenged this view by asking whether the German state of 1870–1914 was one in which civilian control of the military was maximised simply because military professionalism was at a peak and because, while civilian power was concentrated in the Kaiser and Chancellor, military power was divided among several officers. Craig (1955, pp. 218–19) observed that the military in Prussia had attempted after May 1870 to win what they failed to win earlier during the *Konfliktszeit*. That goal of the Prussian military was defined as complete freedom from the budgetary powers of the parliament. The idea of using a coup d'état had occurred to the 'political generals' as a way of escaping from their constitutional difficulties. Rather than embark on that, they reorganised military administration in such a way as to exclude the War Minister, and thus to divide military power in such a way that they could exert some influence. A similar situation had occurred between Bismarck and Moltke in 1870 when they disagreed about their structural and political positions relative to the king during the siege of Paris. It has been alleged that thoughts of a military coup d'état were entertained by certain army generals during the Watergate political crisis in the USA although the story has not been given any prominence. And when Kissinger was the American National Security Adviser, strains developed in the relationship between him and the Army Chief of Staff. It has been widely assumed that the Army Chief of Staff was aiming at influencing policies. Janowitz (1959) has demonstrated that the new technology of modern weaponry very greatly increases the ability of military officers to influence policy decisions on whether to start a war, how far to go, and what strategic weapons to use and when.

Thus, to accept Huntington's position is to underestimate the influence of military thinking on policies. Indeed, such soldier-statesmen as Charles de Gaulle, Franco, Eisenhower and Nasser are deviants from a pure conception of 'professionalism'. Why have such military giants had such a profound influence on politics? Is there not something about the 'military mind' that has implications for politics? (Abrahamsson, 1972)

In further criticism of Huntington's position, Barnett (1961) argued that to listen to politicians and constitutional historians holding forth on the marvels of parliamentary democracy, one would not think that theirs was a civilisation largely born out of wars, and devoted to them. She further emphasised that preparations for war have moulded social organisation in the twentieth century and determined technical and industrial progress.

In fact, according to Barnett, many of the civilian institutions, ways of thinking and techniques of organisation were evolved first in armies or during wars. The Schlieffen plan, according to her, preceded the Marshall plan; staff colleges had come before business schools, and the first schools of engineering and technology were military. In the USA, the army played a crucial role in the opening up of the west of that continent. Currently, many modern technological developments and innovations for peaceful uses have definitive origins in developments emanating from war research. A most significant example is the modern propelling techniques of space travel which grew out of German Second World War rockets. Further, the widely publicised 'military–industrial complex' in recent literature has underscored the impact of war preparations on social organisation.

Mosca (1939, p. 238) in an opposing view to Huntington believes that a standing army could overturn its government whenever it had the resources, training and equipment, number and organisation to do so: 'in a bureacratic state which represents the most complicated type of social organisation, the standing army will absorb all the more belligerent elements, and being readily capable of prompt obedience to a single impulse, it will have no difficulty in dictating to the rest of the society'.

Mosca's view, of course, has obvious weaknesses. He assumed that only 'belligerent' elements in the society are recruited into the army. Even if this were so, would not the process of training and socialisation have remoulded their character? Secondly, his view does not allow for any distinction between legitimate and illegitimate rule. Because Mosca has assumed that 'belligerent' elements are found only in the lower social classes, he tends to confer a position of privilege on the higher social classes. He referred to the military in quite derogatory terms, and by implication to the lower classes too. He argued that the armies of Western Europe played such a small part in politics precisely because the officer corps, who were 'gentlemen', had great affinity with their civilian counterparts and no respect for the 'vagabonds and peasants' who had formed the other ranks. His thesis that the military is subordinate only when recruited from the social class which dominates government finds support in the work of Andreski (1954, p. 107). This thesis may explain why the English army is loyal but will hardly explain the complex situation in Africa where many of the armies have proved 'disloyal' to governments.

Corporate professionalism is not a guarantee against praetorianism (Perlmutter, 1969; Abrahamsson, 1972). It appears that current increased effort at civilian control in America has been in response to the fear of praetorianism. As the military moves in the industrialised Western nations into the centre of defence policy-making, it faces the dilemma of the struggle between the non-partisan tenets of their creed and the requirements of effective participation in the political process. It should be borne in mind that it is the military who must put defence policy to the test of public accountability by exposing the bases for decision to congressional and public inquiry (Lyons, 1961). The dilemma facing military officers in industrialised nations of becoming increasingly involved in policy matters is functionally analogous to the role of the military in the Third World by which they become increasingly involved in political rule.

A second significant point is the role of violence in the political development of Third World nations. Violence and revolution are anathema to the Western democratic theory of society. Systems theory and functionalism which support that position are inadequate to explain the upheavals that have been characteristic of African development. Violence has been part of the emergence of modern African societies. It has been an important element of the folklore and history of many of its cultures (Zolberg, 1968). Where systems theory and functionalism have been unable to accommodate change and revolution, they assert that any society is 'simultaneously a host of tensions and a network of tension management devices ... an aspect of revolutionary potential is its relation with social change' (Feldman, 1964). This means that military intervention, rebellion, and so on are aspects of the same phenomenon–they signify failures, small or large, of the political system. Early studies of political development of African states began with these assumptions; but recent scholarship found that such an approach needs to be revised. Total culture and early socialisation take a violent form in Latin America (for example, the 'Machetismo'). To ignore that is to ignore a basic and most significant factor in the evolution of those societies. Violence may, in fact, be functionally appropriate behaviour. Political violence cannot be regarded as aberrant behaviour in Latin America because there is a compatibility between the values and styles imparted by non-political institutions and the perpetration of patterns of political violence and revolution in Latin American political behaviour (Silvert, 1961; Blankstein, 1960; Fitzgibbon, 1960; Horowitz, 1969). Investigations reveal that violence is institutionalised in the organisation, maintenance and changing of governments in Latin America (Stokes, 1952, pp. 445–68). There is a gradual progression in the quality and quantity of force employed in Latin American societies. The first level is the 'Machetismo', then the 'Guarterlazo', which is a more highly organised way of changing governments, and finally the military coup or 'golpe de estardo'. Stokes (1952, p. 467) has asked whether the employment of violence in organising political power necessarily negates the principles of representative democracy.

While it is an undeniable fact that the military is a conservative institution, and that its organisational structure creates difficulties in its attempt to rule civilians effectively over a long period, some of the conclusions deriving from this tradition appear to have been over-determined and to underestimate the influence of local environment in Third World countries on the role of the military. The local issues which must be examined include inter-élite conflicts, slow rate of economic advancement, corruption and inflation, which are problems that tend to invite military solutions from time to time. Lieuwen (1960) concluded that the eventual removal of the military from politics dépends on the gradual emergence of the intermediate strata and crosscutting status or role positions, economic development, wider catchment areas for officers and political development. Those conditions appear rather imprecise, difficult to achieve and, in the long run, are nothing short of the liberal-democratic model of Western development. In the same tradition, Finer (1962, p. 21) has argued that where public attachment to the civilian institution is strong, military intervention in politics will be weak.

The military élite is part of a comprehensive national leadership élite 'subject to the same influence and pressures . . . indeed the closer integration of the military with their civilian counterparts in new states where the total leadership group is small may be one of the most important reasons for the relatively greater frequency of military coups in developing rather than in developed countries' (Gutteridge, 1965). Horowitz (1966) also maintains that when the popular classes are too ineffectual in changing obviously bankrupt social relations, the élite of the armed forces perceive themselves as capable of filling a social vacuum. No matter the degree of professionalism within the officer corps, the level of technology and the organisational format of a particular military, the military in Africa is always a potential political factor because it can exert some strength in what is essentially a domestic power vacuum (Bienen, 1968). These arguments negate the relatively strong tradition which states that professionalism in the military leads to apolitical behaviour. Closeness to local issues and problems and the existence of a power vacuum are far more crucial in determining the political behaviour of the military than are professionalism, organisational format and level of technology.

In *Changing Patterns of Military Politics* (1962), Huntington took a revisionist position which has rendered the consistency of his position questionable. He said that 'frequent' reform coups are actually a sign of political health since they are mechanisms of gradual change and that, in any case, 'virtually all reforms are produced by coups'. The significant implication of his revisionist position is that democratic consent must include the consent of the military since it is a significant expression of the culture. It is thus recognised that Anglo-Saxon norms of political neutrality may not be appropriate everywhere (McAlister, 1965). Azikiwe (1972, 1973), the former Nigerian President, has started a debate in which he urges that the Nigerian polity consider including the military permanently on its government and future constitutional arrangements.

The First View: the military as a conservative, unprogressive force

The view emphasising the conservative character of the military and its support of the *status quo* is associated with the military professional character. Abrahamsson (1972, p. 106) asserts that military men as a professional group seem to be conservative partly because many of the values and attitudes that are part of the conservative syndrome appear to facilitate, and tend to support, an adjustment to the professional code. Also military values of order, hierarchy and stability as frequent explanations of the military conservatism derive from its characteristic association with the ruling class. This is emphasised by Mosca in his analysis of civil–military relations in Europe and the United States (Mosca, 1939).

Many historical examples have shown that ruling élite and the military usually come to an agreement on the *status quo*, and also on their mutual suspicion of and hostility towards rapid social change. Vagt (1959, p. 30) asserted that traditionally the military has not been in the forefront of revolutions, but has rather chosen to support the *status quo*. To Vagt, the great modern revolutions have been foreign to and remote from armies. He further argued that armies have been closely associated with suppressions, reactions and counter-revolutions. This view argues that the basic values of the military profession have developed from its feudal heritage, from the historical role it has played as the guardian of the *status quo*, as well as from its traditional association with the ruling groups who were bent on preserving the existing order. For example, a large number of the old French army left to join forces with the first coalition to fight the revolution from outside. Also, in spite of the fact that, due to expansion during the First World War, there was a large influx of the peasant class and the intelligentsia into the Tsarist Russian army, the officers were more often found among the ranks of the White than the Red army during the civil war (Vagt, 1959, p. 106). Again, when fascist movements grew strong in Europe, many officers were eager to support them because the fascists favoured policies which brought a number of seeming advantages to the military (Abrahamsson, 1972, p. 107).

The history of military coups in Latin America reveals that only a small percentage of coups are reformist, and that the majority of them support the *status quo*. Lieuwen wrote that 'on the balance, the armed forces have been a force for the preservation of the status-quo; their political intervention has generally signified, as it does today, a conservative action' (1964b, p. 77). Analysing the internal dynamics of coups, Needler (1966) arrived at a series of illuminating conclusions. He argued that military interventions increasingly take place to maintain the *status quo*. He asked, if the military coup is frequently called into play by the workings of the political system, what is its function in relation to social and economic change? He concluded that its purpose must increasingly be to thwart such change and indeed that military intervention is increasingly being directed against legally elected presidents heading constitutional governments, and finally that the army in Latin America is increasingly committed against the liberal party. If Needler is correct, however, we could not establish the proposition that the military who hope to thwart social change and who succeed in seizing power necessarily accomplish their aim (Bienen, 1968). Huntington argues that modernisation is not the product of any one particular group however modernised that group may be in comparison with the rest of the society–'rather it is the product of coup and counter-coup in which military elements play important roles inaugurating both conservative and radical regimes' (1962). The frequent coups and counter-coups in the West African nations of Nigeria, Ghana, Benin and Mali illustrate this point. The Gowon government in Nigeria displayed great ability in reconstructing a broken nation. There was, however, strong evidence of a decline in this ability and of increasingly greater dependence on the federal civil service after 1973. The short Muhammed regime gave a new meaning and direction to development–a situation that was continued by the Obasanjo regime. So there is agreement that each successive coup has brought some change. Huntington further states that the military are neither exclusively harbingers of modernisation nor the defenders of entrenched oligarchies in Latin America. Thus, Huntington's argument does not depend on the military being a comparatively modernised organisation in society. He further asserts that conservative groups are not able to undo change and that radical coup-makers keep extending political participation and emphasising reform and, therefore, the net effect is likely to be one of improvement.

Even though rightist movements and ideas have had greater appeal for military men than the movements and ideas of the left, there are quite obvious exceptions. For instance, in those nations where the armed revolutionary forces have carried on the struggle against landholding, industrial and/or aristocratic élites, the military leaders of these nations have typically exhibited a less conservative orientation than in nations where change has been more gradual or where the armed forces were not involved in the overthrow of the existing order. The armed forces of revolutionary France and of Russia during and immediately after the revolution contained considerable progressive elements. Similarly, in Cuba, Egypt and Algeria the armed forces that overthrew Batista, Farouk and the French regimes respectively contained substantial progressive groups. It must be added, however, that when new regimes are consolidated, the military tends to become an important supporter of the *status quo*. Vagt (1959) has said that the army depends 'upon the order in which it takes form'. Horowitz also maintains that 'the military stands closest to the class and sector that wields power' (1966, p. 355).

Another pitfall in the view of the military as a conservative force is that it tends to generalise its position over the whole spectrum of military activity and relationships. While the military may prefer order and stability to change, it will not be correct to infer that military conservatism applies equally strongly to technological change. For instance, West Point was in the forefront of technical education. In Third World countries, the military has frequently initiated or supported technological research particularly if such research favoured its interests. The successive Nigerian federal military governments have greatly encouraged the establishment of an iron and steel industry in that country.

The Second View: the military as an anti-revolutionary force

The second main view that the military is anti-revolutionary has derived from the recent increased military aid of the 'big powers' to less developed countries in the last twenty years and the character of the international dependence it has generated (Cockcroft *et al.*, 1972). Exponents of this view emphasise the reference group orientation of overseas-trained Third World military officers towards the metropolis, and its preservation of the capitalist *status quo* and antisocialist tendencies. This view assumes a structural dependence of the Third World nations on the metropolitan countries because of technological dependence. Emanating from this dependence is the exercise of undue influence on the policies (internal and external) of the recipients by the donor countries. Foreign aid does induce a definite orientation of the military leadership concerned towards the donor countries' control (Hoovey, 1966). The influence of the tradition of the donor country, suitably fed into the armed forces, may be actually formative of national consciousness in a unique fashion (Gutteridge, 1968, p. 139). Price, applying reference group theory to the behaviour of Third World military officers, noted that the military training which officers undergo can be viewed as a socialisation process within which the recruit's identification with his previous civilian reference groups is broken down and replaced by new ego-involved associations centred in the military organisation (Price, 1971a). The extent to which conformity to group norms and other group processes like the acceptance of group standards are significant in reorienting the new recruit into the group are well documented in the social-psychological literature (Lewin and Grabbe, 1945; Festinger, 1951; Siegel, 1957). It is to be expected that the military recruits from Third World nations will be particularly motivated to adopt the values, and also to identify with the traditions, of the military school in which they now fortunately happen to find themselves. A direct illustration of such a powerful influence is to be seen in the example of Sandhurst-trained Colonel A. A. Afrifa, who led the Ghana coup against Nkrumah in 1966. He wrote: 'I was thrilled by Sandhurst, the beauty of its countryside and the calm Wish stream which separated Sandhurst from the rest of the world. Sandhurst so far was the best part of my life' (Afrifa, 1966). To be trained as a soldier at Sandhurst which Afrifa referred to as that 'mysterious institution' was to learn where one rapidly acquired manly habits and attitudes. Afrifa claimed to have met many boys of his own age for whom there was nothing sweeter than bearing arms in the service of their country. He always looked back upon Sandhurst with great nostalgia: 'It is one of the greatest institutions in the world. Through its doors have passed famous generals, kings, rulers . . . I left Sandhurst, crossed the Wish stream, looked back at my old school, and was filled with boundless gratitude' (Afrifa, 1966). Obviously Afrifa had had his training at a stage in his life when he was highly impressionable. But it would be difficult to imagine Afrifa as head of state looking too critically and negatively at influences emanating from Sandhurst in particular or from Britain in general. For those non-commissioned officers (NCOs) whose promotion did not depend upon formal training in the metropolis, the process of socialisation is somewhat different but the result is the same. Because they were to be promoted into an exclusively European class, and by European officers, they had to exhibit what was considered proper behaviour according to European military standards. Thus, they had to undergo what Merton (1963, p. 265) has called 'anticipatory socialisation'–identification with and concomitant adoption of the values of the group to which the recruit aspires but does not belong. The aid programme offer includes the secondment of training and advisory personnel from the metropolis to the less-developed nation. In 1964 there were nearly 3,000 French officers and NCOs seconded or contracted to the armed forces of independent African states, while 1,500 Africans were undergoing training in France. During the same period, about 600 British officers and NCOs were on secondment and more than 700 Africans were training in Britain (Bell, 1965; Wood, 1966). It is not difficult then to appreciate Gutteridge's proposition that 'the armies of new states tend to retain their colonial flavour, their foreign advisers and their affinity with Europe longer than do the civilian public services' (1965).

My emphasis on European influence in Africa is not an attempt to discount the growing American influence. Wood (1966) said that whereas 10 per cent of America's general economic assistance is allocated to Africa, the percentage of her total military assistance programme directed there is only 2 per cent. Such comparisons mask the strategic importance of the aid and its growing character. US expenditure has been increasing considerably since 1960 and is now approaching $40 million, more than is spent annually by France. However, US expenditure is far more concentrated than French which is diffused through the Francophone states. US aid to Congo-Leopoldville (now Zaïre) was four times greater than that given by Belgium in 1964–5. The other recipients of US aid are Liberia and Ethiopia. Ethiopia and Congo-Leopoldville possessed the largest and potentially dominating armed forces in sub-Saharan Africa (although this ranking has altered since the Nigerian civil war). In Ethiopia, the activity of the advisory groups clearly transcended the traditional understanding of military objectives and spilled over to civic and social 'action' espoused by advocates of 'counter-insurgency' and military contributions to 'nation-building' (Murray, 1966, p. 51).

The concept 'revolutionary' has been interpreted in the body of contemporary literature on military role more or less in a neo-Marxian sense. This interpretation was itself a reaction to the conservative role which the military in many Latin American nations had been playing. This may be as narrow as it is perjorative. However, I believe that any dramatic changes in the accepted ways of doing things is revolutionary irrespective of the source or direction of the promptings.

Many African militaries would not by my definition qualify as revolutionary. Perhaps more recently the Ethiopian military would qualify and this is the prime reason for its inclusion among the states to receive special treatment. The Ethiopian case is a particularly illuminating one. The level of US aid was so high and its influence so intense and pervasive during the last decade of the reign of Emperor Haile Selassie that the military intervention of a few officers was sufficient to orient the society in a pro-Moscow direction. The government of General Andom which was overthrown by Colonel Mengistu Haile Miriam could be said to be under the influence of the United States of America and in supporting the *status quo* was clearly anti-revolutionary. It is assumed here, of course, that certain changes were necessary if Ethiopian society was to overcome its feudal heritage.

At present, the most direct channel through which foreign influence reaches Third World countries is the independent armed forces of the countries themselves, through expenditure on military aid and assistance, but above all in the fields of training and equipment. The commitment to the set of traditions, symbols and values of the metropole is very strong and has powerful behavioural effects on the relationship of Third World military officers to civilian political authorities and on their role as leaders of government when they accede to political power. It seems, therefore, that foreign aid from specific sources has influence on the political behaviour of young armed forces (most African armed forces are young), only the direction may not be predictable. In particular, the training of officers overseas established a new and significantly large element in the educated élite of the country concerned through which new ideas may easily enter from overseas (Price, 1971a, p. 404).

The theoretical issue in this controversy is that there is a conceptual link between the conservative attitude of preserving the *status quo* and thereby of keeping the local population quiescent on the one hand, and on the other hand the objective interest of the donor country as well as its influence on the local leaders. Thus the local leaders, who in the context of this work are the military, become the centrepiece of attention. Does this link always work? Can a local leader not accept aid and turn in the opposite direction to the one intended? That is, how predictable is the influence of aid?

If the military leaders already have plans of their own to change the society in specific ways, aid becomes a secondary factor helping that movement. If, however, the aid comes first then it is predictable that the leadership will be influenced in desired directions.

The relevant issues for this book are, how true of the African military is this first position? How professional are the African militaries and, if they are, how well has this attribute insulated them from participation in politics? Do the African militaries possess the values of order, hierarchy and stability–in short, the value of discipline? If they do, do African societies have ruling classes who possess these conservative values and with whom these militaries may be said to be in alliance? Some of these issues will be dealt with in separate chapters in greater detail. Meanwhile, evidence will be brought to examine the issues in a more general manner at this point.

The age, historical development, type of training, quality of organisation and level of experience of African militaries are nowhere near those of industrialised Western nations. While African armies may possess the same code of ethics as many Western militaries whom they look up to, the historical circumstances under which African militaries have developed have not allowed room for the quality of mature growth characteristic of Western militaries. In Africa, political independence which brought a wider political consciousness in terms of participation, socialisation, recruitment, and so on was matched by a rising political nationalism. The military as a symbol of national consciousness was expanded too rapidly in such a way that the products of the rapid training could not have matched those that were brought up under longer, more settled conditions. Hence, as demonstrated above, the theoretical link between military professionalism and the acquisition of an apolitical attitude is at best tenuous and indeed not applicable to African situations.

Many African military organisations have also been characterised by indiscipline. The Army Chief of Staff in Nigeria in 1978 openly decried acts of indiscipline in the Nigerian army. The same situation is true of the Ghanaian, the Ethiopian and the Republic of Benin militaries. The issue can be looked at from another standpoint: why has there not been a successful military coup in Kenya, Tanzania, Zambia and Malawi in East Africa, and Senegal, Gambia and the Ivory Coast in West Africa? No one single factor is sufficient to explain this. However, there are some common factors which emerge from this comparative analysis. First, these nations are commonly characterised by the strong leadership of one man–a situation that has built up legitimacy for these leaders' authority. In fact, they had been *de facto* leaders of their nations before independence–Banda in Malawi, Kaunda in Zambia, Nyerere in Tanzania, Kenyatta in Kenya, Senghor in Senegal, Jawara in Gambia and Houphouet -Boigny in the Ivory Coast. These nations never have had anything like a Western professional army, so that factor is totally irrelevant. Rather, an attachment and loyalty to a legitimate source of authority in the form of a national symbol seems a more likely explanation. Similarly, Nigeria, Zaïre, Mali, and so on lacked the kind of figure commanding a whole nation which Nyerere had been to Tanzania, Senghor to Senegal, and so on. However, Nkrumah was such a strong leader who built legitimacy as a national symbol – why then was he overthrown? The Ghanaian military was far more sophisticated in training and equipment than either the Tanzanian or Malian army. Could it be this level of sophistication and training, indeed a higher level of professionalism in the African army, that makes them less docile and therefore less apolitical? That is, this higher level may create greater interest and awareness both towards politics and other spheres of life and may thus lead to intervention.

However, obvious gaps exist between the level of sophistication and training of the Ghanaian army, an example of the army of a developing nation, on the one hand, and that of the British army, for example, on the other hand. Yet the British army does not intervene directly in politics. Thus, it may not be the level of training, equipment and sophistication *per se* but the perception of the gap between such levels in a developing and a developed nation by armies of the developing nation which induces them to engage in apolitical behaviour. That is, the more sophisticated an African military becomes, the greater its awareness, hence its ability to reduce gaps between itself and other armies. Murray (1966) argued that congenital susceptibility to imperialist pressures stems from the structural subordination and dependence of the underdeveloped regions in the world market. Conditions of poverty, low capital formation and shortage of exchange make these countries especially vulnerable to externally catalysed political crises. Murray argued that the United States as the capitalist world centre is playing a leading role through the adoption of government policies which are subsequently mediated through the impersonal mechanisms of international finance and commodity markets. Cockcroft *et al.* (1972) claimed that the Ghanaian case clearly illustrates this. In general, however, the Latin American military remains dependent upon the United States for arms, training and political support. Its function has been to maintain 'stability', to 'pacify' peasant populations and urban neighbourhoods on which guerrilla units depend for their survival and to crush insurrections, whether rural, urban, or student. The extent to which the military are anti-revolutionary is the extent to which they represent foreign capitalist interests in their own country. Cockcroft further asserted that the military reform governments of Bolivia and Peru, while anti-imperialist in their propaganda, appear unwilling to break the traditional power-hold of the most advanced sectors of the bourgeoisie, national and anti-national, but on the contrary welcome 'modernisation' and 'developmentalism' within the bounds of state-regulated capitalism and foreign finance. Cockcroft, Frank and Johnson (1972) also emphasised the role of the US military training of Third World officers as a covert, tacit device to use such military officers to protect (sometimes unwittingly) the interest of US-owned multinational corporations in Latin America. According to these writers, the major impetus for the increased militarisation of Latin America came during the administration of John F. Kennedy. It was this same spurt of renewed enthusiasm in the role of the military that gave rise to the third view of the military as a moderniser.

The Third View: the military as the best-organised institution, nationalist and most reliable manager of social change

The 1960s witnessed the emergence of a view among American officials that major assistance to military élites in developing nations could result in mutual benefits. Although American military assistance had its origins in the Truman administration's aid to Greece and Turkey, it was the Kennedy administration that gave the major impetus for reconceptualising the utilisation of foreign military élites in 'modernising' and 'stabilising' roles in developing nations.

The Kennedy administration's response to the Congo crisis and the strategic location of Cuba resulted in a flurry of activities to articulate and co-ordinate counter-insurgency planning. The special forces were accorded increased prestige. President Kennedy himself let it be known that he was familiar with the guerrilla warfare doctrines of Mao Tse-Tung and Che Guevara. The main thrust was the containment of communist upsurge and the indigenous military was thought to be the ideal institution to use. In this context and in the emerging guidelines for coping with insurgency, new or additional possibilities for the utilisation of indigenous military élites in developing nations began to be articulated (Lovell, 1971, p. 161). In 1959 the Rand Corporation sponsored the first intellectual conference on the role of military élites in underdeveloped countries. Hans Speier, chairman of the Rand Research Council at the time, prefaced the published version of the papers (Johnson, 1962) with the following statement: 'In any of the new states that have emerged in the recent era of decolonisation the military play a vital role.' He argued further that as a revolutionary force they have contributed to the disintegration of traditional political order; as a stabilising force they have prevented some countries from falling prey to communist rule; as a modernising force they have become champions of middle-class aspirations or of popular demands for social change and have provided administrative and technological skills to the civilian sector of the countries in which such skills are scarce.

Other scholarly conferences at about the same time produced at the Massachusetts Institute of Technology in Boston the report for the US Senate entitled 'Economic social and political change in the under-developed countries and its implications for the United States policy' (1961). This report contended that the likely social origins of the military group in a transitional society, the nature of their profession and the context in which they operate contribute important elements to their potential for leadership towards modernisation. A conference was also convened in 1961 on 'The role of the military in society and government in the Middle East'. The published book elaborated the thesis of the modernising potential of military élites within a common geographic region (1969).

While the activities of the administration were primarily directed towards encouraging research on the 'new role' of Third World military, other factors also stimulated general interest in the subject. Such factors included (*a*) the rapid development of political system analysis, and (*b*) the production of general or theoretical works which further stimulated interest in the subject.

A spate of propositions followed in the wake of these activities. Johnson asserted that 'the military establishment are now and will continue to be symbols of national sovereignty' (1964b, p. 15). Thus, by implication, nationalism is a most important ideology of the Third World military. It is also Halpern's view that the more the army was modernised, the more its composition, organisation, spirit, capabilities and purpose constituted a radical criticism of the existing political system (1962). If these qualities are added to the 'stabilising' role of the military, then it becomes the only institution with modernising values and capabilities to establish order. Besides, it is the only unifying institution wherein diverse ethnic groups come together in a common bond. Therefore, by implication, it becomes the only institution capable of carrying out political development. Between 1960 and 1965 there were varying scholarly commitments to the modernising role of the military. These commitments ranged from economic modernisation to political institution-building, and to other spheres such as (i) the building of economic infrastructure like roads and bridges, (ii) the performance of managerial duties for the civilian society from its pool of managerial skill, and (iii) the alteration of the social structure in a more modern way due to officer recruitment from the lower classes and identification with the middle classes in order to build a 'democratic' society.

The military indeed possesses quite varied qualities but the analysts who have taken this view appear to have theorised in an empirical vacuum. In Johnson's volume (1962) a theoretical article written by Pye argues that in the new states the military organisation represents the most effective public institution available for modernisation, but the empirical case studies are striking in their lack of empirical support for the theories of military potentiality developed earlier in the volume. McAlister (1966) has commented that in terms of content and substance, the most noticeable feature of recent literature is, with the exception of a very few items, the absence of firm data and of empirical support for conclusions offered. What has really emerged is a set of propositions and counter-propositions about the role of the Latin American military–which are theoretically testable, and about what their role ought to be–which are not.

When one examines these assertions against empirical evidence, the result is a mixed bag. To what extent and in what Third World countries is the military the most modernised institution?–for situations vary from one Third World country to another. Has the military more or less often been a factor of political stability and economic development?

Recent writings have revealed that in many new nations the records of the military have been dismal, for example in Ghana. However, in a few other cases it has ranged from average to successful. Within one nation with a history of more than one successful coup, performances of successive military regimes have varied widely, such as between the Gowon and Muhammed regimes in Nigeria, or Ankrah and Acheampong in Ghana. One must be clear, though, what specific areas of development are to be considered. I suggest that it would be unrealistic to generalise about successes or failures of the military over a wide spectrum of activities.

2
Military Organisational Values and Skills as Modernising Instruments

In this chapter we shall examine certain organisational characteristics and values attributed to the military and the effects of these on societal development as well as on the military institution itself.

In theory it is emphasised that the military is a puritanical organisation, and that the training which men receive in this institution and subsequent military experience inbues them with austere attitudes and a high sense of discipline and responsibility (Huntington, 1962). The military is also believed to possess 'rational norms' far above any other institution in Third World societies. Finally, the organisation of the military is assumed to recognise the universalistic value of the criterion of achievement in the award of honours and promotion. Thus, the values of puritanism, discipline, rationality and achievement orientation of the military are assumed to be much more directly relevant to change and development than the indulgent 'superstitious' and 'ascriptive' orientation of the larger part of the rest of the traditional society.

Those who hold this position have made certain assumptions. The first is that the education and training which soldiers receive socialise them into professional men having those attributes. It also assumes that such acquired values or attributes are transferable into situations or occupational roles which may not be entirely military. The third assumption is that in the process of governing a civilian society, these military values are transmitted to the rest of the society in a way that regulates societal behaviour and consequently changes such societies.

Professional Training

Studies in professionalisation will support the first assumption, particularly for the officer corps, although, as will be seen later, it should be applied to Third World militaries only with considerable caution.

To be a true professional, a person must be fully committed to his calling and he must treat his occupation and all its requirements as an enduring set of normative and behavioural expectations (Moore, 1970, p. 5). In other words, the outlooks and values which are consequences of his special training and activities become what he lives with daily. The training which may produce such a top professional usually is of exceptional duration (Moore, 1970, p. 6). Taking this last point first, the rapid indigenisation of the officer corps in Nigeria and Ghana after independence certainly produced situations where officer training periods were shortened. In 1963 a target date of six years was set for the total indigenisation of all Nigerian officer grade posts in the military services. Almost unbelievably, this was achieved. This situation led a Nigerian major in the army to comment as follows: 'The degree of professional proficiency in the Nigerian army of today has declined many folds in comparison with the Nigerian pre-civil-war soldier' (Ogbebor, 1976, p. 38). The army major attributed this to the piecemeal military training received by over 90 per cent of the officers and men, especially during the war emergency. While the indigenisation in Ethiopia was slower, the emperor kept a wary eye on officer corps that were being trained in an effort to consolidate his own powers. The emperor's attempt to improve on the education and training of military men after the attempted coup of 1960 was not intended to create an open occupational mobility system but to quiet an agitated military.

Apart from the effect of indigenisation, the prosecution of wars (Nigerian-Biafran civil war, the Eritrean War, and so on) created the necessity both for rapid and crash training as well as 'quick' promotions because of manpower needs to prosecute such wars. The administration of a civilian society also created severe manpower needs for fledgeling military organisations which were just trying to find their feet. The movement of more senior officers to man civilian administration brought about premature promotions of more junior officers to act in more senior positions. Rear Admiral Wey claimed that there was an inevitable spate of accelerated promotions and that many officers had no option but to mature in office–'the lack of adequate experience . . . adversely affected and retarded a properly organised growth of the Armed Forces' (Wey, 1979, pp. 19–25). When it became necessary to retard and extend the time-scale for promotions, the military did not succeed in pacifying some of the officers already adversely affected. That is, the Nigerian military was itself aware that it possessed, in its organisation, a sizeable level of mediocrity within its professional officer level and could do little about it. A more serious situation can be imagined in the case of Ethiopia with a more prolonged war, a need to raise social levels of long-neglected groups and the demands and pressures of a rising élite.

Again, some officers earned promotion merely for serving as administrators of civilian societies. Such premature promotions, though not by any means the norm, created a corps of officers who were certainly less professional when compared with military officer corps in the highly industrialised countries.

A good number of the officer corps in many African countries have received excellent training at Sandhurst College and advanced education at the Imperial College in Britain, Mons in France and in the USA. The first generation of African military officer corps were in this category. However, a negligible number of such men, probably less than five, remain in any one African country today. They have either died in coups or been forced to retire. Indeed, second and third generations of trained officers have gone the same way. It may be difficult to find one serving officer of the general staff category in West, Central or Eastern Africa who has been serving in that position for ten or more years together.

Proximity to Civilian Society

The evidence reveals that men of the other ranks in the army in Nigeria live close to the people. The size of the army and the lack of barrack facilities ensure that the education and training of men of other ranks are conducted, to a clearly observable extent, in camps which are not insulated from interference by civilians. Civilians and soldiers mix freely at shops, markets and open spaces to such an extent that it can be argued that there is considerable 'civilisation' of the military. Abrahamsson (1972) has argued that civilianisation of the military as described above could lead to what he called the 'dissolution' of the military ethos. The absorption of military values and attitudes will be ineffective when other social groups can interfere, albeit so indirectly, in the educational and training processes of the military. Therefore, the fact that professional men of high standing are in short supply and professional training has been constrained by several factors in Africa, necessarily makes it difficult to agree fully with the position that the education and training which soldiers receive would socialise them to become professional men with the values of rationality, achievement, and so on.

How Transferable Are the Values?

If, in fact, values acquired through military professional training are available in abundance, there are serious problems about how transferable such values are to the governance of civilian societies. The

difference between a civilian and a military community requires great
adaptability on the part of the commanding officer (now state governor)
whose orders were, on the military fields, immediately obeyed. Many
such officers tended on first assumption of rulership to behave as if they
were still military officers. A good example was the constant effort of a
military governor of Oyo state of Nigeria to 'drill' the state civil servants
by 'disciplining' latecomers to work each morning. This practice soon
died out due to the pressures of civilian administration and lack of
immediate results.

The third assumption is by far the most significant. To what extent do
military values permeate the rest of the society when the military is
ruling? For such permeation to take place, there must be channels of
communication that are recognisable in some way; the recipient society
must also be ready and willing to accept such values. In addition, the
process must take place over a sufficiently reasonable period of time to
permit absorption and final adoption. An example of a channel would
be the lessons learnt from good examples of the ruling military élite by
the recipient population, which population would watch in admiration,
appreciation and subsequent emulation.

In theory, a measure of anticipated role expectations is called into
play. Many an African society had hoped for miracles from the military
who promised to 'wipe out corruption', 'create stability', raise
standard of living, and so on. In other words, the ruling military élite is
looked to to generate new norms of behaviour which will move the
society forward. The example-as-precept model described above is
observed to be true only in the first few months of military rule in Africa.
I have argued elsewhere (Odetola, 1978) that military rulers accede to
political power with great enthusiasm. This enthusiasm mounts up and
flattens to a plateau and declines after a short while. The reasons for this
mode or pattern of behaviour are not the subject of our discussion here.
What is important is that the military soon assumes the 'hue' and
'colour' of the society it is supposed to lead. Inability to maintain the
initial spurt of enthusiasm makes the military incapable of nourishing
and sustaining any new norms that may have been generated.

The military itself needs to create social or political institutions
through which it can execute puritanical policies that are meant to
change societies. Efforts to control extravagance in the society have
rested on legal sanctions such as the banning of importation of luxury
items like champagne drinks and expensive textile materials such as lace
and organza. The Nigerian military government depended absolutely on
its customs control system to ensure the absence of these materials on
the market, and thus by implication to ensure their absence from
people's homes. The resultant thriving smuggling stretched to the limit
the capacity of the Nigerian Customs Prevention Services to control the

smugglers; in fact it induced some of the men engaged in the prevention and control services to participate in the illicit trade themselves. Once the progress of the illicit trade could not be stopped, the initial effort at control was also perceived to have failed. It then requires still more massive efforts to restore the morale of members of the society to its original state before the perception of failure. The resultant decline in morale both of the ruler and of the ruled create a certain amount of resignation. Hence, the inability of the military in Nigeria, Ghana, Ethiopia, Uganda, and so on to 'wipe out corruption' results in the perception that corruption can never be wiped out. Africans begin to believe that they themselves are probably corrupt by nature and nothing can cure them of it. The rise in Marxist ideological beliefs among the élite, beliefs which are looked upon as ways of solving these problems, are probably a result of this malaise.

Structure of Society

If the African societies are ready and willing to be oriented to new norms and values, the structures of the societies do not make for the total permeation of these values to the society from top to bottom. There are few structural links (such as political institutions) between the more traditional segments and the more Westernised groups, between the élites and the masses, between the urban proletariats and the rural peasant masses, between the metropolis or centre (such as Lagos, Accra, Addis Ababa) and the periphery or the interior. Social links through which such values can spread are mere ethnic organisations whose orientations are particularistic. The development of new social institutions and voluntary organisations which can complement political or economic institutions is still at the rudimentary level.

While the political or economic and social structures may be changing with the introduction of new ideals, values and goals, and therefore capable in the future of accommodating rapid changes, the length of time that armies stay in power (assuming that they are constantly institutionalising new values and norms) is perhaps too short for any very permanent changes to take place. However, it is arguable whether the length of stay is the crucial variable. The point at issue concerns the durability and permanence of these norms and values. Considering also the anxiety and speed with which succeeding civilian or even military governments want to erase the memory of preceding regimes, it is important that values be entrenched in the society.

The various values and norms of the military will now be examined in detail with reference to specific comparative examples within the theoretical framework given above. These values and norms are: (1)

puritanism, which includes attitudes to wealth, property ownership and corruption; (2) discipline, which includes order, effectiveness and centralisation; (3) rationality; and (4) achievement orientation. It will be important to see the degree to which these values exist, if at all; how they have affected the society; and how the military organisations have in turn been affected by operating within a civilian milieu. Before proceeding, several factors need to be taken into account in evaluating how puritanical, or disciplined, or rational and achievement-oriented the military is. These factors are:

(a) quality of leadership (commitment and decision);
(b) declared goals of the military junta, and the zeal displayed in pursuing these goals;
(c) national resources at the disposal of the military;
(d) the civil–military relations that obtain in a particular society at a particular time;
(e) the corporate interest of the military; and
(f) the structure of the civil society.

An analysis of these factors will help to explain the varying degrees to which military organisational values are extant both among several African ruling militaries and also within a particular military (for example, among different successive military regimes where there has been more than one successful coup, such as the Gowon as against the Muhammed–Obasanjo regimes).

Quality of Leadership

Each military leader in political power has come with an 'armoury' of abilities and attributes. Some are more dynamic, more mature, more professional, more committed and dedicated to changing their societies than others. For example, it has been argued that General Muhammed was far more dynamic and capable than General Gowon, while Gowon was more cautious than Muhammed. The same remarks are heard when Rawlings and Akuffo in Ghana or Megistu and Andom in Ethiopia are compared. Processes of decision-making within the ruling military élite, like most other decisions, bear the stamp not only of the set procedures for making such decisions, but also that of the leadership. Where such set procedures are more authoritarian than others (for example, a military organisation versus a political party), the influence of the leadership becomes crucial. Thus, I am here taking account both of the personality, commitment, vision and dedication of the leader as well as the organisational milieu in which he is located. As a case in point,

General Muritala Muhammed set the tone for his administration by dismissing or retiring several public and military officers whom his administration considered to be deadwood material. The intention was to clean from the body politic 'useless' or 'unclean' material so as to be able to advance the society forward with little or no deadweight. This has been contained in a speech of his erstwhile Chief of Staff, Brigadier Obasanjo (1980, p. 1).

The military, according to Halpern and Horowitz (quoted above), has the organisational ability to be decisive and move promptly into action. However, the combination of such leaders as Muhammed and Obasanjo operating within the military institution explains the difference between their regime on the one hand and Gowon's regime on the other. Gowon's regime coincided with the period of the greatest oil boom in Nigeria (1973–6) but produced phenomenally wasteful spending, for example, the massive importation of cement and other prestigious construction projects (such as road flyovers) that have come under serious criticism from the society. These will be considered in greater detail below. On the other hand, the Muhammed–Obasanjo regime pleaded for greater austerity and discipline. This was, in part, achieved although that regime, as will also be pointed out, was not without its own serious weaknesses. I shall provide evidence to show that as a soldier (specifically as Inspector of Engineers) Obasanjo has been concerned with discipline and frugal spending.

Similarly, Rawlings caused several past officers (public and private), former heads of state and military officers, to be killed or dismissed. Rawlings claimed (*West Africa*, May 1980, p. 958) that he had prepared the society for a socialist revolution while the succeeding civilian regime had ignored this and decided not to take advantage of it. Mengistu staged a coup to oust General Andom whom he considered slow and unable to lead the society. The swift movement of all of these men is characterised jointly by the vision which they have for their societies and the direction they want them to move. That is, possession of clear goals for their societies by the ruling military junta can be associated directly with ability to employ and show evidence of military values of speed, discipline, and so on. Thus, the possession of 'goals' and 'vision' for their society is positively correlated with the ruling military junta's ability to employ military organisational values to achieve its aims. Can we, then, in theory argue from the other side of the coin and say that those who do not have as a clear vision as others are not capable of using military values to achieve whatever goals they might set? This position will be examined under consideration of the declared goals set implicitly or explicitly by the ruling military.

Goals

In Nigeria, General Gowon was more or less persuaded to accept the headship of the nation. He had not himself come to organise a coup and had therefore no prior set of goals to present. After the civil war he had to begin to map out a set of objectives. Then came the oil boom, and with it a sizeable amount of unanticipated wealth. Along with these, there occurred simultaneously pressures from civilian groups to democratise his rulership. In addition, there was the emergence of an articulate business group that had made some money during the war. Finally, there emerged another kind of pressure demanding that the military should wind up its rule. The varied and myriad pressures began to take a heavy toll on the ability of the military to give a sense of direction and to rule. It can be argued that as soon as the Nigerian civil war ended, and some measure of stability and unity was restored, the lack of possession of an initial set of goals became very evident and the government began to drift. It was observed that in both Ghana and Nigeria, once this drift had set in, it became impossible to arrest the progress of the decline. The ruling military increasingly became dependent on civilian advice as in Nigeria and Ghana, or some form of external support as in Ethiopia, to shore up itself in power.

When such situations have arisen, it is hardly possible that a sudden reversion to military values will solve all problems. More often than not, when societal problems have become compounded and tend to defy immediate and direct solutions, the ruling military begin to look into the civilian society for some kind of help, even sometimes for guidance. For example, during Gowon's regime, several kinds of civilian groups intervened or made attempts to supplement the efforts of the military government to solve problems. Ruling militaries can themselves become as much part of the problem as the solution to it.

It has been easier for Ethiopia's Colonel Mengistu to sustain himself in power and continue to mobilise human and material resources, in spite of the heavy odds of an internecine war, drought and poverty, because he had a much clearer set of goals (setting up of a socialist society) than a Gowon or an Acheampong. Mengistu has succeeded, at least in part, in inculcating military values into the structure of the political and economic institutions (Peasant Associations, service and producer co-operatives, Tenant Associations, and so on) which he set up to achieve his goals. When a military regime assumes power merely to correct a few ills of a former civilian or military regime, the assumption is often made by such rulers that the elimination of one area of corruption, either in whole or in part, will purify the whole of the society. For example, Rawlings, motivated by a high moral fervour, ordered that the large central market in Accra be dynamited as part of the war against speculation. While this was part of the 'house-cleaning' operations of the Revolutionary Council of Ghana, it fell short of a total surgical operation and indeed did no more than scratch the surface. Rawlings, of course, had clear ideas as to what his goals were, but it is obvious that they were never fully carried out. The momentum of the movement towards civilian rule, as well as international pressures and opinions against his style of 'house-cleaning', led to a premature halt to his achievements.

The destruction of a market cannot be said to be part of a general and far-sighted economic policy. It can only be seen as a token of a determination of the ruling military to demonstrate to the public that certain corrupt values need to be wiped out. Token demonstrations are assumed to have effect largely because of their visibility value. The extent to which they can have enduring and permanent impact becomes questionable. Hence, unless the ruling military has succeeded in setting up lasting mechanisms through institutions and structures to perpetuate these values, it may achieve very little. This has been the case in Nigeria and Ghana, where even though the military has ruled for a long time, it has not succeeded in wiping out corruption or inculcating the values of discipline into the society on any appreciable scale. In Ethiopia, the military has succeeded better in entrenching its values through the institutions it set up. Of course the Ethiopian situation is different because it had a smaller middle class capable of resisting military pressures than either Ghana or Nigeria has.

Be that as it may, the point of theory here is that a mild reformist military regime may succeed less than a revolutionary one in inculcating its values into the civilian society merely because the latter alters the structures of the society and builds new and perhaps more permanent institutions. It is arguable, however, whether short reformist regimes do not build lasting institutions or in fact whether the institutions built by a radical revolutionary regime cannot be reversed by new regimes. The answer to that is simply that it is more difficult to alter again what has been radically changed in the first place without incurring the ire of the masses (assuming, of course, that the radical change is in their favour). It is, on the other hand, easier to reverse changes when the reformist regime did not alter the foundations of the social structure.

Resources

The amount of material resources available in a society and the manner such resources are distributed and used can assume important proportions in influencing how capable the military can be in employing military organisational values or inculcating them into the society. In other words, it is assumed that societal resources constitute an external factor to the military organisation which may affect the internal structure of that organisation as well as the ability of that same organisation to influence the society.

In a situation of large societal resources, military men who traditionally and in theory must be frugal and austere begin to compare their own living standards with those of the more opulent civilian society, as General Ocran did in Ghana; or even with their overseas counterparts where, for example, in Europe or the United States of America, general living standards and the level of technological development are so much higher. Such a situation tends to reduce the willingness and ability of the military rank and file as well as that of the officers to remain austere, frugal and disciplined. This becomes more so where the economic and social structures encourage or permit a visible amount of inequality, injustice, or both. In the Nigerian situation, where more opulent wealth is more discernible than in Ghana or Ethiopia, military officers have been caught misappropriating public funds, particularly where they have direct access to it. Even where such misappropriations have not taken place there is ample evidence that many serving or retired military officers have tried to live like rich civilian businessmen, bureaucrats and other élite groups, for example, in the kinds of houses they have built or cars they own. Even if their wealth had been acquired cleanly and legally, the point is that the way in which such wealth has been used has not been in any way different from the way in which their civilian counterparts have sought to acquire or use such wealth.

Again, the very availability of uncontrolled wealth creates a perception of limitless abundance such as occurred in Nigeria between 1973 and 1976. Such a perception created in the mind of General Gowon the need to import massive goods (such as cement) even against the judicious advice of the governor of the Central Bank of Nigeria at that time. It would have been expected that a strict puritanical attitude would dictate immediate and cautious preservation of wealth rather than its ill-considered dispersal. However, one might try to justify Gowon's effort by the declared and explicit need to reconstruct the war-torn nation in a massive and rapid way. But if such extensive importation of foreign goods were placed side by side with the tremendous rise in salaries as evidenced in the Udoji Commission reports, it will be seen that they were ill-advised. The effect on the national society was not one of inflation alone; socially it encouraged bribery, corruption and stealing and, on top of this, it built into the minds of the population the antithesis of puritanism.

It was obvious that in Nigeria, within the military organisation itself, the general rise in salaries had created a near-uncontrollable feeling that national resources are inexhaustible. Policemen, soldiers, airforce men and men of the navy invaded the shops, markets and stores to purchase imported foreign goods. Sometimes they used military force to gain a purchasing advantage over prospective civilian buyers. The military organisation itself was not happy about the situation and had to issue advisory notices in conspicuous places in the army posts and barracks, enjoining the soldiers to spend their money judiciously. Perhaps it is in this ability of the military either to enforce or advise its men together and in one visible location (and therefore with greater prospects of success) that it has a clear advantage over the civilian society.

But how has the military behaved in Ghana and Ethiopia, where resources are obviously more meagre than in Nigeria? It can be argued in theory that a situation of near-poverty would encourage an attitude of frugality and puritanism and that this would accord well with military values. In Ghana, however, successive military regimes have been found guilty of corruption, stealing, misappropriation, and so on, as will be demonstrated below. In that nation, military officers have broken the rules to gain personal advantages. For example, some officers hoarded material goods which were scarce in order to satisfy their own needs or those of immediate relatives. So when they had the opportunity to steal they were not restrained by any internalised values but behaved like the rest of the civilian society. Evidence shows that this was widespread in Ghana. We do not have as much proven evidence in Nigeria as we have in Ghana, probably because the investigations conducted in Nigeria were not as elaborate and open as the probes instituted by Rawlings in Ghana. The situation in Nigeria may have been just as bad as that in Ghana.

The point of interest, however, in the Ghana example is that, in a situation of general national scarcity and need, many military officers were simply incapable of transfering and generalising military values of discipline and puritanism to non-military situations. What took over was the more personal value of greed, and the communal value of 'sharing'. A man of status in many African societies believes that he has obligations to his immediate relatives and this is no less true of the soldier officer. It is to his communal base from which he has originated that he more often than not returns, or from which he draws succour in times of personal stress. The relationship between the single individual élite and his small communal origin has implications for the transfer of military values to the society. This point will be dealt with in greater details below under considerations of the military value of 'rationality'.

However, what accounts for the differences within one nation (General Ankrah or Acheampong as against Flight Lieutenant Rawlings in Ghana, or General Gowon as against General Obasanjo in Nigeria) are the two factors already discussed above–quality of leadership and possession of clear goals. Mengistu appears to combine strong leadership with clear goals even though he may not have been achieving results at the desired level. In such a situation as Ethiopia, where the nobility and the new élite were eager to seize power, it becomes most imperative to succeed, hence the building of several political and economic institutions. Mengistu appears to have perceived rightly the problem as residing specifically with the structure of the Ethiopian feudal society. Can one not argue then that a clear perception of the sufferings of the masses by both Mengistu and Rawlings has been responsible for the disciplined (although sometimes brutal) ordering of their societies; and therefore, further, that identification with a particular social class enables the military to evince those of its values that may enable it achieve such objectives? Further evidence lies in the fact that when the military allies with the upper classes in Latin America, it evinces those of its values that are clearly conservative. This matter will be dealt with in the next chapter.

Civil–Military Relations

Civil–military relations cover the generally broad aspects of the contact between civil and military societies. Among several others, the points of contact include the structure of decision-making and accountability in the preparation for war, general foreign policy issues, education of the military in its relationship with civil education, and ordinary social relationships that emerge from direct contacts between the two either as individual members of the army and civil society or in groups.

Where the civilian society is closely involved with the ruling military in decision-making, it is possible that military precision and other values come to influence such civilian groups. An example is the kind of cabinet that existed in Ghana, Nigeria and even in Ethiopia, where non-military people were involved together with the military officers in top decision-making. It should be noted, however, that where such values have rubbed off on civilian colleagues in the decision-making hierarchy, the effects on society as a whole may not be great since such men are few. In any case, it must not be assumed that this kind of short socialisation will have any permanent effects on such men which are transmittable to the rest of the society.

Another point to consider arises in a situation where many civilians can train together with soldiers in schools or colleges. Such a situation is not common although there are examples of primary and secondary army schools which a considerable number of civilian children attend. Such civilian children soon disperse into the rest of the society with little effect.

An important area of contact will be where a large proportion of the army has been trained in civilian occupations as a part of package training and where such men are released into the society in considerably large numbers. In the Nigerian situation, very little such training was given to soldiers simply because vast numbers of them were recruited specifically for the Nigerian civil war. After the war ended, a proportion (evidently small) of demobilised soldiers joined criminal groups which have since been terrorising the civilian society.

Finally, where some number of retired officers have gone into business and are managing industrial or business concerns, we may begin to see the impact of military training and values on civilian society. The extent to which this is possible depends on the degree of professionalisation. The level of professionalisation of the African military has not been very high, as noted at the beginning of this chapter. Also, we do not have such men in abundance as yet. Even when they begin to arrive on the scene in larger numbers, the fear remains that they may quickly revert to or be easily absorbed into the old civilian way of life.

Military Corporate Interest

When the military is in power, a certain level of military corporate interest is evident in the handling of national affairs. This level depends on the original reason for staging a coup, the amount of national wealth discovered in the treasury and also on civilian pressures. In situations where their corporate interest is paramount, the military tends to move with speed and some discipline. Sometimes, however, the feeling of power and lack of checks and control by any visible force external to itself tend to make militaries proceed beyond what is ordinate and proper in spending public funds for its own ends. That is, it can be speedy in getting its own requirements, but at the same time very unthrifty. Examples of such non-puritanical attitudes abound in the vast sums expended by the successive Ghanaian and Nigerian military regimes to build army barracks and generally equip the military.

The Structure of the Civil Society

The literature on military sociology has pointed out that the social forces operating within the society itself can have an effect on military institutions, and vice versa. These forces are related to ethnicity (Enloe, 1970) and social classes (Nun, 1967; Mazrui, 1973), as well as to religious factors. What has not been significantly faced up to is the problem of how any one or a combination of these factors influence specific dimensions of the military institution, and vice versa. This neglected aspect will be looked at more closely in this work.

Ethnic considerations in the bestowal of favours, promotions, allocation of duties and military postings are particularistic and affect the ability of military officers to be guided by rational norms. Besides, this invites intervention by civilians into the operation of the military organisation since these would seek to protect and enhance the interests of their 'own men'. The theoretical issue here is that ethnicity becomes one of the conceptual linkages between modern and traditional institutions. In some African pre-colonial military institutions, the armies were constituted mostly of men belonging to the same clan or ethnic groups. Wars and conquest were then looked upon by ethnic groups as a means of advancing group interests. In the modern African armies, such a consideration also remain a means of promoting group mobility in a competitive milieu. While it may take the form of subtly pushing your own men up, there comes a time when the competitive milieu produces conflicts, as we have seen in the Nigerian civilian war, the north–south conflict in the Sudan, the wranglings that followed the Rawlings coup in Ghana and similar instances between the northern and southern Ethiopian tribes. The direct and open ethnic conflicts aimed at subjugating each other in pre-colonial armies is re-enacted in modern times by more sophisticated weapons, wider scope and more ominous results.

Such processes themselves produce situations where ethnicity as a social factor is re-examined by governments within such societies (if the societies have not already been destroyed) vis-à-vis national integration, unity, stability and modernisation. A re-examination of that kind may again result in the formulation of new ideals (as in the Nigerian and Ghanaian constitutions) or policies to minimise the influence of such a social factor and may eventually lead to new alignments. In the Nigerian situation, the guidelines written in the latest constitution attempt to enhance opportunities for the formation of political parties that are nationwide and not ethnically based. This came after the civil war. Similar processes are more or less operating in Ghana. The situation is quite different in Ethiopia, the Congo Republic and most recently in Mali where the armies have been busy establishing one-party socialist states. The differences exist because of, among other causes, the different orientation and determination of the military leadership and the goals they have set for themselves. Ethiopia, the Congo Republic and Mali produce interesting examples of political situations where the leadership has consistently eliminated members of the ruling junta who disagreed with the top leaders' programmes. Mali's original leadership group in the ruling military council has been whittled down from fourteen to six between 1968 and 1979, and Ethiopia's has been similarly reduced. In the Congo Republic, Opango has eliminated colleagues in the pursuit of the same original goals. The strength of leadership and commitment to goals have important consequences for the reshuffling and nature of alignments within, and consequently for the organisation of the military institution itself.

One conclusion one can then draw is that ethnicity or class which constituted the building blocks or elements of the social structure of any society are transformed into processes for changing or altering the character of these blocks. That is, the problems of linking modern and traditional institutions within developing societies create situations where elements of the social structure acquire a dynamism to transform themselves into processes to change the society further. This, to me, constitutes an important area of further research if we are to understand social change, social stratification and development in these societies. We can begin to ask such questions as, how does the élite use ethnicity to sustain its own position in relation to the masses in the structure of the society? When does ethnicity become more or perhaps less relevant as a form of social relationship? What effects do any changes in the political organisation of society have on the factor of ethnicity? The relationship between ethnicity and social class will acquire more significant meaning when answers can be provided for some of these questions (Kuper, 1974).

The African militaries, being inspired and created by European militaries, possess what has been referred to as the 'Bible'. This is a book containing rules and regulations, a code of ethics, guidelines on relations and attitude to peers and the public, and the values of the organisation in general. While all soldiers, particularly the officer corps, are enjoined to abide by the letters of the 'Bible', the factors of inadequate training, unduly rapid promotion, incomplete isolation from civilian life, participation in politics, all militate against a strict application of the terms of the military code of ethics. Evidence of ostentatious living, indiscipline, corruption, involvement in crimes, nepotism, and so on abound in the military organisations of African societies.

Puritanism

Like the protestant enterpreneurs of Western Europe, the soldier reformers in non-Western societies embody and promote a puritanism which forms distinctive innovations in their societies (Halpern, 1962). Puritanism embodies an austere, clean, strict and severe attitude towards sin, fun, wealth, property and extravagances as well as a discipline approach to behaviour, the conduct of interpersonal relations and any other actions one may engage in. Thus Halpern (1962) argued also that in contrast to political parties, armies are disciplined; they are well organised and are able to move into action without obtaining the voluntary consent of their members. He maintained that the military is a disciplined organisation without peer. In line with the literature above, Horowitz (1966, p. 362) has also stated that the military is prompt where the society is tardy, it is neatly uniformed where the society is ragged, and it takes direct action where indecisiveness reigns supreme.

Those who hold this view have looked at the military only at the organisational level. That is, the military is taken as a holistic collectivity and then compared with other organisations such as political parties. However, they have neglected to consider individual actions of military officers and soldiers which if derogatory may have serious effects on the image of the collective organisation. Because of its professional code of ethics and its ability to discipline erring members, as we shall see later, the military does possess internal mechanisms which will enable it to project a much more puritanical image than other institutions. Whether it in fact does so by utilising all of these mechanisms is another question.

Ostentatious Living: Attitudes to Wealth and Property Ownership

In Ghana military policy was less than austere. Major General Ocran complained: 'we had to suffer a loss in pay and of certain amenities while the cost of living rose astronomically. One day they [the army officers] were to pay for electricity; the next day they were to lose their travelling facilities . . . we all wondered what was happening to us . . . when the British were here our interests were better protected' (Ocran, 1968). It was clear that the Ghanaian army had intervened in large part to protect its own interests, and certainly austerity was not one of them! Similar complaints were made by the Nigerian military about being housed in poor barracks, about lack of standard uniform and shoes, and so on. The point of interest here is that the military compares its own conditions with the more open conditions of civilian society which are so near and so visible. Certainly the terms of the 'Bible' do not constitute controls capable of restraining military men from indulging in the glamour of civilian life. Hence soldiers 'squander their salaries on [football] coupons, alcohol and other trivial matters' (*SOJA* [magazine of the 2nd Infantry Division, Nigerian Army], 1979, p. 4). General Obasanjo as head of state had warned all soldiers, particularly the officer corps, against 'living ostentatiously beyond our means' (Obasanjo, 1977). So military men either want to supplement their income or get rich quickly through betting. This is a practice that is rampant in the rest of the civilian society: in government offices, corporations, supermarkets, schools, hospitals, among the urban élite, urban proletariat and farmers. In short, the military is no exception, and are thus not in any way any more puritanical than the rest of society in this regard. Hence, as we will argue later, there is no convincing evidence that the military is so distinct from the rest of the society as Huntington has claimed to make it uniquely worthy of admiration and emulation. We must bear in mind the distinction between the performances of the military in instituting economic and political changes on the one hand, and on the other hand the direct effects of its organisational values on itself and the society when it is in power. It requires the small ruling group to bring these changes about while the larger band of soldiers who are in daily contact with the rest of the society may be engaged in activities that are not particularly complimentary to the military institution.

At the level of operations of the ruling military on the wider societal plain, questions can also be raised about military austerity. First, at the instance of military regimes in both Ghana and Nigeria salaries were raised throughout the public service. The Nigerian military established the Udoji Salary Review Commission which made recommendations with extremely far-reaching consequences for Nigerian society. Table 2.1 shows the changes in salary structure.

Table 2.1   *A Comparison of pre-Udoji–Williams and post-Udoji–Williams Salary Scales in Nigeria (in naira per annum)*

Qualifications and positions held in the public service	Pre-Udoji–Williams salary scales	Post-Udoji–Williams salary scales (starting-point only)
Messengers (primary school-leaving certificate)	312	720
Dental hygienists, community nurses, senior industrial technicians	830	2,142
Medical doctors (post-qualification)	1,680	4,668
University lecturers with Ph.D. but with no experience	2,424	5,760
Full university professors	6,000	11,568

Sources: Federal Military Government of Nigeria Estimates 1974–5, Reports of the Udoji Salary Review 1975 and Williams Commission, Lagos, Nigeria, 1975.

Table 2.2 shows the pre-coup and post-coup salary figures for Ghana. Here the percentage increase ranged from 17 to 40 while in Nigeria it ranged from 50 to 200. The direct effects of these increases were to increase purchasing power without corresponding increase in production, to increase imports and to raise inflation levels. The colossal wage rise in Nigeria was due to increased revenue from oil production. While neither case of wage increases portrays the military as puritanical or austere, the Nigerian case is particularly indefensible. It

Table 2.2 *Salary Increases for Selected Government-Employed Professionals in Ghana under the National Liberation Council (in new cedis)*

Occupation	Salary range as of 1965	Salary range under NLC	% increase
Principal state attorney	4,600	6,100	32.6
State attorney	2,940–3,540	4,000–5,000	36–41
Assistant state attorney	1,840–2,240	2,400–3,000	30–34
Senior medical officer	4,940–6,000	6,904–8,320	39–40
Medical officer	3,560–4,240	4,960–5,484	29–39
Principal secretary	5,200	6,084	17
Assistant principal secretary	4,100	4,848	18
Police commissioner	5,000	6,180–6,972	24–39

Source: Report of the Commission on the Structure and Remuneration of the Public Services of Ghana (Accra: State Publishing Corporation, 1968), pp. 67–9, 74, 78; Ghana Establishment Secretariat Directory of Positions in the Ghana Civil Service, January 1967, file no. A2258, quoted in Price, 1971b.

generated new consumption patterns, new hopes and new aspirations in the populace. Table 2.1 reveals that the income of a new Ph.D.-holder doubled overnight, and so did the incomes of several other categories. An unprecedented level of purchasing power by the civilians was unleashed into the society.

Some of the effects of this step on the civilian society were tremendous. First, in Ghana the registration of new private motor vehicles increased sharply when the military came to power. The number of new private cars registered in 1968 was 42 per cent higher than during Nkrumah's last year in power. Most of these cars were in the high luxury car range. Similarly in Nigeria the registration of private vehicles increased massively, as Table 2.3 reveals. Here also it can be seen that the quantity of important footwear rose by about 2,000 per cent in a period of five years. Similarly, the importation of private motor vehicles rose by about 1,300 per cent. These two items are considered luxury goods whose importation have not only harmed national foreign exchange situations and therefore the national economy, but created such new tastes and values as had never before been present in the society. If we examine Table 2.4 we will discover that the amount of money expended on importing private cars in 1973 (76·39 million naira) was more than the capital expenditure of the entire federal military government on agriculture, education and health combined (68·3 million naira). In 1975 the amount spent on importing private vehicles

Table 2.3   *Nigeria: Imports of Selected Items by Quantity*

Commodity	1970	1971	1972	1973	1974	1975
Footwear in thousand pairs	754	1,309	3,183	4,365	11,839	14,904
Private cars	7,488	18,297	35,699	44,526	51,582	95,928
Cement in metric tons	466,055	977,523	720,111	854,459	972,464	1,737,542
Cotton piece goods in thousand square metres	176,503	39,177	36,893	13,321	101,198	19,326

Source: Digest of Statistics, Nigeria, 1976.

(220·299 million naira) was greater than the government's capital expenditure on agriculture (211·2 million naira) in the same year. But at this time, national agricultural productivity in cocoa, palm products, groundnuts, cotton, and so on was declining at an alarming rate. Because money was available in relative abundance in Nigeria, the Gowon regime made it possible for a lower income category than had hitherto been the case to qualify for financial loans to purchase private motor vehicles. Thus, many people whose incomes were insufficient to maintain motor vehicles properly bought them and then ran into serious financial difficulties. The civilian society was thus encouraged to live above its means, and the consequent appearance and image of opulence in the society induced still less fortunate ones to look for crooked ways to make money. It must be pointed out, however, that the Muhammed–Obasanjo regime imposed budgetary bans on the importation of selected luxury items, including certain classes of drinks, and also of motor cars.

Some Military Regimes Compared Internally

As we have observed from the tables, imported luxury items ranging from expensive home electronic equipment, jewellery, textiles and drinks to prohibitively expensive cars (such as the Mercedes Benz 450 SLE costing about 40,000 naira or approximately $73,000) flooded the Nigerian markets. The Nigerian sea and airports were congested and the nation paid heavy demurrage costs. Foreign businessmen had a field-day exporting various items irrelevant to the Nigerian economy in the certain belief that Nigerians would gobble them up–which, of course, they did. This resulted in corrupt foreign exchange transactions.

However, in the 1976 budget speech General Obasanjo warned that there had been some recent publicity about the so-called wealth of

Nigeria because of her oil resources. This, he continued, has led 'to a widespread and unfortunate attitude of mind'. He stressed that while Nigeria 'has great potential, . . . she is not a rich nation', and that her resources from oil are not enough to satisfy the yearnings and aspirations and the genuine needs of her people for development and social services. In the 1977/8 budget speech General Obasanjo banned the importation of all cars over 2,500 cc engine capacity. Cars of over 2,000 cc but less than 2,500 cc attracted an increased duty of 150 per cent and were placed under licence together with cars under 2,000 cc engine capacity. Champagne drinks which in Nigeria had been regarded as a symbol of affluence had already been banned. Placed under licence were canned beer, soft drinks, furniture, carpets, watches, and so on while the duty on some spirits (brandy, whisky, gin, and so on) had import duties on them increased by 50 per cent.

Besides such budgetary steps, the Obasanjo regime had instituted a low profile and fiscal policy by which government and its functionaries were to show examples of simple living and low consumption to the society. This was welcomed by the general populace who had become tired of the conspicuously high level of consumption to which they had no access and were ready for some kind of change. In general this last military regime kept to its policies with the result that big cars were much less in evidence on the roads and the atmosphere and attitudes of mind had at least to some extent become more frugal. Similarly, in Ghana Rawlings's efforts in the short period of his reign had highlighted, by exposing and punishing luxurious consumption and corruption, the ostentatious living of previous military leaders. We can find similar examples in Mengistu's regime as against the regime he succeeded. What explanations, in theory, can we give for these differences among members of the same army, who were probably trained in the same schools, when they come to rule the same nation?

First, two models already advanced are useful here. The stronger, more dedicated the leadership, the greater is the ability of the military to

Table 2.4   *Nigeria: a Comparison of the Value of Car Vehicle Import with Capital Amount Spent on Agriculture, Education and Health (in million naira)*

Amount spent on:	1972	1973	1974	1975
Car imports	45·36	76·39	80·53	176·07
Capital expenditure on agriculture	20·7	35·4	87·4	211·2
Capital expenditure on education	21·3	16·3	134·4	631·1
Capital expenditure on health	11·4	16·6	—	—

Source: Federal Office of Statistics, Lagos, Nigeria.

ensure at least some levels of discipline in the society it is ruling. If in addition it has clear goals and objectives in coming to power, as well as visions of the kind of society it wants, there is evidence that the military can and does adopt its organisational values.

Secondly, the Mengistu, Rawlings and Obasanjo regimes had succeeded military and not civilian regimes. This similarity makes them good examples for comparison. The regimes they succeeded had become unpopular or ineffective or both, and such a situation had tarnished the image of the military in their respective nations. Therefore it is not surprising that Muhammed, Obasanjo and Rawlings expressed the embarrassment and tiredness of the military at the ineptitude of their predecessors. Whether that is the reason they carried out their coups is not directly relevant. What is important is that they proceeded to make efforts to clean the image of the military in the eyes of the public. Again, the results of their efforts have become controversial but our point of theory is that successive military regimes attempt to carry out reforms farther than those they succeed. Successive military regimes become more reformist than their predecessors in some sectors, although whether such strings of reforms can be integrated into meaningful and consistent instruments or examples of development is another question. But in carrying out further reforms, they succeed to an extent in improving the image of the military by initially advocating and using their own values. The effect may be that a military organisation which has been involved in several coups will find among its own members more advocates of the need to inculcate and teach military values within itself. It is not being argued that such a military organisation will evince or always stress military values: in fact the opposite may be true. The effect of the emphasis of the Muhammed–Obasanjo and the Rawlings regimes on puritanism and discipline must certainly be in the direction of making these values operative within their respective organisations.

Another point of interest is that the civilian government that succeeded the Obasanjo regime has reviewed the latter's low profile policy. The task force appointed to carry out the review had recommended that the President of the Federation of Nigeria and some other top government officials should be exempted from the low-profile policy inherited from the military regime (*Sunday Punch*, vol. 7, 8 June 1980, p. 1). This, the committee argued, was because of security implications, stability, durability and weight of higher vehicles, such as a Mercedes Benz vis-à-vis a Peugeot car. An additional reason, the group advanced, is that the Peugeot car is not suitable for receiving visiting heads of state, and concluded that the use of a higher grade vehicle had become 'incontestible'. A Mercedes Benz 600–the biggest in this class – was recommended despite the fact that General Obasanjo himself had ridden, on a few occasions, in buses. Rawlings complained of the reversal of his frugal policies by the new civilian regime. If these two military regimes and the two civilian regimes are typical, the conclusion would have to be drawn that the military institution is more austere and puritanical than political institutions. Such a conclusion would be not only facile but also false. It is sufficient to claim, however, that where the military has succeeded in demonstrating its own organisational values, significant changes have been recorded. We will now turn to the military and corruption.

Corruption

The claim discussed above that the military is the most disciplined institution in Third World nations will now be looked at critically in the light of evidence that will be advanced. First, however, it must be pointed out that such claims unduly raise people's expectations about military institutions vis-à-vis other societal institutions. The result is that any single slip by the military will be perceived by the observing society as a double slip. That is, since in theory the military is expected to be above board, one is not likely to view any weakness with as much of a sympathetic eye as if the particular incident had been anticipated anyway. The general expectation of Third World politicians is one of a greedy, corrupt, inept and vindictive group. If they perform true to these expectations not many eyebrows are raised. But the conspicuousness of military regimes, coupled with these expectations, make any slip on their part inexcusable in the eyes of the general public. While evidence shows that military officers can and do steal public funds, organised corruption based in the military corporate body is a very rare phenomenon. Of course, corporate interest may induce the military to spend public funds unwisely but that is different from organised misappropriation of public funds by political parties to finance their future electioneering campaigns and other things.

Evidence abounds, however, of high-level corruption and graft among top military personnel. In Ethiopia it was discovered that some high-ranking officers had absconded with $80,000 earmarked for relief of drought victims. This particular incident has been selected among several others to represent the depth to which military officers can descend in the effort to get rich quickly. When it is realised that the per capita income in Ethiopia is less than $300 and much less in the drought-stricken areas, the stolen sum is quite sizeable. The fact also that it was destined for dying people renders the stealing inhuman and entirely reprehensible.

In Ghana, General Ankrah, a one-time head of state, was disgraced and had to leave office for taking bribes. The Rawlings administration killed or jailed several top military officers (including two former heads of state) for terms ranging from five years to life in prison after they were found guilty of obtaining loans, properties, material goods, favours and advantages, committing abuses by virtue of their official position in the public service, and intentional or reckless dissipation of public property. A short list of these names, their ranks and punishments is provided as Appendix I at the end of this book.

In Nigeria in 1977, more than twenty army officers of the Second Infantry Division were found guilty of offences ranging from fraudulent misappropriation of public funds to the preparation of false documents and conspiracy. Punishments awarded ranged from dismissal to varying degrees of reduction in seniority. Certainly such corrupt practices were not limited to the Second Infantry Division of the Nigerian army; the commander of a fighting division during the Nigerian civil war was dismissed in 1974 on evidence of involvement in the smuggling of drugs out of the country. It has been reported that under the Gowon regime many military officers held 'bulging bank balances' (*ARB*, July 1975, p. 3695).

Gowon attempted to stem the tide by relieving some civilian politicians in 1975 of their responsibilities, with the result that the issue of corruption in high military echelons became very prominent. His dismissal of Brigadier Adekunle for smuggling drugs was seen as only scratching the surface. Indeed, what exacerbated the situation was that top military officers who were either retired or dismissed became prosperous businessmen, particularly in the contract businesses. Brigadier Jemibewon, himself once a governor, complained of the Gowon regime that 'corruption had reached such a pitch that top public functionaries wallowing in it did not bother to take the trouble to conceal the acts of their corruption from public gaze' (1978, p. 33). He observed that there existed a flagrant display of affluence and open demonstration of corruption in high places. Military governors during the Gowon regime had 'carried corruption to an unparalleled degree in the history of Nigeria', he charged. It is, of course, customary for an incoming military regime to 'expose' the ills of its predecessor. The Muhammed regime set up probes to investigate alleged corrupt practices by Gowon's military governors. Only two of twelve former governors were cleared of corruption.[1] Those found guilty were made to forfeit substantial properties to the state. Such instances serve to set a standard which new military regimes themselves hardly ever meet. The punishment meted out to guilty officers had effects on the society as well as on the military organisation itself. Of what kinds are these effects and what conclusions can be drawn from them?

First, the tainting with corruption and bribery of military regimes in the eyes of the lay public has a deep psychological effect. Since the military has come to be perceived as the saviour of the society from economic, political and social ills (or at least they proclaimed themselves to be so), their fall from grace has had the compounding effect of ensuring, in the minds of the public, that the last hope is gone. The booty, as it were, becomes more accessible, more open and visible, and successive leaders can plunder more and more. It became fashionable in Nigeria during military regimes to become friendly with military officers or to establish some channels of communication with some of these men in order to get contract awards or obtain some favour. The societies in many military-ruled African societies come informally to look upon ruling militaries as disbursers of favour, patronage and even largesse.

In the Nigerian case, several hundred million naira worth of contracts were awarded by the Obasanjo regime in its last five days in power. Perhaps the administrative and routine procedures for the award of these contracts had proceeded and required only signatures in the last minutes of its rule but the apparent rush and the subsequent reversal of these contracts by the succeeding civilian regime gave the impression, however wrongly, that the contracts were improperly awarded. While these are impressions only they do not do great credit to a regime with an avowed aim of stamping out corruption. Certainly, a spate of stealing from the Nigerian Central Bank and other institutions happened during the first few months of the incoming civilian regime and up to the time of writing these thefts (which run into several million naira) are constantly reported.[2] The scandal of the alleged loss of nearly 3 billion naira in petroleum money by the Nigerian National Petroleum Company created a cloud of suspicion. The findings of a commission of inquiry which reported that there was no loss of money has been welcomed with resignation by the society. Such alleged loss was supposed to have occurred under the Obasanjo regime and the rumours go round that the press was merely afraid to report it at that time. The point here is that the press hardly ever reported any official corruption of members of the ruling military or any senior military officials during the life of that regime. If certain military officials were discovered to be corrupt, usually they were dealt with within the military organisation, and the mass media would pick the reports up afterwards. Perhaps some day more official evidence can be advanced to lay bare the degree of corruption that took place during the tenure of the Gowon, Muhammed and Obasanjo regimes. Thus, in the people's eyes no military regime, whether rightly or wrongly, can be held to be above board. Of course, no military regime can make such claims since all have had occasion to deal with the corrupt ones among them through institutionalised channels. Such a perception that the 'best' had not measured to standard, coupled with the psychological resignation that things can hardly be better with any other type of rulers, can only serve to encourage a wave of corruption in the society at large. This is in fact the phase that

Nigerian society is currently going through. The Ghanaian situation is not much different, except for the brief effect of Rawlings, the lack of money in Ghana and the low level of her economy.

The effect of official corruption by the military has had quite significant effects on the military organisation itself. Officers as well as other ranks become as restive as the lay society over corruption by the ruling group. The officers (not those in government) observe and note these lapses and tacitly, sometimes overtly, support the feelings of the public. Jemibewon (1978, p. 30) has noted that 'what the public did not know, perhaps, was their general outcry, which was a popular demand was in fact backed up by the senior officers in the armed forces'. Jemibewon further claimed that the officers had openly demanded that Gowon should change the military governors even in the presence of these governors, at an open meeting. This fact reveals that often the feelings of the public are paralleled by similar attitudes and feelings within the military. Jemibewon also said that while the public were becoming restless with Gowon's administration, 'the army itself was fretting and beginning to complain aloud about the unsatisfactory situation in the army in particular and in the nation in general' (1978, p. 33).

Corruption by the ruling military often becomes, then, the focal point around which other grievances within both the army and the civilian society are anchored. It is seen by the civilians as the mechanism for widening the gap between the rich and the poor. This social division, whether real or perceived, provokes nationwide discontent as observed in Ghana and Nigeria, and does, in fact, result in instability. In Nigeria, in 1974 and 1975, riot events, strikes and boycotts followed the discovery of corruption concerning one of Gowon's military governors and Gowon's apparent condonation of the offence. Similarly in Ghana, the populace openly cried for the blood of corrupt officers and celebrated throughout the streets when these officers were killed. Corruption assumed such importance because it represents an abuse of the trust and high hopes placed in the military and the smearing of its organisational image held by the other officers. It is an issue in which military and civilian ethics coincide and around which emotions and feelings commonly rise. At the same time, it represents a weakness which both of the groups share in varying degrees. The nature of corruption in both civilian and military ruling groups is similar in origin generally, but probably different in scope, depth and use. The corruption consists usually of misappropriation, embezzlement and other forms of stealing arising from non-institutionalisation of proper and effective monitoring channels of public accountability in the bureaucratic system which the two groups preside over and use. It is most widespread in the area of disbursement of public funds particularly concerning the negotiating and award of contracts. It requires men of the highest professional ethics (which are not in great abundance in either civil or military groups) to resist open abuse of office when opportunities to steal stare them in the face and where detection will not be easy.

Misappropriation by military officers tends to be on individual bases and for individual uses only. Whereas this is also true of the civilian political leaders, official corruption can be for the advantage of whole groups such as the political party. As mentioned above, party functionaries attempt to keep back large sums of public fund for party uses. Where the ruling military use public funds unwisely, say for the purchase of hardware, it is usually with public knowledge and can therefore be explained in theory, by invoking military corporate interest. Thus, corruption by ruling military officers is related to individual attempts to move up socially. Once a lot of ill-gotten money has been put aside, most of the military officers retire to a private lucrative business life. This category of men soon join the ever-expanding cadre of Africa's rising bourgeois, making use of the important contacts which they have made while in office.

This situation has significant consequences. First, other officers in the military, for whom individual upward mobility is equally important, look forward to the day when their own opportunity will come. Involvement in military rulership becomes an avenue of undisputed importance to the character of social mobility both within the military organisation and in the society at large. The killing or retirement of all officers above the rank of that of the leadership of a successful military coup cannot be totally divorced from the attraction of the appurtenances and special advantages that go with ruling a civilian society. While the active desire of senior military officers to see Nigerian military governors changed round during Gowon's regime was directly linked to the desire for the improvement of the military image, it is not far-fetched to argue that indeed the hope of personal gain may have been mixed with this enthusiasm since many of those who were called upon to replace the displaced military governors themselves cannot make absolute claims that they have not enriched themselves in office.

Thus military rulership has tended inadvertently to give opportunities for individual as opposed to group mobility in the society at large. This must be seen in the context of group mobility at the ethnic level in the rapidly modernising African societies. The appointment and commissioning of military officers is by a quota system based on state of origin (or largely on ethnicity) in Nigeria. This is true in varying degrees of other African societies. In this way, the commissioning of military officers can be looked upon as an aid to group mobility. However, the trend noted above of retired and even dismissed military officers becoming part of the rising bourgeois class in the final analysis underscores individual rather than group mobility.

Once the leadership of a ruling military junta is perceived as incapable of checking public corruption within its own organisation, serious problems arise about the quality of its leadership. Two obvious cases are the Acheampong and Gowon regimes in Ghana and Nigeria respectively. Brigadier Jemibewon (1978, p. 33) has complained that the 'administration of which Gowon was commander-in-chief, was stinking with gross inefficiency and mismanagement'. Dissatisfaction with Gowon's handling of corrupt military officials had spilled over into other areas of his general administration. Jemibewon further praised the Nigerian army for exercising restraint, patience and self-discipline in the face of such glaring corruption, maladministration and inefficiency.

Once again, the order in which these charges are laid down reinforces our theoretical point that corruption represents a pivot around which other issues of assessing a military rule revolves. The internal divisions caused by the desire to replace a weak or corrupt military leader are reflected in the fact that many coup-planning groups arise during the reign of such a leader. For example, it would appear now, with the advantage of hindsight, that at the selfsame time as the group that successfully brought Muhammed to power in Nigeria was making plans, so were others such as the Bissalla group; similarly, the Rawlings group may well have been planning at the time as the Akuffo group was making plans in Ghana. The issue of corruption tends to reduce rapidly the credibility of ruling military juntas within their own organisation and thus to undermine the legitimacy of their leadership. It is the single most visible weakness of military rulers because they all invariably make promises to wipe corruption out from the society once they assume power. It immediately sets in motion a measure of internal strife within the military organisation which spills over into civil society or sometimes has parallel developments in the civil society. Either or both situations have had serious destabilising consequences for society in general.

General Discipline and Order

Another area in which military organisations claim to be superior to other institutions is the issue of order and discipline. Several scholars (Horowitz, 1966; Halpern, 1962; Pye, 1962) are very strong supporters of the theoretical position that the military is the most disciplined institution in the developing areas. This theoretical position, as noted in Chapter 1, has roots in the attempt by the United States to bolster its military aid to developing nations as a bulwark against instability and communism. Observing that military officers represent symbols of power, authority and sovereignty and a focus of national pride, a Rockefeller Report (1969) claimed that in Latin America 'a new type of military man is coming to the fore and often becoming a major force for constructive change'. The assumption here is that the regular drills, rules, regulations and norms governing the training of a professional soldier will not only qualify him to acquire these values but will be transferred to the governance of civil society. What will be looked at now are examples of the real behaviour of the African military in power as against this theoretical position.

Upon assumption of office, many ruling militaries have indeed attempted to put the values of order into practice. The problem has always been that of their ability to sustain the initial enthusiasm. Muhammed, more than any other Nigerian military ruler, assumed office with the sole determination to make the society more disciplined and efficient. Jemibewon (1978, p. 39) claimed that 'the name of Muritala Muhammed had come to be associated with merit . . . and unparalleled efficiency' in the army. Several of Muhammed's speeches and actions amply illustrated this. His successor, Obasanjo, also emphasised discipline both within the army and in the society in general in several of his speeches. He admonished the military that 'by virtue of our calling, we have a special and sacred duty, no matter under which administration to raise ourselves above board and show to others examples of discipline, modesty and honesty' (1977). In a formal address to graduating officers in Jaji in 1977, Obasanjo (1980, p. 186) said: 'As officers of the Armed Forces, you will understand the import of discipline. To me, discipline implies restraint and self-control . . . It is the axial principle on which my idea of society rests.' Further, he referred to the Nigerian society as undisciplined and complained about several facets of civil life–social, political and economic. He concluded that a society like Nigeria where lawlessness in its organisations is rife, where selfishness and greed are reflected in hoarding, cannot be regarded as disciplined.

Muhammed applied a keen surgical knife to the body politic in Nigeria by retiring hundreds of officers from public offices–for, among other faults, indiscipline and inefficiency. The effects of this were controversial but it has left the unmistakable impression that the military can show very active interest in changing the society. Obasanjo went further in deploying military officers to secondary schools to help maintain discipline and train students in the art of drilling, physical education and general military ways. This practice has been discontinued at the time of writing under civilian government, and thus its effects may not be deeply felt. In the economic sector, several regulations were devised to combat hoarding, profiteering and cheating.

Rawlings in Ghana applied the ultimate sanction by killing citizens found guilty of hoarding and profiteering. The socialist system of government adopted by Mengistu in Ethiopia has gone much further and its actions are more radical than the reforms initiated by Rawlings or Obasanjo. The cleaning up of the body politic in Ethiopia required, under a clear ideological umbrella, that the society be completely restructured.

However, there is ample evidence of gross acts of indiscipline exhibited by soldiers in virtually all African societies ruled by the military. For example, in Nigeria soldiers became a law unto themselves in their inter-relationship with civilians. On several occasions, rather than maintaining law and discipline they themselves constituted the law-breakers. These acts culminated in civil–military disturbances in which lives were lost and much property destroyed. In a particular instance, the Army Chief of Staff travelled to the scene of disturbance, pacified the civilians, castigated soldiers and set up an investigation which recommended that the soldiers in that brigade should pay for the loss of civilian property at the rate of 10 naira per private soldier graduated upwards to 100 naira for colonels. In Ghana, soldiers clashed with the police and killed a policeman, stormed Accra prison and released four of their men serving jail terms for corruption. In Liberia in May 1980, after the successful coup, soldiers in an orgy of indiscipline arrested people en masse, demanded money from them and stole their cars (*West Africa*, 2 June 1980). It was reported that they fired guns at the slightest provocation and harassed ordinary people. The fear generated certainly did not help civil–military relations. The effect on the civil society has been tremendous, and where I have observed it directly in Nigeria, it has been very disturbing. The image and hence the legitimacy of the military was undermined. People justified their own misdemeanours and malpractices by what they observed the military doing. It is important, however, to place these acts in perspective.

These acts were committed by individuals or bands of soldiers, sometimes of course by whole brigades. The point about professionalism becomes an important explanatory tool. Because they were less professional, they were less disciplined. Another point of explanation, however, is that the gap in modern or disciplined outlook between a traditional society and a highly professional military organisation is large. Since large segments of many African militaries can be characterised as not professional, they do not regard themselves as any different from the civil society and are very often ready to 'rough it up' with civilians. Another explanation in theory is the issue of status identification in a rapidly changing society. The general flux that accompanies modernisation makes it necessary that each individual make a point of his own identification. This is especially true of social mobility during modernisation where an upwardly mobile position or status becomes an avenue for getting results. In interpersonal exchange situations in such societies, one's readily identifiable upwardly mobile status is important in the relationship. It might be easier to obtain a confirmation of one's air ticket if one identified oneself as 'Professor X' rather than as plain 'Mr X'. Relationships centring around differences in such statuses may result in conflict situations particularly when all the parties concerned are aiming for the same rewards. Soldiers struggle to get material rewards similar to those wanted by civilians but soldiers make superior claims simply because they are soldiers and are in power. Professionalism and the need to maintain order generally in the society is completely thrown overboard in the mêlée. The need to identify oneself in one's social position in order to struggle with others for the same scarce resources results in a clash of claims, in general disorder and in the undermining of authority and legitimacy. The African military is as much part of this disorder as any other modern institution. This struggle can be observed at a corporate level in the open competition with educational, bureaucratic and other institutions for the annual allocation of resources in the budgetary exercise. This will be dealt with in a separate chapter.

While it can be said that the military have displayed overt interests on the issue of discipline in the society, and that in some cases they have taken positive steps to achieve the aims of cleansing the society of corruption and indiscipline, it is also clear that the achievements have not reached the levels expected of them. The military have not been able to sustain the initial spurt of enthusiasm and in some cases have become perpetrators of open and glaring instances of indiscipline and corruption. The fact of this failure and the ever-increasing problems of corruption brought by the very process of modernisation have served to entrench corruption and indiscipline in the society. In some cases, for instance in Acheampong's Ghana or Gowon's Nigeria, corruption and indiscipline became worse. It has been claimed that even after Rawlings, 'Ghana was not a noticeably cleaner place' (*West Africa,* 2 June 1980).

The mechanisms used by many an African military to cleanse the society are often very idealistic. The open caning of senior public officers for coming late to the office in Nigeria, or of market women for hoarding in Ghana, and the award of punishments when the accused are not even present, do not appear as serious efforts to grapple with the problems. Sometimes they are farcical, and even take on the aspect of an abuse of power. By placing themselves above or outside of the law the military have sometimes contributed to instability and disorder rather than order. The unrestrained exercise of power can itself be very corrupting and produce results that smell of indiscipline.

Where a claim to superior status in a competitive position leads to or is combined with an unrestrained use of power, we have the beginnings of a totalitarian regime, as in the case of Amin, Emperor Bokassa, or the last years of Acheampong. Success in making claims to a superior status in a competitive position creates the need for more power to sustain that position. Perhaps the struggle among competing élites in African societies cannot but sometimes produce authoritarian tendencies or results. The consequences and implications for modernising societies are that there is often a reversal economically, politically and socially through inability to consolidate initial gains. Neither Uganda nor Ghana has yet found its feet after the regimes of Amin and Acheampong.

Perhaps the efforts of the military to cleanse the society are merely moralistic attempts. The effects of caning or killing wrong-doers may not achieve discipline nor even cleanse the society. It may merely make the masses rejoice (as has often happened) that the 'cheats' are being dealt with openly.

In theory, there is a difference between 'morals' and 'discipline'. Morals concern precepts about a sense of right and wrong. Discipline is more predicated towards training either of the mind or the body. While standards of moral codes do discipline the mind, the acquisition of discipline in certain directions may not be justified by a sense of right and wrong, justice and injustice. Indeed, it may be entirely unjust, wrong and lacking in any virtue, as exemplified by the precision and discipline displayed by a well-orchestrated robbery exercise. The openly demonstrative, or rather moralistic, attempts by some of the ruling African military to cleanse the society has made these efforts appear idealistic and incapable of being translated into lasting and practical measures. The false conclusion may be reached that the actions of military élites will enhance the establishment of discipline and order simply by observing military attitudes and behaviour which shows a great concern for the maintenance of order. Lovell (1971) has argued that such a conclusion confuses intentions with results.

Any serious effort to wipe out corruption or to cleanse the society of indiscipline needs skilled sociological research, as well as long, detailed and careful planning. Research and planning were carried out in those instances where the African military has been fairly successful in establishing some mechanisms that have proved useful. In Nigeria some social sciences research was done before the recommendation to deploy military personnel to secondary schools to improve discipline, and to establish the Public Complaints and Corruption Bureaux. The fact that some of the institutions created to carry out these reforms are continued in Nigeria by the succeeding civilian regime raises the hope that they will be permanent and bears testimony to the need for careful planning and research. Unfortunately, the image of the military as a speedy and no-nonsense organisation may encourage its leaders to shun cautious planning and research in the belief that those steps will be slow and defer rapid results.

Evidence reveals once again major differences between successive military regimes in any particular nation in the way the issue of corruption and indiscipline is handled. In Nigeria, Gowon appeared weak, ineffectual and moralistic in the face of serious cases of corruption among his own men. Addressing his Cabinet once he declared: 'if there be any of you who has abused in any way the confidence I and the nation reposed in him to enhance some unworthy ends, I leave such a person to his conscience and to his God and to posterity' (*ARB*, January 1975, p. 3494). The effect of that homily on the society was fast and galvanising. The press, sensing that some Cabinet men had obviously been found to be corrupt, seized on this for public disclosure of commissioners' assets, and the whole nation became restless. The demonstrations, boycotts and riots that followed left Gowon virtually helpless. The society had rejected this weak plea to his Cabinet and had demanded action.

On the other hand, Muhammed's firm, decisive if sometimes drastic measures to rid the society of indiscipline and corruption came from an understanding of the problems and greater insight into how to solve them. He declared that 'the indiscipline in our national life are all symptons of a deeper malaise at all levels in the territory' (*ARB*, October 1975, p. 3787). Proceeding to dismiss several public officers, in contrast to Gowon he said that commissioners and public officers who were found to own assets over and above what could reasonably be computed to represent their legitimate earnings would forefeit all such excess assets by confiscation. The precision of Muhammed's statements and actions in contrast to Gowon's left people wondering whether they belonged to the same army. After careful planning, Muhammed took the following two steps: (*a*) he established a corrupt practices bureau; and (*b*) he restructured and enlarged the Federal Public Service Commission and the Police Council in order to enable them to cope with those responsibilities. Explanations for these differences in approach are provided by our theoretical model discussed above of the differences in leadership styles and goals each military ruler has set for his society. In addition, it has been emphasised that each succeeding military regime attempts to wipe out the poor image of its predecessor and to carry reforms some steps forward.

Rational Norms and Achievement Orientation

An important dimension of the alleged 'progressive' attitude of the military is the orientation of its members to be rational and to abhor ascriptive considerations in their judgement and actions. These attributes are considered by several scholars of social change and development to be crucial to modernisation. The military training and professional socialisation coupled with the acquisition of the values overseas is assumed to be the source of these attributes. Levy (1966) has argued that universalistic criteria based on physical fitness and mental ability are more predominant in recruitment to armed forces organisation than elsewhere. Pye (1962) claimed that the military possesses rational and achievement norms far and above any other organisations in Third World societies. Pye further claimed that because of these values the military can speak more convincingly than most other institutions about the changes a society requires to defend itself.

It is arguable whether the military stands out so uniquely in societies with an emerging civilian middle class or with a trained civilian bureaucracy as in Nigeria and Ghana; or indeed whether the military stands above the ascriptive standards of ethnic loyalty. In contrast, however, Levine (1968) has found the military in Ethiopia to possess these rational norms far above the ordinary civilian society there. He found the Ethiopian military to be more secular and more modern oriented than the rest of the population. The Ethiopian population has been essentially feudal and rural and does not possess the level of education, sophistication and general technological advancement that can be found in either Ghana or Nigeria.

Those who argue that the military possesses rational values at a more abundant level than the civilian society have not taken full account of the influence of religion and ethnicity–two most powerful factors in these societies bearing on the military's ability to be rational. Sometimes the emergence of the military on the political scene has meant a reversion to the traditional form of government, as in some Middle Eastern societies. Shlomo (1970) claimed that within the Arab context, military rule has not signified a breakthrough to modernisation. Rather, government based on the Islamic religion accepted and revered by Arabs for fifteen centuries came to ascendancy. It cannot, however, be argued that the influence of religion, particularly Islam, is all-pervasive, for Turkey under Ataturk became secular. It is perhaps the strength of Ataturk's leadership and the subsequent ability to control the situation, coupled with a strong vision of a modernised society, that was in part responsible for his success. Ethnic considerations in promotions and other rewards have been observed to be as strong in the military as in civilian society. In the Congo People's Republic as well as in the Sudan, Ghana and Nigeria, rivalries exist in the army between northerners and southerners. To counteract discontent from the south, the Congo Republic's strongman Nguoabi appointed a southerner, Major Louis

Goma, as Prime Minister in the military government. Goma's appointment did not, however, lead to a cessation of tribal hustling and jostling within the army. In Nigeria, Rear-Admiral Wey (1979) claimed that towards the end of 1965 it was known that some service personnel, officers and men had access directly or by invitation to some politicians for promoting their personal interests in the service, on a tribal basis. In both Ghana and Nigeria, rumours abound of the promotions awarded to military officers on a purely tribal basis. Ethnicity, as we have earlier argued, is a concept that links a modern Western institution with the traditional society. These observations, Wey said, signified the time that politics started penetrating deep into the Nigerian armed forces. The invitation to the military by the civilian Nigerian government in 1963 to quell the Tiv riots created additional political inroads into the armed forces because partisan and political issues were the causes of the crisis. The inroads culminated in the constitutional tussle for power between President Azikiwe and Prime Minister Balewa in 1964 when both had called in the various service heads and handed down widely differing interpretations of their powers. The meaning of the above is that the military harbours non-rational norms as does the civilian society. The consequences are the disintegration of the armed forces as a unified institution through civilianisation processes noted above. The military institutions and the civil society become progressively more coincident in values as the military comes to rule these societies. The saving grace is that a new military regime may attempt to save images by arresting the progress of the decline.

Rawlings in Ghana and Obasanjo in Nigeria banned public officers from joining secret societies, and those who were members were enjoined to resign. Secret societies have been alleged to be responsible for a great deal of corruption at all levels in national life–in court proceedings, in the award of contracts and in the granting of bank loans. Secret societies are alleged to foster a kind of selective fraternity which encourages discrimination against the ordinary citizen. Even if they have not wholly succeeded, the military has taken positive steps. Another special advantage the military organisation has over the civilian is the means it has in its formal and laid down procedures to prosecute within itself abuses of non-rational norms. One such institutionalised procedure is the weekly 'disciplinary order' held by each commander of various units in the army to try offenders and apply justice. Such procedures, however, have serious limitations for the trial of more senior officers (sometimes the commander himself) who might be guilty of the offence. In other words, the internal mechanisms for applying sanctions within the military are inadequate to cover situations that may arise when the military is in power.

Military Organisation as a Repository of Skills

The organisation of research which preceded the establishment of foreign assistance for Third World military by the United States gave birth to a body of intellectual knowledge that was supportive of the ability of the military in those nations to use their skills for direct national development projects. This body of knowledge also stressed the role of the military in spreading general education and literacy to these societies. It has been claimed that 'the skills inherent in military forces–those skills that are needed to perform normal military duties and which include specialists whose talents are health and medicine, public works and engineering, transportation, safety communication, administration, education are skills beneficial to a developing nation' (Slover, 1963, p. 48). A special report in 1967 by the US special warfare school said: 'the level of skill usually is greater among professional military personnel than among the population as a whole. They have been exposed to technology, logistics, and training in modern organisation. This training gives the military man a modern outlook which is not often an outstanding characteristic of the civilian elite.' Janowitz (1964, p. 85) himself claimed that the military serves as a training ground for technical and administrative skills, and that the military manages economic enterprises to meet its own requirements and for the need of the civilian society. This claim rests on the assumption that the gap between civilian and military occupational structures is diminishing and that the professionals in each group are becoming increasingly interchangeable. Janowitz found that the proportion of civilian-type occupations (technical, scientific, maintenance, and so on) among enlisted men in the US military increased from about 7 per cent at the time of the civil war to roughly 70 per cent in the post-Korean war forces. Daalder (1962) said that the many skills of the military are the more crucial because many ex-graduates of special military colleges return to use their acquired skills in civilian employment. Obasanjo (1975), himself an engineer, consistently stressed the civil role of the military, and said that 'in Africa, where there is dearth of many skills, the military has within its ranks quite a number which are vital for development'. Earlier, in 1974, he had insisted that whether one likes it or not, the Nigerian army cannot help departing from its conventional role of involving itself in the present national struggle by building for the future; and whatever it builds must be capable of numerical calculation. The Nigerian army, he charged, cannot restrict itself to worshipping professional idealism like the Royal British Army (Obasanjo, 1973). Such bold statements were never translated into the kind of practical measures for which they had raised expectations. This is due not only to the fact that skilled men are few but also because military-operated projects were dwarfed, that is, made to look pale, by civilian skills.

It has also been claimed that the military is an agent of socialisation at large because their training runs from basic literacy instructions to more sophisticated management techniques and the operation of complex equipments. New recruits, it is said, learn to acquire new habits of dress, literacy and a new personality; it is said that they achieve physical, social and psychic mobility–the army becomes a major agency of social change as it spreads new skills and concepts into the hinterland. This apparently pervasive ability of the military seems to parallel civilian ones at every turn. If this were so, it would give the military an extra capability to mobilise societal resources over and beyond its coercive character; and possibly therefore to substitute their own skills for a length of time even when workers' groups go on strike.

The ability of the military to perform these roles in some forms is incontrovertible. Janowitz (1964) found that the military has contributed to development works in Burma and Pakistan. It has also helped to develop basic education in Ethiopia, Korea, Iran and Guatemala. In Nigeria it has helped to build bridges, roads and contributed to other capital projects. Most of the activities of the Nigerian and other militaries have, however, been limited to constructions in and around the barracks. This includes the construction of officers' messes, the expansion of offices and stores, and the building of sports fields, quarters and shooting ranges. Only rarely do they undertake civilian projects. While some of these are large projects, and can save the government some money, they are relatively small in scope when compared with the massive and gigantic projects undertaken by civilian engineers and technicians. Some of the road projects undertaken in Nigeria have either taken too long to construct or have not lasted long.

There are, in fact, many more engineers, architects, medical doctors and other technicians in the Nigerian and Ghanaian civil society than in their respective armies. A substantial proportion of these skilled men in the military are those who transferred from the civilian services to the military. The military has been and is in constant search for this grade of men. The colonial experience of Nigeria and Ghana (which is lacking in Ethiopia) has conferred this opportunity. Ethiopia has also had a long experience of feudalism, authoritarian rule and poor educational development which have together prevented the growth of these skills in the society. To support the position above, the military has had to look into the civilian society for skilled men to supplement its own inadequate resources particularly in times of emergency. African armies are generally small armies and only a few of them have the kind of complexity of organisation that the Burmese, Indian, or Turkish armies have. Only the Nigerian, Ethiopian and Zaïrean armies are over 25,000 in strength. This is a ratio of military to civilian population of 1:1,131, whereas it is 15:1,000 in the USA, 10:1,000 in the UK and 5:1,000 in the Magreb states (Grundy, 1968, p. 299). Also, there are a few African nations where the military has these skills in greater abundance than the civilian society, such as in Mali and Niger, but the rise in educational levels even in those nations has been rapidly reducing the gap.

Even if we assume a great enthusiasm on the part of the military to modernise their societies by their own skills, we may begin to assess what changes these military activities are likely to bring about in the African societies. It has been claimed for example in Latin America that such activities 'fall into the category of welfare rather than infrastructure'. That is, they are not likely to have any lasting or cumulative effect (Barber and Ronning, 1966). In Nigeria, the road development projects undertaken by the military come under the category of emergency road programmes: that is, the military is not part of a long-term and comprehensive programme of development and these activities are, therefore, at best only temporary. Also, such civic activities may raise expectations which cannot be fulfilled; they may represent one-shot forays of the military into a rural area; they may be fragmentary and not fit into an overall social and economic policy. The specific area where lasting changes may be felt is in adult or literacy education. This is scarcely undertaken at all by the African military but experience has shown that in South Korea, where military recruits and civilians have been given. adult education, thousands have moved to the already overcrowded capital city of Seoul, and thereby created urban unemployment. In Turkey, where literacy education has been undertaken, Horowitz (1969) found that the effect has been exaggerated, noting that no more than 3 per cent of the illiterate rural males learned to read and write.

Many African armies, particularly those of Nigeria, Sudan, Ghana, Ethiopia, Sierra Leone, Zambia, and so on, are career armies. This fact slows down and restricts the feedback to civilian life. The majority of retired military officers in Nigeria and Ghana have become private businessmen. This fact alone practically excludes any substantial impact of the trickling down effect on the society.

Emphasis on civil action by many scholars, particularly in the USA, has regarded it as a component of counter-insurgency. It was primarily conceived by the US government to assist in the prevention and elimination of insurgencies inimical to free world interest through the improvement of the relationship between the military and the population. Pauker (1959) suggests that it is only the military in South-East Asia who can prevent the spread of communism. Although Barber and Ronning suggest, in support of Pauker, that experience in Bolivia,

Peru, Ecuador and Colombia show that military civil action can be a deterrent to insurgency, they feel that the expansion of military capabilities and programmes may not succeed in eliminating the primary source of frustration and discontent. African societies do not experience insurgency on the scale that Latin American and Asian societies do. The most obvious example of the use of the military for counter-insurgency in Africa has been provided by the situation in Zimbabwe, although that situation was in itself anomalous. The government was white and the bulk of the military's other ranks was black fighting against black liberation movements.

In conclusion, it must be borne in mind that no matter how sanguine scholars, politicians or even some military officers may feel about military civil action, there is a limit to which the military is willing to be converted, according to Horowitz (1966), from a sword to a ploughshare purely out of professional considerations.

Unchecked civil action by the military may encourage militarism within the population. Neither as a concept nor as a process should military civil action depend on insurgency or counter-insurgency (Glick, 1967). It has to do with the social and economic activities of the military *per se* and is related to arguments about the role of the military in developing areas within a broader context than that of internal war.

Summary

We have found so far in this chapter that the theoretical position upheld by an earlier generation of scholars (Pye, Halpern, Johnson, and so on) that the Third World military has modernising values and skills needs serious modification when applied to many African societies. It is true that the professional training, socialisation and other experiences expose young officers to the values of puritanism, discipline and order and to a variety of technical skills. It is also true, however, that the professional socialisation of many African armies is inadequate or of insufficient duration and quality to uphold the theoretical position. It has also been demonstrated that there are intervening variables between the level of professionalism and the ability of the ruling military to demonstrate such values and skills. These variables are the leadership qualities of the ruling junta, its declared goals, the resources available to the society, the corporate interest of the military as well as the structure of the society itself.

While some military regimes have demonstrated these values in varying degrees, others have not. The explanation for these differences resides in the influences of the variables mentioned above. The explanation also resides in the fact that successive militaries, upon assumption of office, attempt initially to improve on the 'tarnished' image of the military created by the previous military regime but do not themselves prove capable of maintaining the initial enthusiasm. The declining enthusiasm or capability is due both to the pressures of ruling a civilian society and to increasing disintegration within the military organisation. The coming to political power of the military does tend to bring the cleavages within civilian society into the military organisation. The inability of the military to handle such cleavages through lack of coping mechanisms tempts the men within this organisation to look outside for help, thus tending towards further civilianisation of the military. Military professionalism which, it is argued, gives rise to various values itself breaks down in the face of tensions arising from the management of a civilian society. Hence, many top African military leaders have been guilty of as much indiscipline, corruption, and so on as civilian politicians. However, the military makes attempts where strong and committed leaders have emerged to rebuild its image by internal punishment and reorganisation. We have also found that such internal arrangements have often been inadequate in general to cope with situations arising not from internal sources but from external problems of ruling a civilian society. The military in power, I believe, needs constant and dynamic regeneration of its values by means of institutionalising new processes of coping internally with externally induced problems. One way would be to increase efforts to achieve much higher levels of professionalism so as to keep its internal values intact or nearly so. It appears that the alternation of more or less committed military regimes (Gowon–Muhammed and Obasanjo, in Nigeria; Ankrah–Acheampong–Rawlings in Ghana) tends to keep alive the need to strengthen military organisational values. This gives the military a kind of resilience on which it can build.

One reason that the effects of the values of the military have been so weakly felt in civil society is that the military do not establish or institutionalise procedures for enhancing or fostering such values, but rather displays one-shot, short-time, highly demonstrative energies towards restoring order and discipline in society. Where careful sociological research and planning has been done, for example in some instances in Nigeria, the results have been manifestly marked. The military may then be able to move away from apparent moralising to the real institutionalisation of discipline. Once the demonstration effect of these 'displays' have worn off, the society not only reverts to its original level but also tends to decline further. This is because the society which is made to believe in the apparently extraordinary ability of military regimes to rid it of its evils of indiscipline and corruption finds itself doubly disillusioned.

In the Ghanaian and Nigerian military organisations, the level of technical skills found in the civilian professional groups is higher than those in the military, particularly in the engineering and medical fields. In those two nations, the military organisation is only just developing its professional skills because it is only in the last two decades that the military organisation itself has become modernised. The long colonial experience of both nations ensured the availability of these skills. On the other hand, the Ethiopian society lacks these kind of skills in its military organisation because of the long neglect of education in that erstwhile feudal society, as well as, in contrast, the recent high speed and volume of technical assistance given to the Ethiopian military by the USA and more recently by the Eastern bloc countries. Thus, for the purpose of assessing differential skill levels between the military organisation and the civil society, there are two categories in Africa: those nations who through long colonial experience have acquired some level of these skills through the training of its citizens in Britain and France; and secondly, those more or less neglected nations like Ethiopia. It is not being argued that colonialism is the explanatory variable, since after all Liberia was not so colonised. The essential factor is the external contact which gives some opportunity for training, and which may have been obtained through other avenues that are not necessarily colonial.

Notes: Chapter 2

1 The results of the probe were published in the national newspapers. The names of officers found guilty and their assets forfeited are provided in Appendix II.
2 These reports appear to be on the increase since the civilians came to power. It can be be said that Nigerians are no longer surprised by these reports.

3
Military and Social Classes

There are two principal angles from which we can examine the relationship between military ruling élites and the structure of social class. These are, first, the effects of social origins of military élites on social mobility in the stratification systems in order to see whether lowly or aristocratic origins would influence ability to move up and hence, in turn, the effect of changing mobility on the class structure of societies. In addition to this there is the effect of social origins on attitudes, on political behaviour and modernisation, on political stability, economic development and social change in Africa. The nature of the alliances which the military élite makes while in power are of crucial importance in determining the outcome of development efforts. Does the military élite ally with the conservative oligarchy, the middle classes, the radical left, or the centre in terms of ideological orientations and political behaviour; or with separate groups of bureaucrats, politicians, or intellectuals in societies with rudimentary social class developments? The second analytical area concerns the pattern of recruitment as an act of deliberate policy in many African societies based on ethnic or regional groupings.

Social Origins, Stratification and Political Behaviour

General Considerations

In much of the European tradition (Prussia, France and Britain), the bulk of the officers were recruited from the upper classes (see Craig, 1955). One good illustration of recruitment from the nobility was that carried out by King Frederick William of Prussia in the late eighteenth and early nineteenth centuries. Frederick William personally selected the young noblemen who were to enter the cadet corps in Berlin. He believed that it was the sons of the nobility that protected the state; to him that category or race (as he called it) was so excellent that it deserved to be protected in every way. The notion of honour, he firmly held, was to be found only in the feudal nobility and not at all in any other class. By 1806 in Prussia out of an officer corps of 7,000 only 695 were not of noble blood. The middle classes and bourgeoisie he believed were narrow in their views; they were subservient to authority and were only interested in gain. The peasantry had no ambition and were no different from animals. Thus, the noble social origins of a military that exercised tremendous state power led to a rigid class stratification. Craig (1955, p. 20) has argued that the institutional framework of the absolute military state did not permit the members of the middle and lower classes to identify themselves in any real sense with the state machine. The unusual dependence on this class as an origin of the officer corps put a great burden on it. When it could no longer supply men at the required level, Frederick turned to foreign nobility as his source. The rationale for this tradition was that since the military officers emanate from the same social class as the ruling élite, there would be correspondence of values, attitudes and hence political behaviour; and that this would augur well for political stability and development, because the military becomes subordinate only when it is recruited from the ruling class. Mosca said that by virtue of family connections and education, army officers retain close ties with the minority which by birth, culture and wealth stand at the peak of the social pyramid (1939, p. 233). In echoing Mosca's position, Andreski (1954, p. 107) claimed that closeness of the military officer corps to the ruling classes has been effective in subordinating the military institution to civilian control, because the military élite and the ruling classes share a common interest in the preservation of the *status quo*. The findings of Otley (1968, pp. 84–108) confirm that until recently the British army élite has been recruited almost exclusively from the propertied class and the higher professional strata. Otley's research on the British army élite led him to conclude that social affiliations and loyalties of army officers do not provide a sufficient explanation for the political record of the army officer corps; rather, he argued, they constitute merely one set of factor which predispose officers to look unfavourably on politicking. Finer (1962, p. 40) argued that social origins have little to do with an officer's political loyalty. This thesis sets aside the effects of professional training and other exposures and experiences which may distinguish the officer corps from the ruling élite. It also neglects to consider the changed structural position of the military vis-à-vis the upper élite when the military comes to power, and the pressures to which they are subject. In its efforts to consolidate its position by strengthening the state apparatus in Latin America and Africa, the military élite does encounter serious opposition and varied pressures from different classes. Its reactions often are not then based on class similarities but sometimes on the requirements of nation-building where there is a strong commitment to nationalism, and also sometimes on corporate interests.

In most of Asia and Africa, recruitment to the officer corps is not from any feudal aristocracy. In South-East Asia, Pauker (1959, pp.

339–40) found that the officer corps are not products of a social class with a feudal tradition. Mazrui (1973, p. 1) described the Uganda military élite as the lumpen-militariat comprising a class of semi-organised, rugged and semi-literate soldiery which is now claiming a share of power and influence in a society that would have been totally dominated by the educated élite. In Ethiopia, Levine (1968) has also found that most military officers are from humble families, although there is evidence that recruitment has also been carried out from the nobility. The same is true of Ghana, Nigeria and the Sudan although an occasional officer has emanated from aristocratic origins, such as General Muhammed in Nigeria. The bulk of recruits in Nigeria and Ghana have humble origins and the first generation of officers rose from the ranks. Only after political independence from colonial masters did formal secondary education, and now, more recently, university education become a criterion of selection to the officer corps. Even those who have become officers by virtue of educational advantage have originated largely from humble backgrounds. However, it is beginning to be the case that children of the newly emerging educated class are those who are the better qualified to gain entry for training into the officer cadet courses and corps. The rise of the less educated within the military organisation hardly goes beyond the level of sergeant-major which is strictly speaking not part of the élite corps.

Education thus becomes one significant factor in examining the relationship of social origins to the development of the officer corps in the African military organisation. In this way it becomes a useful analytical tool in a general examination of the changing patterns of social stratification and also of the structure of political power among African élite groups. There are two aspects to this. First, the educational level at which a prospective candidate seeks entry into the officer corps in the Ghanaian and Nigerian military organisations has risen in the last twenty years. Whereas forty years ago a soldier with full primary education could reasonably expect to get to the top, advanced level in passes in the General Certificate of Education would today be required for similar expectations to be met. A person with a university degree in the humanities, or better still in one of the professions, has a much higher chance. Such candidates are found in relatively large numbers in both West African countries today. In other words, there is an increasing convergence between the civilian requirements of upward mobility and those that are currently operating within the military organisations. The effect of this growing convergence is to reduce the gap or differences among the various élites in African societies. Military engineers, doctors, dentists, and so on usually register their names for professional practice with civilian professional groups, thus emphasising their interchangeability. Secondly, the kind of training that prospective officers undergo while in the army can be so intense and of such quality and duration that they receive the equivalents of degree certificates or are at a level comparable to university graduates by the end of such courses.

While in the past only a few military officers had climbed through the ranks and because of their lower level of education had reason to feel inadequate in the presence of western-educated bureaucrats and intelligentsia, today the relationship both at the social and professional levels is tending to become one between equals. This argument contradicts the position held by Mazrui (1973). Mazrui hypothesised that the emergence of the modern army in African countries has broken the correlation between political power and Western education by interrupting the trend towards the dictatorship of the educated class in modern African history. He argued persuasively by the example of Amin, who had less than full primary education but rose to be his country's ruler, supported by a band of semi-illiterate soldiers. These soldiers, Mazrui alleged, had become very powerful. His hypothesis does not find support in the evidence of many other countries, particularly those of West Africa where I have demonstrated that the level of Western-type education in the military organisations is rising and that there is an observable tendency of the convergence of educational levels between the military and civilian elites. The thinness of Mazrui's evidence, therefore, has led him to a conclusion which is incapable of being generalised to many African countries.

Moreover, a coup is a one-time event. It allows the successful leaders to wield some power for some time. It does not permanently interrupt the system of stratification unless political and social institutions are built to link the seizure of power with the permanent exercise of power. Even when the military seize power, the bureaucrats are still the *de facto* wielders of power behind the scenes, for it is they who often initiate advice and policy and see that these are carried through. That is, the extent to which the temporary character of military coups make military officers a separate and permanent social class must be viewed with some caution. It is important also to argue that the nature of political pressures on military rulers ensures that local and national politicians still have considerable influence. Therefore, the immediate and constant influence of the bureaucrats, politicians and business élites on the ruling military dictates that the military must build its own institutions to make any lasting impact on the structure of stratification. The Ethiopian and the Congo military élites appear to have established more lasting political institutions than those of either Nigeria or Ghana. In addition, the almost complete absorption of retired military officers into the business world in African societies emphasises the inadequacy of Mazrui's position. If political institutions have been built while the military were in power, it becomes easy for retired military élites to occupy leadership positions in such institutions. In the West African experience only the former French colonies of Mali, Benin and Togo which were ruled by military élites are experimenting with the formation of political parties by the ruling military. A similar situation obtains in Ethiopia and the Congo Republic. Perhaps the type of French political education that encourages an African élite in a colonised state to look towards France encourages him to believe in a diffuse role. That is, the explanation for the peculiar French connection in the above examples lies in the fact that Kerekou and other leaders believe they are accountable both to France and their people and thus must see their programmes carried through by establishing political parties. This explanation may not be far-fetched. However, the more plausible reasons which embrace factors that are common to Ethiopia and the Congo Republic as well as these former French colonies are that the pace of modern élite development has been slow, the level of education has been low and the countries have been relatively poor. The turnover of élite is therefore at a much slower pace than in Nigeria or Ghana and those who hold power may retain it longer. It does also help to explain why Houphouet-Boigny and Leopold Senghor have been able to retain power for so long.

The group of retired military officers in Ghana and Nigeria who made wide social and political connections while in office are wielding significant influence in the world of business. It is much easier for them to obtain import licences and foreign exchange than it is for others, but at the same time they help other civilians to obtain these privileges. They have, in this way, the opportunity of commingling effectively with the businessmen. Upward mobility in military organisations procures and ensures a place in the business world. It appears then that the individual military officer, sensing what opportunities may await him after retirement, struggles to move up in his organisation. The higher he was before retirement, the more the influence he can wield later.

The struggle for individual mobility advantages within the military organisation calls into question the general theoretical point that in the process of modernisation, individual mobility of men from lowly origins implies the desire to help others to move up. Shils (1962) claimed that the lower-class origins of new officers in the less developed societies make them painfully aware of the distance which separates them from the wealthy and powerful; that once these officers accede to power they become unsympathetic to big businessmen and conservative politicians; and that by implication they will be favourably disposed to the redistribution of wealth. The question arises whether the experiences of marginality, poverty and degradation together with the poverty of lowly origins which these men may have experienced before entering the military instils a broader concern for the not so lucky ones. As we have seen, there is an alluring aspiration and impetus for individual mobility which may reduce concern for collective mobility. Nordlinger (1970, p. 1142) supports this position when he says that 'undoubtedly the iniquitous and inequitous experiences of some officers were sufficiently poignant and their memories vivid enough to maintain concern for *los de abajo* throughout their careers. But despite the importance of socialising experiences we cannot assume that they are generally more salient than adult, class and status positions'. The strong support that Rawlings in Ghana, Mengistu in Ethiopia and Ngouabi in the Congo Republic have declared for the lower and working classes is not so much a reflection of lowly origins as an attempt to remove the tarnished image of the military brought about by the acts of the previous ruling military élites. Such acts include open corruption, stealing, nepotism and enrichment of a particular group by the military. These acts present an antithesis to the declared goals of the military. The knowledge that the military is so corrupt will tend to deepen a sense of injustice felt by the exploited classes.

Alliance of the Military with Other Classes

Charges that the Latin American military have often allied with the landowning classes to exploit the peasants abound in the literature (Lieuwen, 1962; Cockcroft, 1972). Such a position has derived from the recruitment of military officers from the aristocratic class, as discussed above. Johnson (1964) has noted the changing source of officer recruitment in Latin America (from upper aristocratic to lower middle class) and that this change is responsible for the increasingly modern attitude of the military. Since more officers are coming from the lower and middle classes 'the armed forces may be expected to be more inclined than formerly, to gravitate towards positions identified with popular aspirations and to work with the representatives of the popular elements' (Johnson, 1964b, pp. 152–4). He further argued that the increasing radicalism of the Latin American military means that the industrial commercial bourgeoisie will be surrendering control of the armed forces which were maintained by their taxes. Whereas political and historical conditions differ between Latin America on the one hand and Africa on the other, it is argued in the literature that the participation of the African military in the process of modernisation will produce an officer corps that is not likely to become the natural ally of feudal or other vested interests because their natural propensities are progressive (Pauker, 1959).

In the Middle East, Halpern (1963) has noted that the officers showed an acute awareness of the chronic ills of their country because they joined the military to escape from the economic frustrations of civilian life. The general thesis in the literature, then, is that because the social origins of the military are not high, they will be aware of social ills and become more progressive than their predecessors. To be progressive in this sense, according to the literature, implies concern for changing the conditions of the lowly and modernising their societies. In support, Pye (1962) has argued that above all else the revolution in military technology has caused the army leaders of the newly emergent countries to be more extremely sensitive to the extent to which their countries are economically and technically backward. When they accede to power, he said further, they can hardly avoid being aware of the need for substantial changes in their own societies. Thus the desire for social and economic change arises from an awareness of backwardness brought about by improving military technology. Halpern (1962, p. 258) has also hypothesised that the more the army was modernised, the more its composition, organisation and purpose constituted a radical criticism of the existing political system.

It seems plausible to expect that overseas experience of training or duty would make military officers eager to have their own countries progress. However, the link between social origins and political behaviour is one that is difficult to establish. How, for instance, do we operationalise the natural propensity of the military towards progress? The unprogressive character of some military rule makes little sense of such assertions. It is not difficult to agree that lowly origins, later middle class attainments, may create antagonism towards aristocratic or upper class and feudal members of the societies. In theory such a development would merely reveal the antithesis between achièvement and ascription. But the fact that there is no simple positive correlation between one's origin and how progressive one's attitudes are does not allow us to conclude that ruling military élites will be concerned with socio-economic change. Nordlinger (1970) argued persuasively that to oppose the upper classes is not necessarily to support the lower classes, especially in the zero-sum political arena and in the context of economic scarcity. To hold on to such a position restricts the field of investigation. It also prevents the evaluation of the significance of external factors which may be important in determining the behaviour of the ruling military élite. Abrahamsson (1972) has observed that in spite of the social changes in recruitment to the military profession in the direction of more middle and lower working class, the European military has retained its élitist perspectives, especially in its political conservatism and the stress on authority in interpersonal relationships. He noted that in Norway and Sweden the officer corps has become the most democratic profession with regard to its social recruitment but the attitudes and outlooks of the military have lagged markedly far behind the ideological changes in the population at large. Inferences from military origins to military political behaviour become less valid to the extent that officers are subject to pressures and expectations from other groups. This is particularly so in Third World countries and especially in Africa. The increasing politicisation of the military profession helps to develop a politicised ethos. Hence it is to be expected that social origins would become a less valid predictor of behaviour today than in the time of Mosca. When outside pressures mount and politicisation increases, the spectrum of options open to the military élite group and the values attached to each alternative will play a greater role in determining actual behaviour than will social background. The process by which an occupational group develops professional characteristics involves many features that tend to diminish the impact of social origin. Since the political role of the military is expanding, it is expected that they will be more dependent on an increasing number of pressure groups and that they will be adjusting their political roles to the needs and contingencies of day-to-day bargaining and *ad hoc* alliances with other groups. We will examine below the nature of the alliance or general relationship which the military has struck with the African masses (peasants, lower class workers, and so on) and also with the emerging middle classes made up of the new élite groups.

Before this, however, it is important to raise issues linked with the supposed connection between the officers' technical orientation and the hypothesised modernising motivations. It is argued that the officers' technical orientation and anti-conservative social backgrounds predispose them to carry out programmes of economic and social change, and that this combination of attributes will make them natural allies of the progressive classes. There is a theoretical problem in defining what is 'progressive' in Third World societies. There is the old school that advocates the increase in middle-class values as a bulwark of progress (Johnson, 1962, 1964a; Pye, 1962). The more recent and more fashionable position is to regard the neo-Marxist, leftist group as the more progressive (Frank, 1971). The debate is still an ongoing one and my contribution will reside in the empirical examination of the African situation below. The position assumes, at the outset, that there is a conceptual link between technical orientation and anti-conservative attitudes. Conservatism comprises several attitudinal dimensions, some of which in practical application to Third World societies may signify progress. For example, a policy of careful disbursement of public funds may result in the best development strategy in a situation of scarcity. What, on the other hand, appears 'progressive' may be so destabilising as to result in net retardation. The assumption here is not that stability always induces progress: the opposite may well be the case. Indeed, the school of conflict theory has established that frequent change, which may appear destabilising when considered in isolation, often augurs well for progress. The general position which links technical orientation together with anti-conservatism as productive of change also ignores other factors such as military corporate interest. Corporate interest, as amply demonstrated about the first military coup in Ghana, can exercise such a powerful effect upon officers' motivation as to overshadow their possible modernising predispositions. While Janowitz (1964) was ready to argue that the officers' technical education and their opposition to religiously defined traditions incline them to act as modernisers, he did not show that these predispositions are sufficiently pervasive and powerful to overcome other factors. What this theoretical excursion underlines is, first, the weakness of the basic unquestioned assumption by the neo-Marxist school of a deep but unanalysed conceptual link between lowly origins, aspiration for upward mobility through education and a leftist orientation culminating in a progressive attitude. Evidence will be brought to demonstrate that not only can this connection fail to be made some of the time, but also that there are several intervening variables which may determine the supposed progressive attitude. Secondly, it exposes the weakness of the theoretical position of the functionalist school in a rather interesting way. The middle class has not always been in the forefront of development; and popular revolutions have been led by men from middle or upper classes in Africa. Development is paramount in Africa and no social class has a monopoly of leadership. Thus, to attribute to a particular social class an absolute progressive attitude is to misunderstand African development problems and aspirations.

Relationship with the Peasants and Lower Working Classes

While most successful military uprisings proclaim that they have come to save the exploited classes, only two appear to favour the peasants and the working classes. The two are Mengistu's and Rawlings's successful coups in Ethiopia and Ghana respectively and an attempt will be made briefly to compare them.

On 21 March 1975 Mengistu proclaimed: 'Today is no time for the Ethiopian people to be guided by a monarchy–a system of creatures who claim to be descended from heaven' (*ARB*, May 1975). Declaring the socialist state, he continued that the kind of government which passes from father to son has no place in socialist Ethiopia. Further, he charged that the people themselves would set up a peoples' government in which they would be their own masters, and there would be no appointments of people through heredity. He concluded by saying that the avenues for social mobility would henceforth be through the possession of the attributes of conscientiousness, trustworthiness and progressiveness, and not heredity. The highlights of Mengistu's declaration are the need to destroy ascriptive channels of social mobility and create a more open society by emphasising achievement values. Such a need arose from the feudal and autocratic rule of Haile Selassie.

On 4 June 1979 Rawlings seized power in Ghana and declared that 'justice, which has been denied to the Ghanaian workers will have to take place. That I promise you. Some of us have suffered for far too long' (*ARB*, June 1979, p. 5307). In an interview when he was no longer the head of government, he characterised the revolution he led as the common man's revolution–'for once, a rebellion comes from common man's level in the interests of the common man' (*West Africa*, February 1980). He appeared to be over-concerned about the common man and referred frequently to the works of Fanon. Rawlings did not emerge from as humble an origin as most of the other ranks or even as several other officers. His motivation for the emancipation of the common man appears to spring from the suffering which the rank-and-file Ghanaian soldier was experiencing through generally poor national economic conditions, as well as through ineffectual organisation of the military and the open corruption of the élite officer corps who had been in power in the nation. Rawlings wanted to lead the rank and file against the senior officers, hoping that by drawing a parallel between them and the lowly civilian workers, all lower-class people, whether civilian or military, would rise together against the 'exploiters'. He believed that the revolution in the army would shatter the fear which the junior man has for the senior man and that similar results would happen on the civilian front–'now a similar situation is developing on the civilian front, workers demanding the heads of their bosses, wanting people's courts in their yards' (Rawlings, 1980, p. 169).

There was not the same kind of suppression of a total population in Ghana as under feudalism in Ethiopia. That is, the target of frustration of the common man in Ethiopia (the emperor) was more obvious and visible than in Ghana. Rawlings's inarticulated position focused the attention of the masses on a disparate group of 'exploiters'. That can only result in mobilising anger in a diffuse direction as against what happened in Ethiopia. The Ethiopian emperor had not allowed a sizeable élite to grow. Those who had moved up he had sought to use for his own ends. Therefore the peasants, the salaried lower classes and the emerging élite were kept down. In Ghana the situation was different. A sizeable number of the élite in the professions, trade, and so on had grown up with a substantial store of skill, experience and influence. A revolution that will bring the masses to rule will need first to examine how to deal with that class but, more important, what to do with that pool of skill and wealth of that class which the nation may still need. It was easier, therefore, to pull down the structure of the Ethiopian society than it was in Ghana. It was also easier, thereby, to build new political institutions based on the needs, values and aspirations of the masses in Ethiopia. The resistance of the feudal class in Ethiopia has not amounted to much precisely because they lack the pool of skill, knowledge and experience which the emerging middle class élite in Ghana and Nigeria possesses. The chances of a revolution of the masses are reduced in proportion to the growing strength of the emerging élite groups of knowledge, professions and business. One reason a revolution or even a proclamation of any of the military rulers in Nigeria has not come anywhere near that of Rawlings in Ghana or Mengistu in Ethiopia is a fear of the quality of resistance which could be offered by this emerging élite. In consolidating their own position, this élite group of the professions can hold the nation to ransom by withholding their skills, as happens frequently in Nigeria when medical doctors go on strike. Thus, beside other considerations, a useful area of research in political sociology and the sociology of development would be to examine the rising level of skill in relation to such other factors as the élite–mass gap, the level of societal awareness, and so on. To support the above positions, I will now turn to a more detailed examination of the class relations in Ethiopia both shortly before and during Mengistu's leadership.

Class Relationships in Ethiopia

The general fabric of social relationship in Ethiopia was based on the land through the systems of landholding and land tenure. There were generally three types of land tenure system: the 'Rist', the 'Gult' and the 'Madeira' systems. In brief, the Rist system derived from descent group membership or communal village landholding as obtains in most of traditional Africa. The traditional checks and balances, such as the relationship between age and landholding right, preserved some element of fluidity as well as the burning hope that the landholding right would one day pass to most individuals. Regardless of other weaknesses in this system, the generality of the peasantry was committed to it because they believed that it prevented the feudal gentry from exploiting them and that it served to limit unequal chances of land distribution. The attempts to change this system in 1944 and 1967 had been strongly opposed by the peasantry who feared that any such changes would lead to freehold and land scale. This they believed would, in turn, result in increasing the economic dominance of the powerful and 'cut off avenues of social mobility now open to every man' (Hobben, 1973; Bailey, 1979, p. 27). The general effect of that attitude was to dampen the development of class consciousness. This was quite opposite to what a revolutionary leader who may want to overthrow the feudal system would expect. That is, the mass of the peasants would be expected to feel cheated and be ready to be mobilised.

In a similar manner, the Gult system, which permitted the holder to serve the nobility in a number of functions and capacities such as in raising troops and pack animals, generated strong vertical ties between peasants, local gentry and feudal lords and preserved a belief among the peasantry that the system allowed social mobility.

The Madeira system which permitted conversion to freehold tenure encouraged, as in the Nigerian example, the nobility as well as the emerging middle class of bureaucrats, businessmen and military officers, who were beginning to 'identify their interest with the development of commercial agriculture', to own land with government support (Bailey, 1979, p. 45). Through this system, the emperor had granted a lot of land to these élite groups. This new commercialisation of agriculture within a capitalist framework resulted in the creation of an increasing number of rural proletariat. However, the emperor had, by creating this new élite class, weakened the strength of the nobility. He had built up his own bodyguard, and stopped the formation of any regional army. He had also found new sources of revenue by collecting tax on the Djibuti–Addis Ababa railway and thus had become progressively independent of the nobility. Thus, before the military coup the emperor had played one social group against the other, making each new one believe that he was fighting its cause. In this way he had been able to control the state machinery by obtaining the loyalty of the new though small educated élite. Clapham (1969, pp. 76–7) stated that the educated élite in Ethiopia 'had not seriously affected the foundations of the imperial system of education. The emperor was not prepared to put as much premium on national development as he had put on loyalty to the crown . . . Thus a traditional oligarchy had been maintained in which the development of self-respecting modern intelligentsia has been effectively restrained and its decisive ascendancy as a new élite had been prevented.' The emperor had built up and encouraged a new but small middle class élite only to deny them any powers or grant them any measure of independence. The new Ethiopian state which began to grow as a result of this in the late 1960s did not represent any agent of social change. Rather it was 'an apparatus of repression in defence of the status-quo' (Bailey, 1979). All the efforts of the emperor to build this new state amounted to an imperial design to consolidate his own authority.

It is evident from the above facts that the operation of the land tenure system prevented the development of class-consciousness among the peasants. It gave them a false idea of the opportunities open to them for upward mobility. But it certainly created a large peasantry ripe for education in a new way, towards new goals and new aspirations. In a similar way, the denial of a real role to the growing and educated middle class paved the way for radicalism. The combination of an increasingly radicalised middle class and students on the one hand, together with an exploited peasantry on the other, ensured the success of a popular movement. Mengistu had ridden on the crest of these waves although the general directions of his goals were not clearly defined initially. The initial impetus was built on the general consensus that exploitation by the feudal regime must be checked. The enthusiasm created by the popularity and success of such steps created the euphoria which immediately began to obscure the goals of the military. In Ghana, Rawlings seized upon the popular resentment against Acheampong and his successor to whip up sentiment but himself lost his sense of direction in the ensuing euphoria. In Nigeria, Muhammed also achieved a measure of success as a result of a general resentment of the last years of Gowon's regime. All three of them–Mengistu, Rawlings and Muhammed–had the idea of changing the decrepit image of the military. The three men have presented themselves not only as peerless leaders but also in a grand style as the panacea for all the problems of society. The expectation is therefore very high that from now onward there will be a happy life for everyone. This hope of a good future which everyone now holds creates a problem of fulfilment. This is because the expectations which are now held can only be fulfilled in the future. To create high hopes for the future by present pronouncements is to play the game of futurology. Therefore, there is an anti-historical dimension to the attempt of the military to create a millennium for the society. We shall now return specifically to the situation in Ethiopia before the military coup.

In Ethiopia there are about 122 million hectares of land and only 40 million of these are fertile. The bulk of arable land is in the south. The emperor had owned 15 per cent of this land, the church between 20 and 25 per cent, the aristocracy 20 per cent and the government 25 per cent. However, 90 per cent of the population worked on the land but had to share between them only about 15 per cent of the arable land; and it is interesting to note that this 15 per cent of arable land contributes 47 per cent of Ethiopia's total Gross National Product (GNP) (Bailey, 1979). It would seem, therefore, that some kind of land reform was imperative. It is in the context of this that Mengistu, on 4 March 1975, proclaimed the Land Decree. By this decree all agricultural land was nationalised. Collective farms which were to be not less than 800 hectares were to be created throughout the country. Collective farms would be open to all farmers who wish to join them. Smaller plots of ten hectares would be distributed to individuals, and such individuals must farm the land personally. All litigations involving dispute over land ownership became null and void. Also, all lands debts owed to landlords by tenant farmers became null and void. Tenants could retain from their previous owners all agricultural tools and at most one pair of oxen, but fair compensation must be paid within three years.

To implement this proclamation, the military created Peasant Associations for each 800 hectares of land. The Peasant Associations were to carry out the land reform programme and to attempt to distribute the land as far as possible equally among all the farmers. All tenants, hired labourers, landless peasants and landowners of less than 10 hectares were entitled to membership of the Peasant Associations. Owners of 10 hectares or more could become members only after their lands had been redistributed. Thus, the Peasant Associations became the distributors of land as well as possessing the right to carry out certain other functions. These other functions include the establishment of marketing of the producers' marketing co-operatives, the settling of land disputes, the administration and conservation of all public property and the undertaking of 'villagisation programmes'. To encourage the peasants to join the Peasant Associations, certain incentives were created. These incentives included the reduction of land tax for co-operative members. Secondly, no income tax was charged on the first 600 Ethiopian dollars of income received from the co-operatives. Thirdly, if they retained the profit of the co-operatives, they were exempt from corporate taxation. They also received organisational and book-keeping assistance from the government and banks were established to help them. The effects of these measures were tremendous and galvanising: the land reform had at last ended the feudal system of land tenure which had existed in Ethiopia for centuries.

Under the old system, most farmers were tenants who give up to 75 per cent of their crops to the landlord who was an 'absentee farmer'. The immediate result was that large farmers were hard hit. For example, owners of coffee estates in the Kaffa province were badly hit. However, the movement was a very popular one. The next day after this land reform was declared, 25,000 peasants demonstrated in Addis Ababa alone. Real power had now shifted from the hands of the aristocracy and the new bureaucracy or the middle class to the peasants and the urban proletariat.

Beyond the land reform the military had taken certain other steps which were designed to undermine the power of the middle class. They had introduced the income tax law amendment which placed the highest burden on those earning the greatest income. Besides this, 25 per cent income tax was introduced on dividends and 40 per cent on all royalties. Very importantly also the means of production were nationalised. For example, commercial houses, banks, and so on, were also nationalised in an attempt to destroy the economic power of the growing capitalist sector and petty bourgeois entrepreneurs.

Another major step introduced was the producers' incentives policy which particularly favoured the peasants. Holmberg (1977) has said that by accepting this policy, the new government of Ethiopia took a big step towards eliminating the exploitative urban–rural relations that had prevailed in the past. He also argued that, finally, a positive incentive to produce for the market would be provided for the Ethiopian peasants.

While in the central and south-western Ethiopian rural areas, the land reform has generated groups which gave government a support base, the result is different in the urban areas. This is because the military government has failed to generate real economic growth in the urban areas. In fact, it has led to a reduction in the living standards of the urban people because of the emphasis on rural developments. It has been argued that the unwillingness of the military to share power with civilians has resulted in the alienation of the urban population (Bailey, 1979).

It would appear that while the military has established itself as the champion of the cause of the peasantry it has not paid equal attention to the urban proletariat. The creation of the Housing Associations called Kebeles did not give a broadly based opportunity for the creation of a class consciousness. First, while the military has established itself as the champion of the peasants, it has not sufficiently integrated the interest of the urban groups along with that of the peasantry. Certainly we would have expected that a proper mobilisation of the various interests of these groups, in the Marxist sense, would have helped to establish a proper base for class consciousness among the lower classes. Thus, the alienation of the urban groups from real power has highlighted the failures of the military to lead a proper class revolution in Ethiopia. The southern and central provinces have accepted the implementation of the land reform but in the northern provinces, where the Rist system predominates, the peasants have themselves opposed the land reform. It has been argued that this opposition from the peasants is due to the strong vertical link between the peasants on the one hand and the rural nobility on the other. Another argument is that the Rist system contains within it aspects that are egalitarian.

Opposition to the land reform has come, as expected, from the middle class of retired army officers and civil bureaucrats, as well as from the nobility. In the third week of April 1975 several military officers from the headquarters of the army third division were arrested because of their opposition to the land reform. Included among those arrested officers was the head of the security services as well as a top intelligence officer. The second and third army divisions, who were fighting the Eritrean liberation front, had become very uneasy about the land reform.

Through the establishment of co-operative farms all individual ownership of land had vanished. However, many retired soldiers who had owned lands therefore hated the land reform. In the first week of April 1975 officers of the second and third army divisions gave an ultimatum to the ruling Military Council members that they should return to their units and stand for election. It appeared that they had had enough. The plan of these officers who were calling for an election was to reinstate the emperor, release some 350 imprisoned officers, start negotiation with the ELF and, significantly, to institute changes in the land reform policy.

Apart from the opposition from the military officers there were opposition groups established in the north. There were many other scattered incidents of opposition to the land reform. For example, 120 miles north of Addis Ababa two brothers named Mend and Meffin Beru seized control of the Shoa province; also in the north, another landlord took possession of the tourist centre at Nanibela for a few days. Similarly, the hereditary ruler and former governor of Tigre province called Seyoum formed his own liberation front. In Gouggem province, some farmers began to co-ordinate their efforts to resist any changes in the traditional extended family landholding system. Some army units, it should be noted, refused to fight the rebel landlords. By October 1975 the Ethiopia Democratic Union had been formed. This was to unite a broad spectrum of progressive and democratic forces opposed to the bloodthirsty nepotism of the Derg (Bailey, 1979). The executive members of this union were General Iyasu-mengasha, the former Army Chief of Staff, as well as General Mege Jegejine, Divisional Army Commander and also the emperor's son-in-law.

To implement the land reform the military had not only established a Ministry of Land Reform but they had also deployed the students to campaign among the peasants to make them aware of the need for this land reform. However, these students saw the campaign as an opportunity to increase political consciousness and class struggle. In addition, the students had wanted the peasants armed. However, the military government thought that the students' radicalism was going too far and therefore decided to suppress the agitation of the peasants. This move was perceived by the students and the intelligentsia alike as a non-genuine attempt by the military to raise class consciousness. Students started to demonstrate against the military; 1,200 students were detained and the university in Addis Ababa was closed down. The students became disaffected and later joined the anti-PMAC Ethiopian Peoples Revolutionary Party. This new party was later joined by the university lecturers and the intelligentsia in general. By the summer of 1976 it had constituted itself into a very active opposition; the newly mobilising opposition was growing more articulate while the military was becoming less so. While the military had showed a new interest and concern for the improvement of the living conditions of the masses of the peasants it had not succeeded in carrying all of the peasants with them. The situation had clearly demonstrated the weaknesses of the campaign system as well as the traditional hold of the feudal aristocracy and the rural nobility on the consciousness of the peasantry. After all, tradition and customs die very hard. The opposition mounted by the students as well as the radical left had also pointed up the lack of clarity in focusing the class struggles. For example, the struggle was not clearly focused against the feudal aristocracy as evidenced by the motley of groups and the strange bedfellows that have grouped together in opposition against the military. Class struggle and the restructuring of class relationships therefore need, as history pointed out, a clear definition of goals and a consciously designed programme of action. The question then arises whether the military, particularly in Africa, can undertake such programmes. I believe that the military has the apparatus to undertake these jobs. What the African military appears to lack is clear goal definition by a committed leader who will be able to build the institutions to carry out his programmes. After all, a programme and campaign of modernisation had succeeded in Kemalian Turkey.

Identification of the New Military with the Middle Classes: the Notion of 'Democratic' and 'Progressive Development'

Both the more traditional literature and more recent views regard long-run development as dependent upon the emergence of a middle class–which is considered the only group capable of guaranteeing long-term development. This is because, by its very nature, it is dedicated to the support of political stability and democratic institutions (Janowitz, 1964, pp. 49–58; Shils, 1962; Halpern, 1963).

It is Lieuwen's position (1962) that the main character of Latin American history is the struggle for democracy and, within a democratic constitutional framework, economic development and social reform. This can be accomplished according to him basically only by the middle class. Halpern (1962, p. 279) observed that only the new salaried middle class, clustered around a core of civilian and military politicians and administrators, seems capable of leading the quest for status, power and prosperity by taking control of the state apparatus. Perlmutter emphasised that stability is hardly possible in the absence of the middle class: 'the absence of a strong cohesive and articulate middle class is another condition for the establishment of a praetorian government. The middle class has historically acted as the stabilizer of civilian government during modernisation' (Perlmutter, 1969, p. 387).

In Latin America, the officers newly recruited from the middle classes have been observed to ally closely with the middle-class leadership of social democratic movements, as in Guatemala, El Salvador, Honduras and Venezuela (Von der Mehden and Anderson, 1961). Johnson (1964a) noted that since 1930 in Latin America the orientation of the politically active officers has been away from that of the old ruling groups towards that of the civilian middle classes. Their alliance with a class (most often the dominant class) is both necessary and inevitable (Horowitz, 1969).

What are the theoretical bases for the action? It is argued that there appears to be a set of ideas held by the young officers and held in common by large sections of the middle classes. Even though it is not believed that military training is an exact copy or complement of civilian experience, it has been argued that skills are transferable to middle-level civilian administration. However, the notion is strong that sufficient modal patterns of experience exist to ensure sympathy between the two groups (Janowitz, 1964). Emphases have been laid on the primary socialisation and education patterns of both groups, and the structural relationship of the bureaucratised military and the officers vis-à-vis the politicians, especially in African and Asian countries, which is usually one of antagonism. On the other hand, the military and bureaucracy appear to get along well together.

Because both the bureaucracy and military were organised in relatively rigid hierarchies with limited scope for initiative and relatively ordered promotion, they have conservative attitudes. They both show firm interest in ordered modernisation and economic growth, and both are well placed to get what the politicians have often failed to get. It has been claimed that the army and bureaucracy are alternative élites committed to growth, unity and stability (Coleman and Price, 1962, pp. 308–405).

Another general theoretical element is that the bureaucracy and the army belong to organisations benefiting society at large based on Blau and Scot's categorisation of the criterion of who benefits most from an organisation. Both can enter into coalitions to further their own interests or to defend them when attacked (Blau, 1962).

There is empirical evidence to support the theoretical position above. Coleman and Rosberg (1964, p. 676), reporting on the Sudan, said that 'experiences have shown that the authoritarian rule of the military in conjunction with a civilian bureaucracy, is not necessarily an ephemeral arrangement; indeed it may be a substitute for party government'. In Pakistan, the transfer of power from a politician-dominated regime to a military one may have the paradoxical result of reinforcing the influence and authority of civilian administrators. The contention here is that each group needs the other and that they have a great deal in common and can work together. It can, however, be argued that statements regarding co-operation and coalitions between the bureaucracy and the military institutions may under critical examination be unsatisfactory because they are too general. This is because there are different types of bureaucracy as well as different types of armies. Policy decisions relating to monetary allocations, to wars and also to general administration may cause strains in the relationship.

The Ghanaian example is illustrative of the notion that the military can become an effective instrument in the hands of the middle class. By 1966 the army and the civil bureaucracy were totally Ghanaian-manned. Nkrumah had by this time increased the level of taxes, imposed high taxation on luxury imports and enforced savings through bond-buying. Thus the gains made by the bureaucracy were being cut down (Tiger, 1963). At the same time, Nkrumah attempted to bring the military to heel by firing two top officers and by introducing party cells into the military. When Nkrumah was ousted by the military, the bureaucracy and the entrepreneurial group gained back lost ground (Rathbone, 1968; Austin, 1966). Thus, the social group which had expected to inherit the political and administrative kingdom of British colonialism did so with the help of the armed forces. If the alliance of the two groups is an accepted fact, to what extent can we accept it as having developmental characteristics in general military sociology?

Nordlinger (1970, p. 1143), while agreeing with the general hypothesis that the military acts to protect middle-class interests, advanced a supplementary hypothesis. He said that 'soldiers in mufti will protect the status-quo only where the middle class interests are seen to be threatened'. Flowing from this, Nordlinger claimed that it would be expected that where modernising changes and mass political participation are not seen to be threats to the middle class's material and political interests, the military would not oppose them. While the attempt in Ethiopia to stimulate mass political participation would destroy the feudal *status quo*, it would also in the long run be opposed to the interests of the emerging though small and inchoate middle class. The government of Colonel Mengistu, however, ignored such middle-class interests in order to generate political institutions that would stimulate mass political participation. Glimpses of this trend were seen in Rawlings's short-lived revolution. While both men may be seen as attempting to change the 'poor' political image of their predecessors, it is more important to conclude that the apparent sloth of these predecessors added time to the lateness of the development of these societies. That is, the longer it takes for development to come to a society, the less is the need to rely on the middle classes to support a stable growth. The speed with which Muhammed took off in Nigeria may be seen as an expression of his impatience both with the 'slow' civilian efforts and the pace of development under the rule of his immediate predecessor. Other situations such as difference in power distribution may actually determine how the military would behave in particular instances. Thus the military will initiate or accept change sometimes and oppose it sometimes. As Nordlinger himself has claimed, his hypotheses does not allow us to predict the critical points on the continuum where the military's class-defined interests and identifications may undergo a marked change (1970, p. 1143).

Nordlinger made use of data from Adelman and Morris (1967, pp. 74–6) to arrive at certain conclusions on the relationship between the middle classes and the military. I would like to critically re-examine these interpretations and show that some of his conclusions are inapplicable to the African scene. Table 3.1 illustrates the correlation between the political strength of the military and economic change according to the size of the military. In this table Adelman and Morris measured the size of the middle class by the proportion of the active male population in commerce, banking, insurance, technical, professional, managerial, administrative and clerical employments. A country was considered to have a medium-sized middle class if at least 20 per cent of the male population held such jobs, small middle class if 10–19 per cent, and minuscule middle class if less than 10 per cent held such jobs. Nordlinger inferred from the table that in the first two categories the military failed to sponsor economic change because the correlations are weakly positive or even negative. He concluded that officers act to conserve the perquisites of the middle class since real change may involve redistribution of wealth.

Thus he had associated medium- and small-sized middle classes with low economic change; then he had attributed such a relationship to the action of the military officers. But he had already concluded that the military officers act to conserve the perquisites of the middle class. The assumption made, then, is that economic change is not in the interest of the middle class. But, it must be observed, rate of growth of the GNP and changes in industrialisation may not always involve the 'redistribution of wealth'. In fact both of these economic factors may enhance the relative position of the middle classes if they can succeed in retaining the new wealth in their own hands.

Among the countries with a minuscule middle class, Nordlinger further argued, the political strength of the military is positively correlated with the growth of the GNP (0.34), with industrialisation (0.44) and with educational expansion (0.34). He claimed that as aspiring members of a class that is not as affluent as its foreign counterparts, and anxious to improve their wealth and prestige, the military élite will permit change whose end product will be the increase in size of the middle class. In addition, the masses are not a threat since, with a minuscule middle class, only a negligible proportion has been

Table 3.1 *The Political Strength of the Military and Economic Change According to Size of the Middle Class*

	Rate of GNP	Change in industriali- sation	Change in agricultural productivity	Expansion in education	Change in tax level	Investment level	Leaders' com- mitment to economic development
Medium-sized middle class (N = 12)	-0·17	0·05	-0·12	0·12	0·01	0·19	0·17
Small middle class (N = 33)	-0·06	0·17	0·04	-0·18	0·07	0·48	0·02
Minuscule middle class (N = 29)	0·34	0·44	0·17	0·34	0·09	0·07	0·04

Source: Adelman and Morris, 1967.

brought into strategic economic and political positions through the process of urbanisation, commercialisation and industrialisation; and any perceived threat to the military élite's interest would be found among defenders of the traditional order, making soldiers reformers and agents of change.

Thus, Nordlinger is permitting the military some claim as reformers only in special situations perceived by the military as sufficiently innocuous. Such a position attributes an inordinately high level of political astuteness to military officers and assumes that political pressures do not develop to change the pattern of development independently of military manoeuvres. It will certainly not explain why Mengistu proceeded to face up to the gathering opposition of the minuscule but growing Ethiopian middle class.

One could put various interpretations on the figures. The low positive and negative correlations between educational expansion and medium-sized to small middle class may indicate the intention of the military to frustrate the development of such a class. It could also mean that since education would benefit everybody in general, it would be better to maintain the *status quo*. The latter interpretation appears to be contradicted, however, by the (0.34) positive correlation between minuscule middle class and educational expansion.

Nordlinger completely overlooked the commitment of successive African governments, be it civilian or military, to education. This is attested to by the fact that the Gowon (military), Obasanjo (military) and Shagari (civilian) successive governments in Nigeria were each committed to free primary education for all children. This is quite apart from the fact that states controlled by the Unity Party in Nigeria have instituted a programme of free education at all levels for all of their citizens. Education is a critical form of investment for development.

Nordlinger argued that in a predominantly agricultural country, the GNP could be raised by industrial or agricultural expansion or both, but that if the military were acting in their class interests they would support industrial over agricultural expansion because the former has a greater impact on the size and consumption patterns of the urban middle classes. This intriguingly appears to be the case, as the figures (0.44 to 0.17) reveal. But I suggest that the people themselves perceive industrial growth as the greatest and most visible indicator of modernisation and often urge the military to undertake more projects along these lines, and the government may be reacting to such a perception. Secondly, the military would rather support industrial expansion than other forms of development because of the military corporate demand for hardware. That is, they may not be specifically acting in the interest of any particular class.

Again, there is a zero-order correlation with change in tax level–a situation that Nordlinger says may be interpreted as harmful to the middle classes. An interesting set of figures is seen where we have a 0.34 correlation with rate of growth of the GNP and a –0.04 correlation with leader's commitment to economic development. One way in which Nordlinger interpreted this is that economic growth is in the interest and bolsters the prestige of the officers who are always seeking identification with the middle classes; and since they have achieved it, there is no real incentive or commitment on their part for change.

In Ghana, Nigeria and Ethiopia, military governments have increased taxes in such a way that the middle classes have been badly hurt. Aggregate data such as the ones under discussion tend to obscure real variations which are the substantive essences of a comparative analysis. Indeed, as arbitrators of struggles among various African élite groups, African military rulers sometimes go out of their way to enact legislation which hurts large sections of the growing élite groups in the psychological attempt to enforce their own authority and thereby legitimise their own roles.

Thus according to Nordlinger the military's perception of their stake in society is shaped by the 'distribution of political power as well as the class structure . . . and where the stake is thought to be endangered through the acquisition of power by the peasants, workers, or disadvantaged ethnic groups demanding governmental response to their economic aspirations, military officers act as conservatives; and where the threat from below has not yet gathered strength, the officers allow for economic change'. This is in accord with Huntington's position, who claims that in oligarchical societies, the military is radical; in societies dominated by the middle classes the officers act as arbitrators among middle-class groups; and where mass political participation is soon to be realised, the soldiers protect the existing order.

The theoretical issue which neither Huntington nor Nordlinger considered is the reason for coming to power, and importantly the goal the military has set itself to achieve. The establishment of Peasant Associations and of a socialist political party in Ethiopia belies the theory that where political participation is soon to be realised, the soldiers will protect the existing order.

Table 3.2 reveals the high positive correlation between educational expansion (0.34), change in industrialisation (0.42) and change in agricultural productivity (0.60) in tropical Africa. This is in contrast to the figures obtained for Latin America and Asia, and even the Middle East and North Africa which may be regarded as slightly more advanced than tropical Africa. The demand for development is greatest where the need for it is greatest. While the political strength of the military may be important in determining these outcomes, by far the more crucial factor is the obvious and pressing need for development to take place. One

Table 3.2　*Political Strength of the Military and Economic Change in Four Geographical Regions*

	Latin America (N = 21)	Middle East and North Africa (N = 15)	Asia (N = 15)	Africa (N = 23)
Mean size of the middle class	71	62	51	37
Mean level of economic demands	66	47	37	27
Rate of GNP	0·01	0·28	0·03	0·45
Change in industrialisation	0·16	0·03	0·02	0·42
Change in agricultural productivity	−0·06	−0·03	−0·39	0·60
Expansion in education	−0·43	−0·12	−0·31	0·34
Change in tax level	−0·14	−0·11	−0·09	0·07
Investment level	−0·38	−0·32	−0·26	0·06
Leaders' commitment to economic development	−0·43	−0·16	−0·17	0·08
Mean correlation	−0·18	−0·14	−0·17	0·29

Source: Adelman and Morris, 1967, quoted in Nordlinger, 1970.

would really wish to know what it is about the political strength of the military that is responsible for the poor correlation with growth.

José Nun (1967) provides a most excellent critique of the notion of a 'progressive' middle class and its military ally. He asserts that the middle classes in Latin America lack a clear social, programmatic or ideological cohesion. He argues that the military is not a threat to the middle class in Latin America, nor does it substitute for its absence. The middle class is weak, inarticulate and inchoate. The military attempts to represent that class and compensate for its inability to establish a well-integrated and hegemonic group. He accounted for this by citing the early professionalisation of the military. This resulted in the alliance between the incohesive middle class and an articulate military organisation. Secondly, the middle class had not worked out a satisfactory relationship with the oligarchy when it was faced with the problem of the rising lower classes. It thus played a second-rate role to the oligarchy. That is why it raised no protest when the Chilean government handed over to foreign companies the exploitation of the nitrate deposits which it had cost the country five years of war to acquire, nor when the Brazilian authorities frustrated the energetic attempts at industrialisation made by Viscount de Maua.

Thus, the growing middle class did not attempt to change the structure of the system. All it asked for was recognition of its legitimate right to play a role in it. Its aspirations did not transcend the desire to participate in political affairs and for a defence of its moral rights (Nun, 1967). Nun observed that 'the most interesting features of this process were the speed with which these aspirations were satisfied and the instrumental role of the military'. He concluded that it was the armed forces which assumed the responsibility of protecting the middle classes. It was with their support, he claimed, that the middle classes achieved, at the beginning of this century, political recognition from the oligarchy; 'it was with their protection that it later consolidated itself in power; and now it is with their intervention that it seeks to ward off the threat posed by the popular sectors that it is incapable of leading'. Nun concluded by saying that the military in Latin America is not a progressive force because its relationship with the middle class inhibits social change and development. The significance of Nun's and Needler's arguments is to cast doubts on the military as a force for national unity and development through its identification with the middle classes. If this is the situation in Latin America with a substantial and older middle class, one would logically expect it to be worse in Africa and Asia with an even less cohesive middle class. But this may not necessarily follow.

4
Military Nationalism and State Power

The modernising role of the military has been based, in the body of the literature, largely on the formal organisational model which relates to the ideology of the military officers. It is claimed that certain ideological themes inhere in the military as a profession. These themes, it is argued, are grounded in the social composition of the officer corps and in their education and professional experience. One of the most central and pervasive of these is nationalism. 'At the core of these themes', Janowitz states, 'is a strong sense of nationalism and national identity, with pervasive tones of xenophobia' (1964, p. 63). Finer (1962) argued, in the same vein, that by the very nature of the appointed task of the military (that is, national defence), the military is, and has to be, indoctrinated with nationalism. Nationalism forms the distinctive military ideology. The whole *esprit de corps* of the military, without which it would have no fighting spirit, is founded on the supposed heavy emphasis on the national identity.

If this characterisation is true of the Western military model, how true is it of the Third World military, particularly of the African military? To what extent have the Third World militaries espoused nationalist values? If they have, what is the character of these nationalist values and what may account for differences or similarities with those of the Western world?

Nationalism connotes more than merely an anti-foreign orientation. Revolutionary fervour born of anti-domination attitudes, values and actions is but one dimension of nationalism. This concept, in its more traditional meaning, emerged during the building of the nation-states in Western Europe in the eighteenth and nineteenth centuries and implies a kind of commitment, loyalty and dedication to the building of a new society as well as the generation of obedience to one central focus of authority (Odetola, 1978). European nationalism was due, in part, to the rise of the bourgeoisie and the merchant class whose activities, interests and demands began to transcend the local communities and which situation required the establishment of large centres.

Nationalism in most of the Third World reflects not only a feeling against domination but also is an index of efforts to build viable nations, sometimes out of widely disparate groups and communities. It therefore entails competition of some kind among the various institutions that are capable of performing such a task (for instance, political parties, the bureaucracy, the military, and so on). The task of building the nation in the Third World brings into the fore adversary relations between any one or a combination of the above institutions on the one hand, and other groups such as the middle classes, whether they are serving foreign, domestic or their own interests, on the other hand. This nation-building task also may set these institutions themselves on a clear collision course. Thus, political modernisation creates a dynamic relationship among societal institutions which in turn affects what kind of state we have, and what kind of state power is established. Therefore, the second line of inquiry in this chapter will be the influence military regimes have had in Africa on the autonomy and power of the state as an entity. There are two hypotheses guiding this chapter. First, most of the African military regimes have espoused nationalist rhetoric but the evidence provided by their action and performances gives a mixed picture. The second hypothesis which relates to nationalism, nation-building and state power is that in many African nations, the military, in displaying a sense of nationalism, has stood as a pivotal force among several competing adversary institutions, classes and ethnic groups.

In writing of the Middle East armies, Halpern (1963) stated that the military has served as the symbol of national sovereignty and is committed to nationalism and social reform. These militaries, he further asserted, have served as national standard-bearers when others who claimed that role have proved ineffective. They are possessed with a sense of national mission transcending parochial, regional or economic interests or kinship ties and these qualities seemed to be much more clearly defined here than elsewhere in the society. The Middle Eastern armies, Halpern wrote, constituted a unity in the face of the corrupt and unprincipled competition of domestic interests and the threats of foreign imperialism. Pye (1962) believed that the army is an unambiguous symbol of national authority. Levy (1966), arguing in favour of the military, stated that the military harbours radical feelings about the status of the nation as a whole.

It is true that in 1948 the Arab state militaries believed themselves to be more disciplined, co-ordinated and morally dedicated than the rest of the society and therefore entered into a war with Israel. This may be regarded as a true nationalist feeling. But it is, on the other hand, true that the same military struggled against domestic forces which were in turn fighting for more rapid social and political transformation of the society (Bienen, 1968). Political analysts have based such internal repression on the support of the same military for some external agency.

Many Third World militaries, because of their structural dependence (for arms, training and assistance) on the armed forces of the metropolitan nations, may not find it easy to espouse true nationalist feelings. Horowitz (1966) emphasised that military assistance undermines the purpose of independence and that even though the military in the Third World may think of itself as distinctively nationalistic, it still carries on the traditions of the old colonial armies. McAlister (1966) noted that the new imperialism in Latin America is conducted largely through US military policy whose principal instrument is military assistance. Latin American nations were thus faced with the cruel choice of either supporting the USA's policy for developing counter-insurgency capabilities and thereby jeopardising their self-created images as national redeemers, or supporting national redemption and jeopardising foreign aid. Horowitz (1966) has concluded that what has taken place is the external foreign management of internal conflicts.

In Africa, Murray (1966) asserted that the role of the military is straightforwardly counter-revolutionary. Murray used the term 'revolutionary' to mean truly nationalistic change in the social structure. The first Ghana coup, Murray argued, was a case of returning Ghana firmly into the capitalist orbit. This he prophesied would encourage the formation in a new way of a powerful local bourgeoisie and, that privatisation would proceed since it was immediately announced after the 1966 military coup that nine of the state corporations were to be dismantled. Murray further argued that the whole long-term economic programme of the Convention People's Party of Ghana would be negated and that Ghana's economic future would be effectively managed in the interests of an international condominium of creditors. Murray's prophecy was fulfilled in the activities of General Akran and his council whose collaboration with foreign interests ended in disgrace.

In fact, the values and orientations of the officers who led the coup were decidedly anti-nationalistic. Colonel Afrifa and Major General Ocran displayed a strong and deep personal commitment to the British military tradition and this competed very markedly with whatever nationalistic feelings they possessed. In discussing Ghanaian military history Ocran wrote that its members stood, fought and died as soldiers who were loyal to the call to defend the 'Commonwealth, their country and Africa's freedom'. One would have thought that for a true nationalist, Africa's freedom should precede the Commonwealth in order of priority but the answer can be found in Afrifa's account of the Ghana coup (Price, 1971a). One of the reasons for his bitterness against Nkrumah's rule was that Nkrumah paid lip-service to Ghana's membership of the British Commonwealth of nations and that Nkrumah had proceeded to undermine 'the bonds that bind us in this great union of peoples' (Price, 1971a, p. 404). Afrifa further argued that as far as the Commonwealth was concerned, Ghana should be no different from Canada, Australia and New Zealand, and that Nkrumah had proceeded to discredit the British Commonwealth of nations under the guise of African unity and a policy of non-alignment. Price has argued that both men perceived the end of colonialism in their own country (an occasion for deepest nationalist feeling) in a non-nationalist way. General Ocran argued, in an obviously patronising way, that the British acted with good intentions in handing over power and said rather disparagingly that those who received the power (Nkrumah, and so on) had had grandiose aims. Afrifa, in the same vein, wrote that Nkrumah played hard on the illiteracy of his fellow men and women and had rather impetuously insisted on immediate self-government. The British, he suggested, had no alternative since a step-by-step process was unacceptable to Nkrumah.

Afrifa also violently disagreed with Nkrumah on the issue of independence for Rhodesia. He believed that the UK government was capable of dealing with the Rhodesian issue. He felt Nkrumah was making an unnecessary fuss about the matter and that Nkrumah's attempt to break diplomatic relations with Britain and thereby threaten the existence of the Commonwealth was a part of Nkrumah's grand design for self-glorification. Afrifa perceived the Ghanaian military role in the Congo crisis as merely interventionist.

Many African leaders and people have regarded the Congo issue as a test of African nationalism against imperialism and white racism. But many Ghanaian officers before General Acheampong have demonstrated very positive sympathy with British traditions (Price, 1971a, p. 416). A highly significant point is that Afrifa gave precedence to his UN role and resented pressure on himself as a defender of Ghanaian national interest.

The body of the literature in recent times has concentrated on the dependency model (Frank, 1971; Furtado, 1964; Rodney, 1972; Cardoso, 1967). The lack of development of African nations and also of the rest of the Third World countries has been explained not by internal factors in these societies but essentially by the economic and political needs of the imperialist metropolitan powers. In other words, African underdevelopment has been defined in terms of the capitalism of Europe and the exploitative and monetary needs of these societies. For example, Rodney (1972) has said that the Western nations tied the fortunes of African nations to the highly exploitative loan terms which they gave to these countries. That is, the surplus production of these nations which would have been used to develop the societies were used to finance these loans. It is also true that during colonial times, Britain tied the production and surplus external trade of her African colonies to her own international money market. Thus she made it impossible for these colonies to develop any independent external trade system.

Such an approach as this presents a great deal of information about external trade, and also about the processes by which these nations have been exploited. However, it offers very little information about the internal processes that may aid or generate these external exploitations. In other words, this approach has made it very difficult to explain the variations among African nations, and this is the function of this chapter. What I will be focusing on particularly in this chapter, therefore, is the attempt to explain these variations among some African nations in terms of those nations' relationship with the rest of the world economy and also in terms of the relations of class structure and ethnic demands to the apparatus of the state.

The literature on African development has neglected to consider, on one hand, the structure of class relations and the pressure of ethnic demands and, on the other hand, the need to mobilise resources and to enhance the power of the state. In almost all African nations the development of an industrial bourgeois class is weak, and therefore the state must break down class barriers to industrialisation and either create, greatly strengthen, or substitute for an independent entrepreneurial class (Horowitz, 1976). One of the greatest problems facing African nations after colonialism has been the mobilisation of internal resources, and since, as we said earlier, the bourgeois class is weak, the state has to assume great power in directing and controlling the economy of these nations. Hence, the role of the military in African nations over the past fifteen years has been in the direction of strengthening state power in an attempt to create the preconditions necessary for development in African societies. We can then ask the question, to what extent is the state apparatus centralised and autonomous because of the special role it has to play in development and change?

In spite of its negative results and effects in so many African nations, one can say that the history of military coups and military rule in African nations is the history of an attempt to build state power for development. Since the entrepreneurial bourgeois class is so weak and the need to build a powerful state apparatus imperative it becomes necessary to consider the relations of top civil and military élites with the class and ethnic structure of society. In Nigeria and Ghana, the top bureaucrats and top military officers, while they have not been recruited from the dominant industrial and commercial classes, have vested interests in the means of production in their societies. For example, in Nigeria today a large number of retired civil servants and military officers own farms with extensive acreages, and they also have large interests in the production of petroleum, in industrial development, and so on. This is also true of Ethiopia. Therefore, there is an alliance between the bureaucracy and the rising bourgeoisie.

Therefore, the issue is that the state apparatus in the nations under consideration is not autonomous. The attempt in Ethiopian society to create an autonomous state apparatus is a feeble one. All the military regimes have depended on the bureaucracy (or civil service) which has a deep interest in controlling the means of production and of distribution. In African societies which are particularly geared towards the distribution of imported goods, those who own the means of distribution are as important in the development process as those who own the means of production. For example, the decay of railway transportation in African societies has occurred, in large measure, because of the lack of attention given to this state-wide and state-controlled means of transportation. Rather, loans have been given to businessmen to establish transportation industries which have taken away the profit of the railways. A state apparatus which has the potential for playing an innovative economic role is centralised, efficient and, most significantly of all, autonomous (Horowitz, 1976). A bureaucratic state apparatus can be considered autonomous when those who hold the highest civil and military bureaucratic positions satisfy two conditions: (1) they are not recruited from the large commercial or industrial classes nor do they have personal vested interests in the dominant means of production, and, we can add, of distribution in Africa; (2) they are not controlled by or subordinate to any party apparatus which may represent the dominant classes or ethnic groups (Horowitz, 1976). It is possible, however, to make a clear distinction between state power and class power if the state is an autonomous state.

We will now briefly make a theoretical excursion into the relationship between state autonomy and development. Horowitz claimed that the control of the governing apparatus is a source of power which is independent of that held by a class because of its control over the means of production and of distribution. That is, if the bureaucrats own the apparatus of government in a state, they are independent of the business class because the bureaucrats control the means of production and distribution in a state-directed economy.

In modernising agriculture in Nigeria, it is the bureaucracy which distributes tractors, fertilisers, and so on as well as dictates the price of the commodities which the farmers produce. It is also the bureaucracy which gives import licences to the business class.

It is interesting to note, therefore, that those who control state power in African nations are personally committed by their vested interests to the present organisation of the economy. In a counter position, Huntington (1969) emphasised the role of the political party as the instrument to create an autonomous polity. But we can ask the question, what about the political party which articulates capitalist interests and makes it appear a universalistic interest of the entire society? (Miliband, 1969; Horowitz, 1976). While Poulatzas (1970) sees the state as controlled by economic forces, Huntington perceives the polity to be independent of economic forces.

The issue now is, how does the relationship between state apparatus and the dominant classes or ethnic groups acting as independent variables determine the type and rate of economic development in African nations? We must say at the outset that in Africa it is not easy nor even clear how to determine the class base of power. It is clear that no élite is now dominant; that is, there are competing forces which gave rise to an unstable state autonomy.

The conflict among the various élite groups can also be seen in terms of the desire of each group to have a share in the control of state power which in turn controls the economy of the nation. It is important, therefore, to see the role of the military as a pivot and as an arbiter to determine and enhance the apparatus of state power in an attempt to ensure that the conflict does not destroy the nation.

We can argue certainly, and with a great many examples, although with some modifications, that in African societies the military can guarantee the state autonomy far more than can the parliamentary liberal-democratic system. Examples have shown that in many African nations, where the military regime is not in power the one-party authoritarian system has taken power. In Senegal, for example, we have President Senghor ruling with a one-party system for over a decade; similarly in the Ivory Coast we have Houphouet-Boigny. We had Nkrumah in Ghana and presently Kaunda in Zambia and Nyerere in Tanzania. The military bureaucracy functions to guarantee state autonomy for two reasons: (1) the military is more likely than civil servants to be free of ties to the economically dominant class or ethnic group; (2) force is usually needed to break internal and external class alliances that stand in the way of real development (Horowitz, 1976).

Therefore, the argument is strong that the military acts to liberate the state apparatus from class and ethnic fetters in order to promote development. This, however, does not make the military a clean, non-corrupt organisation. The argument we are making is different. It is simply that the military comes to perform functions which the liberal parliamentary democratic system has failed to perform. Horowitz has argued further that liberal parliamentary regimes controlled by either the landed class in Latin America or bourgeois interests in some parts of Africa have proved unable to promote development in the Third World for a number of reasons: (1) the liberal system permits the bourgeoisie which is tied to external capital to dominate the state apparatus; (2) the bourgeoisie finds it safer to invest externally (in many

African nations the capitalist class have invested quite a sizeable amount of national surplus in Swiss banks); (3) international capitalism guarantees some measure of security and therefore the African business class or bourgeoisie are not in any way, as we argued earlier in the beginning of this chapter, comparable to the earlier European entrepreneurial bourgeoisie. The comparison can be invidious here since in the state-directed capitalist mode of development, such as will be seen later in describing the Nigerian and Ghanaian situations, the military itself has not entirely succeeded in limiting the activities of the national bourgeoisie.

Again, we cannot argue that many individual military officers have not put away national wealth in Swiss banks. Such acts by these officers are quite unpatriotic. But we are arguing that, as a nationalistic organisation, the military has succeeded in breaking more sharply with imperial domination than the party systems have done. In terms of their effect on national development, there is a great difference between the amount of money stolen by individual military officers, on the one hand, and the general inability of the African business classes to take the necessary risks for entrepreneurial development, on the other.

The next logical question we may ask, therefore, is, what during the military era constitutes the posture of African states towards external capitalism? In answering this question, it is necessary to state first that the ethnic conflicts as well as the fluid situation among the élite groups have rendered the internal polity of African nations weak. Therefore, my answer is that the posture of African societies to external capitalism is weak not simply as a result of the economic dependence of those societies on European and American societies, but simply as a result of the political weakness and dependence that operates internally in these societies. Therefore, in order to achieve the twin goals of effective national cohesion and integration, the military assumes and fully expresses nationalism, and therefore becomes the focal pivot of rule. In doing this, the military has to contend with various pressures in fostering economic development.

As I have maintained, important among these pressures are ethnic pressures and pressures from emerging élite groups. I will therefore argue that the varying strength of ethnic and class forces and the ways in which the military governments in Africa relate to them are the crucial factors with which to measure the variations among African nations today in terms of their development and change. The military cannot but take these forces seriously into account. This will be discussed more fully in the next chapter.

We will now turn to see how the military has used the state apparatus to foster national development. There are two main ways in which the military has done this in Africa, the first of which is the state-initiated national capitalist development. First, the features of this type of development are as follows: the state apparatus is controlled by the military and civil bureaucracy; and, as we can see, in Ghana, Nigeria and many other African nations it is controlled by the military. Foreign firms are nationalised, and at the same time the military encourages some measures of foreign investment in these societies. Successive Nigerian military governments have come with decrees which nationalise or limit the participation of foreign investment in Nigerian trade and production. Taxes and banks, and so on, are established to aid national development. In Nigeria, the capital tax was introduced in an effort to limit the transfer of Nigerian money overseas as profits. National bourgeois investment is also encouraged.

The situation outlined above greatly enhances the position and power of civil bureaucrats. For example, in both Nigeria and Ghana we have had situations where super-permanent secretaries developed. During the Gowon regime in Nigeria, a few permanent secretaries became so powerful that they more or less assumed the role of executives plenipotentiary. While retired civil bureaucrats, ex-military officers and the like have joined the national bourgeoisie, the state bureaucracy, however, still dominates or manages the growing national bourgeoisie. One way in which the Nigerian state bureaucracy has attempted to limit the power of the bourgeoisie is to encourage the enactment of certain decrees and laws banning the participation of academic and several other competing groups in national politics. This has effectively limited the ability of groups other than the bureaucracy to exercise power over the growing national bourgeoisie. Even in post-military Nigeria and Ghana, where the bourgeoisie dominate the political party and the national assemblies, the civil service or bureaucrats still effectively control and regulate the new assemblies. Therefore the banks, industries, and so on, have remained concentrated in fewer and fewer hands. A recent example in Nigeria today is the attempt of men in the national assemblies to gain control of the means of distribution. There has been recent evidence in the national daily newspapers in Nigeria of attempts by national assembly men to obtain import licences and corner a substantial sector of the distribution network.

Therefore, it is possible to argue that this mode of development may result in greater inequality than before. Thus, while in general in Africa the military may succeed in establishing state power as an autonomous entity, it is quite possible that the bureaucracy gains an independent means of power in this way and consequently directs development in a direction that is initially unanticipated. This is what is happening in Nigeria and Ghana today. In Ethiopia, the military consciously mobilises the working class to combat the growing bourgeois power. For example, they have established the Peasant Associations as well as mobilised urban salaried groups in housing associations called Kebeles.

In Nigeria and Ghana there is a new working class emerging from urban salaried groups which may eventually challenge the political system. The argument here is that one way in which the military can sustain the state power that it is establishing is to build alternative bases of power such as are found in the mobilisation of Ethiopian peasant groups, the urban proletariat, and so on. Horowitz (1976) argued that autonomous bureaucrats have never succeeded in organising a mass political party, although it is apparent that they can have a hand in controlling the economy of the nation. One important feature of this mode of development is the eventual alignment of the national bourgeoisie with external financial capital which eventually may begin to stifle development, a situation that is observable in Ghana and to some extent in Nigeria. This is simply because production is stagnating as distribution and importation of external goods increases. This situation often leads to military coups and instability unless the military builds its own base of support.

The second type of development is the state-directed socialist development, such as in Ethiopia. This type of development attempts to destroy feudalism and take over economic development projects, as well as to mobilise the working classes and the peasants. Examples of these efforts to destroy the landed feudal classes abound in Latin America. A similar example has been Mengistu regime's taking over and destroying the property and the power of the landed gentry and nobility in Ethiopia. However, we must note that while this appears Utopian and clearly different from what is going on or has gone on in Nigeria and Ghana, the masses have never really succeeded, as I shall discuss later, in directing the processes of development. It is true to say that the power base created by the Mengistu regime in Peasant Associations and in mobilising the urban proletariat have not resulted in yielding real power to the urban proletariats and peasants. It may indeed be correct to say that participation is to some extent limited to the top military officers and bureaucrats. One other feature of this type of development is the greater use of coercion. All the attempts by the leftist and other groups to stand up to Mengistu have been crushed by very strong coercive force.

It is also to be noted that where national resources and markets are not large enough, as in Ethiopia and Cuba, to support autonomous development of the state, then crisis ensues. Such crises may be limited to outward migrations of the national bourgeoisie, as in Ghana, or continued internal wars, as in Ethiopia. What happens then is that the state becomes increasingly dependent for its economic and political resources upon an external power. This is clearly demonstrated by Mengistu's attempt to ally with the Soviet Union, and the same condition has been demonstrated earlier in Fidel Castro's efforts to move towards Russia. Even in civilian-controlled states, where attempts have been made to strengthen and stabilise state power, this trend has also been noted. For example, in Tanzania where resources and the market are small Nyerere's efforts have been directed towards an alliance with some great power, for example, China, even though he claims to be totally independent of alignment with any nations. Also, in the former French West African nations of the Ivory Coast and Senegal dependence on France is still very great.

We have seen in the two models described that the military and the bureaucracy have become very powerful. Thus in Africa as well as Latin America, which preceded Africa in terms of development, the military and the bureaucracy become powerful when the need to mobilise resources and strengthen the state becomes imperative. We can argue, therefore, that one feature of modern development in these nations is that the later development comes to them, the more powerful the apparatus of the state bureaucracy. Thus we can argue with Horowitz (1976) that the power of modern states is defined not by the power of the bourgeoisie under capitalism or of the proletariat under communism but by the distance which is put between political power and economic classes and/or ethnic groups. Horowitz has claimed that in this respect Hegel is more important than Marx. The state controls the claims of ethnic groups and of emerging élite groups and social classes. It has been more responsive to the more powerful ethnic groups in the societies. But basically, the emerging Nigerian, Ghanaian, Ethiopian and for that matter any African state is deriving and legitimising its own power from limiting ethnic and class power that may tend to disintegrate the nation. Very clear examples are in the military attempt to stop the secession of Northern Nigeria in 1967, as well as the four-year war to prevent the Biafran secession. Thus we can argue that the Nigerian state has adequately taken care of the ethnic interests of the north and the east both by limiting them and by incorporating them. One feature of military rule in Ethiopia that has been neglected is the effort of the military to strengthen the state by preventing secession and encroachment of its borders.

One comparison we can make between Latin American nations and African nations is that the state in Latin America is developing where there is already a mature and developed class system, and this situation in Latin America limits the power of the state. On the other hand, in African nations the state and the classes are growing together. This more or less simultaneous development of class and state has been hastened by the military regimes which came to centralise state power at a time when the national bourgeoisie was rising fast in African nations. Thus, unlike in Latin America, the state in Africa can effectively subordinate the national bourgeoisie. General Muritala Muhammed immediately attempted to arrest the growing power of the bureaucracy when he came to power. He in fact instructed specifically that permanent secretaries and civil servants should not be present at certain important decision-making meetings of the Supreme Military Council.

In Nigeria today, under a civil presidential democratic constitution, the National Assembly and the national bureaucracy are attempting to limit the power of the national bourgeoisie. This does not contradict the position or compromise the interests of the men in the National Assembly itself. For example, the committees of the National Assembly have invited several business groups and top trade unionists to come before it to testify in the effort to pass bills designed to limit the power of the national bourgeoisie. However, this situation is creating a new type of conflict. For example, when the men of the National Assembly in Nigeria attempted to establish high salary grades for themselves, the nation protested. The National Assembly therefore contacted several top businessmen to find out how much they were earning in an attempt to fix their own salaries. The furore that followed this in the newspapers underlined this new kind of conflict. On the other hand, working-class organisations, though sizeable and somewhat encouraged by the military in Nigeria and Ghana, are not powerful enough like Latin American trade unions to hold the state to ransom. Also the African peasantry has not developed any revolutionary fervour strong enough to challenge the state. The point I am trying to make, therefore, is that the military in the African context has built or is building the strength of the state in situations which favour it.

Is the military enabling the state to fulfil its tasks of growing and, therefore, developing a strong posture towards Europe and North America? Because of competing goals of ethnic and class interests in development, many African nations can now concentrate on developing the power of the state which will eventually help to develop a nationalist posture. Whereas in Latin America the military is trying to liberate the state from the bourgeoisie, in African states the military is also mediating ethnic versus élite group claims. We can argue, therefore, that the spate of military coups in Africa is a function of the rise of state power. That is, the need to centralise power over and against the claims of ethnicity, class and religion in African nations is important in determining the rate, strength and length of military regimes. The military creates the opportunity to achieve national unity by stimulating nationalism. Identification with nation becomes more important than identity with ethnic or class claims. This is not to say that there is no tribalism in the military organisation, but that the military is an institution capable of generating national cohesion and integration. Failure to achieve that goal can be due in large part to structural relations among various social groups in the society in their attempt to control state power. As in Latin America, the military in Africa acts as a pivot guaranteeing state autonomy and this is a condition for development. I am saying, therefore, that a state has come to function as a coercive mechanism which will not tolerate those who may attempt to limit its growth on behalf of any ethnic, class, or religious interests. And as a champion of autonomous state power, the military in Africa assumes an increasing role in development and change. It thus becomes a focal point for creating the preconditions for development.

The military remains in a formal alliance with the bureaucracy in African nations because it is the bureaucracy which manages state power. Ethnic and élite group interests in Nigeria and Ghana and feudal and ethnic interests in Ethiopia bargain to protect and enhance their own share of the national cake. In Ethiopia, Emperor Haile Selassie attempted to create a small élite group of military officers and bureaucrats but he got more than he bargained for. It was precisely the small élite group he built that later formed the bulwark of the bureaucracy which the military came to depend upon so much. In Nigeria and Ghana, the rising national bourgeoisie sought military protection for securing their own system in 1965–6 but were themselves removed from power for thirteen years in Nigeria and somewhat intermittently for shorter periods in Ghana. Therefore, the military can function both to coerce and mobilise and also to check the power of those who installed it in power in the first place.

Ethnic and class forces in African states are so powerful that they cannot be ignored by any aspirants to power. They are, however, not powerful enough to monopolise state power. Through the imposition of taxes, restrictions on licences, and so on, as well as the limitation of political choice, the African militaries have sought to narrow the powers of rising national bourgeoisies. For the Nigerian business class, successive military budgetary controls have banned the importation of item after item, and created the special and allegedly obnoxious Form X which has severely limited the economic profits of the externally oriented and dependent capitalist business class. Similarly in Brazil, Schmitter (1973, p. 79) has argued that military rulers have followed policies depriving most political actors of their autonomy and proceeded to narrow the area of permissible political choice, as well as seeking to eliminate all alternative systems except self-perpetuation in power.

We may then ask, how in Nigeria and Ghana, for example, is the national bourgeoisie growing and how well is it doing? What the Nigerian military has done in spite of oil wealth is to clamp down on ethnic chauvinism through the use of coercion and to stimulate economic development and limit what the bourgeoisie is gaining in this respect because it is assumed that wealth will trickle down from the top.

On the other hand, the peasantry is stagnating and losing. Agriculture, which has been the mainstay of the economic growth of Nigeria, has declined rapidly. Even though banks and loan systems were established for farmers, the advantages have not been felt by the peasantry. On the other hand, the national bourgeoisie are skimming off the cream by taking charge of the distribution of fertilisers and other products that the farmers need. In Ethiopia the military has clamped down completely on the gains made by the bourgeois class but has not succeeded in limiting bureaucratic power. In other words, differences between Nigeria and Ethiopia can be explained by the varying attempts of the military to strengthen state power by making it autonomous of class or ethnic power. It can be stated, therefore, that the institutionalisation of authoritarian systems by the African military will lead to a move towards increased nationalism.

The state in Africa performs more than the mere functions of integrating various groups and group interests and providing the basis for national cohesion. It also allocates revenue to state and local government as well as allocating imported goods such as milk, rice, fish, meat, and so on, to national or sub-national groups. State capitalism performs these functions where the market forces have not established their own networks of sales distribution and allocation. Thus the military in Africa guarantees a place for the state which it would have been difficult to establish through the liberal-democratic system. In general, therefore, in spite of its weaknesses in many other directions, the role of the military has been mainly geared towards strengthening national claims on the one hand and checking the claims of imperialism on the other hand. I am arguing again, as I have done elsewhere (Odetola, 1978), that we cannot claim that political democracy is superior to military rule in gaining the desired end in development and change.

It has been shown that military rule can establish nationalism which in turn can strengthen state power over the claims of other national and sub-national groups in creating the preconditions for development. Even though the military may not succeed in achieving visible and measurable development, or indeed may show evidence of economic decline in real terms, it must be clear that it has made efforts in several African countries to achieve the precondition for development. The unfortunate thing is that the body of the literature has confused military rule with totalitarianism in the effort to show it inferior to political democracy.

5
The Military and National Economy

The literature on military sociology dealing with the economic performance of ruling militaries has hardly gone beyond critiques of the role of military rulers as economic managers. Such works have often compared the performance of military rulers with that of civilian politicians, usually by the use of aggregate cross-national data (Nordlinger, 1970; Adelman and Morris, 1967; McKinlay, 1975). This approach has tended to arrive at negative conclusions about the military. For example, McKinlay (1976) concluded that military governments have proved no more economically competent than civilian ones. Nordlinger (1970) also said that the military are poor economic managers.

It is, of course, true that the record of the military in dealing with economic crisis in Africa has often not been good, for example in Ghana, the Central African Republic and Mali. It has been claimed that military training does not include the control of the money supply (*West Africa*, November 1980, p. 2344).

Therefore, since we can claim that military officers have not been trained as economic managers, it will probably not advance theory to concentrate further on how poor economic managers they are merely by examining cross-national economic indices. My aim in this work is to go one step beyond this level in order to see what structural changes the militaries have instituted and what factors have acted as constraints in achieving the goals they have set for themselves and with what consequences.

More often than not, the military in Africa have assumed power to handle crisis situations in the economy and in the polity. One should therefore not expect overnight miracles. This is why my attention will not be restricted to the economic results attained but will also extend to the mechanisms and processes adopted to institute changes: what these changes are and why they were instituted in the first place; and even whether the military was merely holding the economy in check by temporarily halting the introduction of any innovative policies.

An analysis of structural changes would focus more on the policies made by the military and less on the minutiae of day-to-day handling of the economy. That is, an emphasis on the framework of military orientation may reveal more about the nature and character of military institutions since merely examining results of economic management through such indices as Gross National Products (GNP) does not make any clear separation between the activities of other élite groups like the bureaucrats and the businessmen and those of the military. We will thus be better able to understand why the military rulers have failed where they have, and vice versa. We will also be able to relate economic changes with other societal changes such as changes in the stratification system (mass–élite, rural–urban relations, and so on) and with other sectors of total development such as national integration and nation-building. Policy orientations and decisions reveal the visions the actors have for their communities.

Development of theory in this area has concentrated on the military ability to carry out certain programmes by means of applying the military organisational attribute of coercion to mobilise resources. To advance theory in this area, I will examine the effect of this attribute on economic change but more significantly explore the relationship between coercion, military nationalism, the military desire to build state power and military corporate interest. It is my contention that these factors acting in some combination will explain variations in military economic performance among military-ruled African states.

In Chapter 4, I have proposed and argued the thesis that military nationalism is primary to military effort at state-building. Coercion has been the basic instrument which enables the state-building process to proceed. First, however, I will examine each of the variables of coercion, nationalism and military corporate interest from a theoretical standpoint as they relate to economic development. Then attention will focus on the two types of development (state-capitalist and state-socialist models) in the military-ruled African nations discussed in Chapter 4. This is with a view to explaining in detail the varying emphasis on public as opposed to private sector development, to explain the different priorities accorded to heavy as against light industrial development as well as to industrial as opposed to agricultural development, and to explain money flows, processes of inflation control, taxation, and so on.

Coercion and Economic Development

The organisational characteristic of coercion in the military is very effective in mobilising resources and achieving a breakthrough in economic development (Levy, 1966; Halpern, 1962). It has been argued that when there is no single-party apparatus with a unified goal, 'the military may be the only group capable of preparing the ground for further economic breakthrough and that the civilian sector appears even less able than the military to spur the processes of development' (Horowitz, 1966, p. 334).

There is for Third World nations a wide and real disparity between democracy and development. There is a high congruence between coercion and even terrorism on the one hand and development on the other and a far lower congruence between consensus and development (Horowitz, 1966; Odetola, 1978, p. 22). Theoretically, therefore, a relationship between the political structure of coercion and economic development can be posited. The element of coercion is itself directly linked to the character of military domination. The structure of coercion, Horowitz has further argued, involves relationships among the productive sectors of the economy; the military encourages the public over the private sector and the public sector character of Third World economies will make them more subject to military pressure. Thus, since decision-making is in the hands of the state, the ability of private industry to perform a countervailing power role is severely circumscribed. Therefore, the military attempts to mobilise all sectors by embracing them in an overall consensus based on the needs of the whole people (Horowitz, 1966, p. 364). The ability to mobilise all sectors and resources in a 'national' cause quickens production and limits consumption and it derives from the centralised, hierarchical and disciplined nature of the military. As will be discovered, however, mobilisation may have the unanticipated effect of raising purchasing power and therefore of increasing consumption.

Horowitz (1966) brought empirical evidence to prove this position. The data involved growth rates and per capita GNP output between 1960 and 1967. He grouped developing non-socialist nations into three clusters: (*a*) single-party countries under military rule with high developmental outputs and a high GNP rate over the decade; (*b*) democratic or relatively democratic states with low GNP levels; and (*c*) countries that do not reveal any clear patterns in terms of conflict and consensus in development. He found that a cluster of countries in the high-developmental high-militarisation group were the following countries, with their annual average percentage increase in GNP figures over the period of analysis: Israel, 7·6; Libya, 19·2 (even though oil has contributed to the figure it is still impressive); Greece, 7·5; Nicaragua, 7·5; Iraq, 6·9; Iran, 7·9; Taiwan, 10·0; Ivory Coast, 7·5; Jordan, 8·8; Bolivia, 4·9; Thailand, 7·1; South Korea, 7·6. From the above line-up of nations, Horowitz concluded that development correlates well with authoritarianism. While figures in the data are self-evident, it will be observed that no variables were controlled for, to show that the relationship remains unchanged after the control. Such variables could be (1) degree of urbanisation, (2) sudden discovery of new resources and (3) pattern of international trade.

At the other end of the scale are countries which represent a far less militarised category (although some of them have become militarised since the period of analysis). These are: Venezuela, 1·0; Argentina, 1·2; Uruguay, 1·0; Honduras, 1·8; Colombia, 1·2; Guatemala, 1·9; Brazil, 1·2 (increasing to 9·2 under military rule between 1964 and 1971); Dominican Republic, 7·0; Senegal, 1·2; Ecuador, 1·1; Tunisia, 1·5; Paraguay, 1·0; Morocco, 0·3; The Philippines, 1·0; Ceylon, 1·3; Kenya, 0·3; Uganda, 1·2 (no figures have been available after Amin). The conclusion drawn from this set of figures is that a low rate of development can be associated with non-military character of political mobilisation in the second category of countries. The third group of nations constitutes a kind of middle group and includes Chile, 2·4; Jamaica, 2·1; Mexico, 2·8; Gabon, 3·2; Costa Rica, 2·4; Peru, 3·2; Turkey, 2·7; Malaysia, 2·5; Salvador, 2·7; Egypt, 2·1; Pakistan, 3·1; and Ethiopia, 2·7. This last cluster represents the 'most experimental politically' and Horowitz emphasises the experimentation in Pakistan, Egypt, Costa Rica and Chile. The conclusion was that it is not quite clear what this middle cluster represented, but that it is distinct. Clearly, factors other than the political character of internal conflict in consensus must be significantly operative. Both Pakistan and Egypt were either constantly in a state of preparedness for or were actually engaged in war–a situation representing a constant drain on resources. While Jamaica was at this time involved in a federation experiment and Egypt in an empire-building attempt, the internal orientations of mobilisations (which is the crucial factor) were different–Egypt was more socialist and more military while Jamaica was definitely less so on both counts.

I have found strong support for Horowitz's position with respect to Nigeria. Between 1964 and 1966 (the civilian regime), the GNP level was 4·2; in 1969–71 (the military regime) it jumped to 9·1 and in 1972 to 12·1. For each of the three years of the military regime, the GNP rose above the projected figure for 1985. The findings become more impressive when it is realised that it is not only the highest GNP in tropical Africa but among the highest for any Third World country during any period of its development even when the contribution of oil is deducted (Odetola, 1978). What is the theoretical explanation for those cases where Horowitz's argument appears to have failed? The operation of military coercion reveals that coercion must achieve national consensus for reaching desired national goals. One such goal, it is assumed, is the creation of effective state power. Linked to this is the assumed public character of Third World development. State power and the public nature of development are positively correlated. Hence national consensus, state power and, therefore, the enhancement of the public sector can be achieved by means of the coercive character of military rule. Sometimes, of course, it may be difficult to contain or circumscribe the countervailing influence of the private sector such as businessmen and trade unions, or of other social groups such as the intelligentsia, politicians, bureaucrats or ethnic and sub-national groups who may be determined to subvert national goals. Where these are powerful, as in Ethiopia, the declared national goals of socialism can be subverted. Indeed the unusual dependence of the African military on the bureaucracy quite clearly lays open military goals to the possibility of subversion.

The problem that may be faced in reaching such consensus to my mind explains why Nigerian and Ghanaian ruling militaries have chosen to adopt the model of state-controlled capitalist development rather than an outright socialist one. In Nigeria, the successive military governments have openly avoided discussing the issue of a national ideology (Obasanjo, 1980) and have enshrined private sector roles for businessmen in the new constitution. The problems that would be raised by social groups, for example, ethnic groups as well as the emerging élite group, may be too formidable to be solved all at once. In theory, coercion must not only ensure that norms of behaviour are enforced, but must also perform norm-setting functions. Where agents of coercion have been observed to fail in any or both of these roles, they have often failed to generate the desired force that would create consensus so necessary to resources mobilisation. Thus, as we have demonstrated, the military has often failed to enforce its own organisation norms, much less generate new norms in the society. However, where there has been appreciable success in performing these roles, the general populace has showed great enthusiasm to reach this consensus. The level of enthusiasm that welcomed Muhammed's purge of the Nigerian public service, of Rawlings's killing of proven corrupt officers and Mengistu's land use reforms is sufficient testimony to this. Even where there is a modest effort to enforce norms, as in the redeployment of military governors by Gowon in Nigeria, evidence of support by the population at large is clear. The African societies appear ripe to be mobilised for development–only a sustained effort to achieve this appears inadequate or even lacking.

In general, the achievements of coercive efforts towards national consensus can be subverted by the rising national bourgeoisie, and also by the inability of the agents of coercion to properly enforce or create norms which are the essence of coercion.

Contrary evidence to Horowitz's position has been provided by Nordlinger (1970). Culling data from Adelman and Morris (1967) he advanced the hypothesis that the politicised military do not act as agents of modernisation. He added a corollary that where the military has been found to encourage industrialisation, it has done so for reasons of corporate interests. Seventy-four non-Western, non-communist countries were selected. The first group were those in which the military was in direct control during some part of 1957–62; in the second group the military was an important political influence but not in direct control, and in the third group the military had little or no political influence. The political strength of the military (independent variable) was correlated with some economic factors commonly viewed as indicators of economic and social change. Table 5.1 shows the relationship hypothesised.

Table 5.1 *The Political Strength of the Military and Economic Change (N = 74)*

Rate of GNP	0·13
Change in industrialisation	0·29
Change in agricultural productivity	0·07
Expansion in education	0·08
Change in tax level	0·04
Investment level	–0·11
Leaders' commitment to economic development	–0·22

Source: Adelman and Morris, 1967.

Nordlinger concludes that the mean correlation is 0·04 and two of the correlations are negative. The only one that is contrary is 0·29 for change in industrialisation. He explains this by asserting that the military would encourage industrialisation because it is the only dimension of economic change that benefits the military corporate interests. Nordlinger further concludes that the absence of positive correlations calls into question the support for the military as a powerful agent of economic development. The zero-order correlations in Table 3.2 (p. 86 above) suggest that the officer politicians do not make any efforts or contributions to economic change.

The following objections could be raised to the interpretations above: for any modernising or development programs to show effect, some years should elapse after their implementation; and it will be premature to assess the cumulative value of on-going projects. Nordlinger argues back by saying that even during the period of study, the correlation of the independent variable with leaders' commitment to economic development was –0·22 and investment rate –0·11. He further argued that if his position was wrong then those countries that had military rulers for a longer time would show marked improvement over those whose rulers were relatively new since the cumulative impact of their modernisation efforts would have begun to show. According to him, an examination of the data for the two groups of military-dominated countries does not reveal any linear increase in rates of economic growth when the length of involvement is taken into account.

Could the level of administrative skills of the bureaucrats have been a factor that could render the observed correlation spurious? Adelman and Morris tested for this, and commented that if the zero-order correlations were spurious, positive correlations between the variables should have been found among those countries that had a higher level of bureaucratic competence. Since this was not the case, Nordlinger concluded that the officers' motivation must be held accountable for the absence of any significant correlations. Other variables like level of political stability and wealth of country were controlled for and no change was reported.

However, there are other criticisms to which ready answers may not be found. First, all aggregate data have the inherent weakness of concealing substantial local variations, which greatly limits their applicability for specific purposes. It is important to bear in mind that methodologically, studies on military role have suffered from lack of intensive local case studies from which comparative generalisations could be derived. It would be masking considerable variation to group Brazil and Guatemala together. Secondly, some of the economic indicators used refer to the period 1950–62, but the military variable covers the period 1957–62. This discrepancy in overlap is significant. Thirdly, a basic assumption of the study is that changes in economic variables are due to governmental influence. My point about the significance of local and regional differences is brought out by the set of figures presented in Table 3.2 (p. 86).

From Table 3.2 the general impression is inescapable that the military in Asia, North Africa, Latin America and the Middle East either fail to contribute to economic change or oppose modernising demands where they exist, while the situation is different in tropical African countries. There is even a wide variation among the first four areas, since the aggregate Latin American figure would mask the Brazilian case. Thus, it is important to examine more critically than has been the case hitherto the political and economic situation in each area. Nordlinger argues that the military allows economic change in Africa because it does not feel threatened by the low level of political change and also because it appreciates the need to increase the size of the middle class. He further argues that since African armies are small and new, their corporate interests detract only slightly from modernisation efforts. I would argue in reverse that Nigeria has one of the greatest demand levels for change as well as one of the largest élite groups (that is, middle class relative to the total population of the African group) yet exhibits the greatest growth rate. Again, the Ghanaian military, as has been demonstrated, presents a clear illustration of the effect of military corporate interest, yet it is small and new. Nordlinger's argument becomes weak when the special circumstances of poor economic resources and reference group orientation combine in any military. The Ethiopian military does not feel constrained to increase the size of the middle class; it is, in fact, striving to reduce it.

Corporate Interest and Economic Development

The distinctiveness conferred on the military institution by virtue of the kind of professional training received in it generates an ethos and *esprit de corps* in its members. The legal monopoly of the use of physical force endows their activities and experience with a special character. The physical separation of their abode adds to a sense of corporate belonging that makes its members share an almost unique fellow-feeling which distinguishes them from the rest of the society and underlines the dichotomous concept of civil–military relations. More important, however, is the realisation by top military men of the need for their organisation to possess, research for and to some extent manufacture its own hardware (Odetola, 1978). The dependence of Third World and particularly African militaries on imported hardware increases such need. In other words, a sense of nationalism is mixed with the corporate desires of the military and cannot be divorced from it. This need is expressed in the desire of ruling militaries to foster the development of heavy and petro-chemical industries over that of softer wares or even of agriculture. The military does begin, therefore, to appropriate funds for development in those areas that benefits it most. It is also claimed to appropriate scarce capital to develop other facilities such as uniform, barracks, and so on to the neglect of other priority areas. For this reason corporate military interest may under the ability of military coercion begin to hinder a national consensus.

Both Horowitz and Nordlinger and other analysts agree that military corporate interest deters economic growth. For a number of reasons surplus resources are diverted to military means and since such resources cannot be used to support an advanced industrial labour force, the military retards development. The argument that such a retardation may be offset because idle soldiers are used to perform useful economic tasks is weak. I have demonstrated in Chapter 2 that the civil uses of military personnel are quite limited. In Latin America, military budgets often rocket. The capital that goes every year to the armed forces' salaries, and so on, contributes very little to the economic development of the country. It appears that one way a military élite could be successful in bringing about economic development is by restricting its own growth as well as the importation of military hardware (Bienen, 1968). While I do not justify an inordinate appropriation of development finance by the military and for its own use, we must realise that the military is also an interest group and its role should be constantly evaluated. This is why the traditional literature emphasising military normative role has been inadequate. In recognition of the above, S. E. Finer (1962) stated that 'the military is jealous of its corporate status and privileges which can lead to the military demand to be the ultimate judgement on all matters affecting the armed forces . . . these certainly include foreign policy and invariably includes domestic economic policy'. Alba (1962) has rightly noted that the possibility of action by the military in defence of its own interests or of the class to which it is allied is crucial. The issue to be decided upon then is not whether the military appropriates money on its own behalf but the extent to which such a measure harms economic development. The latter will determine whether the military has in fact intervened to serve only its own interests and the degree of its genuine commitment to economic growth. Thus, Nordlinger's highly critical position again comes in for examination.

Nordlinger (1970) has advanced an argument remarkable for its tightness but laced with strident undertones. He stated that the military in Third World countries has always assumed power only to serve its own interests. It is these countries' most powerful 'trade union'. While he carefully advanced the position that military budgets limit the size and extensiveness of health, education and economic programmes he was wrong to characterise the military role in general as 'socially unproductive'. Certainly not all Third World countries increased their budgets when they assumed power. Ataturk reduced his (even though there are those who argue that Ataturk led an essentially civilian army). To argue that all military heroes proclaim far-reaching changes which they never achieve is to argue that the military do not face serious problems of administration that may debar them from reaching such goals. Such an argument also assumes that civilian regimes have performed better than the military in achieving their aims.

Nordlinger provided a set of figures to illustrate his contention that military politicians actively pursue their corporate interests and do so in a way that detracts from economic and social change. In Latin America in countries with a politically non-involved military, the level of defence expenditures as a proportion of central government expenditure is 9·3 per cent; in countries with an officer corps that has intermittently entered politics the figure reaches 18·5 in countries dominated by the military since 1960. The last group of countries also averaged a rise of 14·0 per cent annual increase in defence spending since 1960, while the 'intermittent' countries showed a rise of 3·3 per cent, and where the military was not involved, the corresponding figure was 2·8 per cent. He also used data from Russett's (1964) *World Handbook of Political and Social Indicators* to show that where the military ruled between 1957 and 1962 (*N* = 18), the average percentage of GNP spent on defence was 3·6; but the corresponding figure among those countries in which the military ruled intermittently was 3·4, and 1·9 in countries where military power was neglible or absent. It appears from the above that the budget in military-dominated countries is twice as large as in countries with civilian rule. The conclusion seems inescapable that when the military accedes to power, its interests become paramount. However, the question is, how injurious to economic development is the increase in military budget? It would be necessary to compare defence budgets with capital allocation for other sectors. This becomes a matter of evaluating data for individual countries and such data have not been provided. Another point is that increase in military expenditure may itself have spill-over effects on the total economy (for example, enlarging the engineering or communication corps or the navy) although how much and how significant is a matter for determination in each case. The case of Ghana provides ample support for the Nordlinger position while the Nigerian case provides contrary evidence. Table 5.2 illustrates the Ghanaian budgets during the military and civil rule. It shows a dramatic decline in industry and the infrastructure–transport and communications. The decline in agricultural investment, while not so dramatic, is very significant, while at the same time the budget for defence has gone up sharply when the country was not faced with or threatened by war.

Table 5.3 shows a yearly breakdown of the increase rates and confirms the observation above. The Ghanaian military ostensibly came

Table 5.2 *Comparison of NLC Budgets with Last Nkrumah Budget Amounts Allocated (in cedis)*

Sector	1966 (Nkrumah)	1968–9 (NLC)	% Change
Defence	39,933,920	48,387,000	+41·4
Industries	24,504,933	5,495,000	–77·5
Agriculture	33,319,125	23,895,760	–28·3
Transport and communications	23,902,310	12,539,630	–47·5
Trade	3,927,722	1,481,700	–62·2

Source: Government of Ghana's Annual Budget, 1966 and 1968/9, quoted in Price, 1971b.

Table 5.3   *Comparison of NLC Budgets with Last Nkrumah Budget 1966: Percentage Change in Allocation from 1966 Level*

	1966–7	*1967–8*	*1968–9*	*Average*
Defence	+4·0	+20·0	+41·4	+22·0
Agriculture	–16·5	–36·7	–28·3	–27·2
Industries	–56·2	–77·4	–78·2	–70·6
Transport and communications	–9·8	–54·1	–47·5	–37·1
Trade	+3·6	–65·2	–62·3	–43·7
Foreign relations	–25·0	+27·7	+22·4	+8·4

Source: Government of Ghana's Annual Budget, 1966 and 1968/9, quoted in Price, 1971b.

Table 5.4   *Capital Expenditure under the Military Regime in Nigeria 1968–70 (in million naira)*

	1968 % of total	*1969 % of total*	*1970 % of total*
General administration and defence	11·1	12·1	24·8
Total economic service	66·0	38·2	43·0
Agriculture	0·6	3·7	5·5
Transport and communications and education	21·7	21·1	30·9

Source: Federal Office of Statistics, Lagos.

to power to improve the economy and clean up corruption but its record has revealed the satisfaction of corporate interests and a dismal failure to achieve its declared aims (Price, 1971b).

In contrast, the Nigerian military presents an example of dedication to national unity and economic development. Aside from the great rise in the GNP level noted above, Table 5.4 is quite revealing about the gradual rise in defence expenditures.

The Military and Economic Nationalism

I have dealt in some detail with nationalism as an ideology of the military in Chapter 4. Here I will elaborate on its specific significance in relation to economic development. It is in the sphere of economic development that military nationalism is most visibly expressed. In its efforts to build state power, the military intervenes massively in the economic sphere by encouraging the public sector and by limiting and controlling foreign investment and participation as well as attempting to limit the power of the rising bourgeoisie. There is an inherent conflict in this role of the military. To limit foreign investment while expanding growth involves either a massive injection of state capital or an equally great encouragement of massive investment, or some of each. There will, however, be some conflict between encouraging private investment and limiting the power of the bourgeoisie. The military managers will have to be experts at controlling the economy in order to avoid absolute reliance on the expertise of the bureaucrats. To rely completely on the bureaucrats creates the basis for adverse relations between them and the business elite, a situation that creates problems for national cohesion and for reaching the goals of national consensus. These problems have become visibly expressed through such issues as the issue of import licences, price control and the creation of government-sponsored national supply agencies. As we will see in the evidence to be provided below, this conflict results in controversies that do no less than hamper economic performance. Meanwhile let us examine some of the proclamations and rhetoric of economic nationalism.

In the 1970–4 development plan, the Nigerian military government declared that the Nigerian federal government would occupy the commanding heights of the economy in the quest for a purposeful national development. It was also determined to provide the 'leadership and honest administration necessary for the attainment of a national sense of purpose' (Nigerian National Development Plan, Federal Government of Nigeria, 1970). The proclamation further said that the government would intervene to protect the public interest. According to the military government, economic nationalism does not imply the restriction of internal trade, but is directed at the progressive elimination of foreign dominance over national growth.

In stating development guidelines in 1975, Acheampong declared that his government would promote national economic independence and would not allow international trade to compromise national integrity, sovereignty and declared foreign policy (*ARB*, January–February 1975, p. 3397).

In Ethiopia, the Provisional Military Administrative Council (PMAC) declared that it would gain control of the means of production by nationalising the commanding heights of manufacturing, commerce and housing in order to destroy the growing capitalist sector and petty bourgeois entrepreneurs. The military proclamations have similar content in African nations: foreign dominance would be reduced or eliminated, and the public sector would be developed. But the rhetoric, as pointed out above, has neglected the power and skills of the growing bourgeoisie and its ability to sabotage declared national goals as well as the lack of sufficient resources in these nations.

The above analysis reveals, in general, that military nationalism cannot be divorced from military corporate interests. For example, the need to encourage the development of heavy industry arises out of an interest both to build solid foundations for the national economy and to promote the manufacture of military hardware.

State-Directed Socialist Development in Ethiopia

We have noted above that Ethiopia has adopted the state-directed socialist economic development model. In this section I shall investigate why this has been so, what are the main features of this socialist development, what the results have been and what the consequences and implications of these results have been, not only for the economy but also for relationships among various social groups in the society. The United Nations classified Ethiopia as one of the ten poorest countries in the world. Ethiopia has been under the feudal aristocratic system for centuries. It has a very large traditional subsistence sector; it also has a small modern sector, and an agricultural sector which provides a livelihood for slightly more than 85 per cent of all the people of Ethiopia. Agriculture also contributes more than 66 per cent of the Gross Domestic Product (GDP) and accounts for at least 90 per cent of the export earnings of the nation. That is, the major bulk of external trade revenue is derived from agricultural produce. In fact, 75 per cent or more of manufacturing industry is engaged in the processing of farm products, 98 per cent of cultivable land in Ethiopia is in the hands of the farmers, while 98 per cent of the food consumed by the public was produced by the farmers in 1979. Therefore, any improvement to be undertaken in the economy of Ethiopia must be based on the agriculture of the nation. We will now see what has happened since the military took over in 1974.

There has been a general decline, and this decline became severe between 1977 and 1978, particularly in agriculture. There was a breakdown of infrastructure, notably in the transport section, due to the internal strife in Ethiopia, and men were lost to the army. The weather has not been particularly favourable. Price incentives to farmers have been relatively poor and there has also been a decline in international reserves due particularly to increases in the army budget. There have been deficits in the budget and these deficits have been made up by borrowing from domestic banking systems as well as from external sources. In 1977 and 1978 money supply was expanded by about 16 per cent and prices rose in 1977 by 16·6 per cent and 14·3 per cent in 1978.

It became obvious that the economy had to be diversified–a situation that has not been seriously taken account of; as in many developing nations, there have been shortages of skilled workers and managers. How well has the economy and the nation done since the proclamation of socialism?

On 20 December 1974 a socialist proclamation of Ethiopia was made to ensure the following: (1) equality of all Ethiopians regardless of sex, race, language, religion and ethnicity; (2) paramountcy of community interest over private gain; (3) right to self-administration of every nationality in Ethiopia; (4) respect of human labour and its dignity; (5) unity of the Ethiopian nation as an element of sacred faith. Of course there was no direct mention of Marxism or Leninism or other types of socialist analysis. The military immediately proceeded to carry out certain reform programmes, as follows: (1) land reform in urban and rural areas; (2) nationalisation of important sectors of industry, commerce and banking; (3) reform of labour laws; (4) establishment of local democratic institutions such as Peasant Associations, Urban Dwellers' and Housing Associations. Later in 1979 service co-operatives, which were merely a structural beginning on the road to building a socialist economy, were established, and later producer co-operatives were also established. It was believed both by the military themselves and by outside observers that the establishment of Peasant Associations and co-operatives would be a solution to the country's problems. In fact, despite the nationalisation of land in 1974 and several years of fighting, the military did not succeed in halting individualism and motivation of personal gains. In other words, the earlier proclamations of 1974 were followed by further proclamations which were designed finally to turn the society into a socialist one. The aim of the establishment of the service co-operatives and peasant co-operatives in 1979 was gradually to bring privately owned means of production under common ownership with the permission of the owner and completely eliminate exploitation of man by man, to raise production by using modern agricultural techniques, and safeguard the peasants' political, economic and social rights by building a socialist state in the countryside. In order, therefore, according to these proclamations, to eradicate the idolatry of private gain, to protect economic development and public interests and to destroy the economic power of the growing capitalist sector and petty bourgeois entrepreneurs, the military delineated economic activities to be reserved for government ownership exclusively, some for joint venture and a small section for private enterprise.

Joint ventures were to be encouraged where capital and technological requirements exceeded Ethiopian capabilities, and private enterprise was to be permitted where the enterprise was small in size. The declaration further stated that those resources either considered crucial for economic development or of such character that they provided an indispensable service to the community were to be brought under government control of ownership. This document put emphasis on the development of the public sector in line with the socialist orientation of the Ethiopian military. In the industrial sector early in 1975 the military government nationalised seventy-two foreign and local companies and became principal shareholders in twenty-nine other companies. These included fourteen textile companies, thirteen food-processing industries, eight beverages including Coca-Cola and Pepsi-Cola, eight chemical industries, five iron and steel works and four printing firms. Among those sectors which came directly under government control were prospecting for precious metals including gold and radioactive materials, large-scale salt-mining, petroleum-refining and natural gas, drugs and medical equipment, tobacco, rail and air transport, radio, television, post and telecommunications. Earlier in December 1974 the government had already nationalised banking and all insurance companies in the nation, and it had controlling shares in oil, furniture and sugar-manufacturing. The following areas were left for joint government and private investment: prospecting for carbons, mining of ferrous and non-ferrous metals, mining of fertiliser materials, pulp and paper, large construction works and tourism. The following were left to private enterprise: food-processing and canning, marketing, bakeries, small-scale weaving, repair of vehicles and small-scale inland water transport. In addition, in the public interest the government set up or instituted restrictive control mechanism on all locally manufactured goods which became effective on 14 January 1975, and distributorships and supermarkets were also nationalised and replaced by the Ethiopian Distribution Corporation. I will now go on specifically to the improvement in agriculture, manufacturing and trade.

Agriculture

The cardinal principles established to improve agriculture were based on the Peasant Associations which among other things were to establish producer co-operatives and service co-operatives, distribute land, adjudicate land disputes and administer and conserve public properties. By 1978 the Peasant Associations themselves had organised over 2,000 service co-operatives, 43 agricultural producer co-operatives and 443 small-scale industrial co-operatives. Other equally important measures included the establishment of state farms which were supposed to be complementary to the development and establishment of the Peasant Associations. In addition, the government instituted certain policies such as the producers' incentives and price control policy. The producer incentive policy which increased prices to the farmers was an excellent idea. Holmberg (1977) said that in accepting this policy the new government of Ethiopia has taken a big step towards eliminating the exploitative urban–rural relations which had prevailed in the past and that a positive incentive to produce for the market would be provided to the Ethiopian peasants. We will now proceed to examine how well the Peasant Associations have performed as well as the state farms and compare these groups in performance. We will then proceed to examine the reasons for this level of performance in agriculture and what steps the government later took to analyse the problems facing the improvement of agriculture. General production in most agricultural crops fell between 1974 and 1979. Coffee, which is the main export crop, reflected this decrease. Output of coffee fell from 193,000 tons in 1966/7 to 190,000 tons in the 1977/8 crop season, representing about a 1 per cent decrease in production. In 1974 coffee accounted for 30 per cent of export earnings, but it accounted for 75 per cent of export earnings in 1977 and 75 per cent again in 1978. This rise in value, of course, is not due, as we have seen above, to any substantial increase in production but to the general rise in prices internationally. The official reasons for the decline in coffee production were security reasons and adverse weather. The level of crop production estimates in 1977/8 was below that of 1976/7. In 1977/8 the total quantity of crops produced, including those from state farms, co-operatives and private individuals, amounted to 47·5 million quintals grown on 5·5 million hectares of land. This is against a total yield of 49·2 million quintals of crops produced on 4·6 million hectares of cultivated land in the 1976/7 crop season. In other words, while the hectarage has been increased, from 4·6 million to 5·5 million, production has decreased by about 2 million quintals. Besides the official reasons of war and adverse weather, one must now ask the question whether the Peasant Associations and the state farms have been performing well, and if they have not, why this is the case.

In the 1974/5 season about 40 million quintals of cereals were produced, as shown in Table 5.5, increasing to only about 41·5 million quintals in the 1977/8 season. Similarly, 5·7 million quintals of pulses were produced in the 1974/5 season decreasing to about 5·4 million quintals in the 1977/8 season. The figures show that there was a 2·1 per cent decline in the production of cereals in 1977 and 1978. Pulses also decreased by 14·3 per cent in the same period. Table 5.6 reveals

Table 5.5   *Ethiopia: Cereal Production (in thousand quintals)*

	1974/5	1975/6	1976/7	1977/8
Cereals	39,750·0	46,890·5	42,422·4	41,520·3
Pulses	5,682·0	5,047·2	6,461·4	5,432·5

Source: National Bank of Ethiopia, Annual Report, 1978.

Table 5.6   *Ethiopia: Value of Major Exports (in thousand birr)*

	1975	1976	1977	1978	% change 1977/8
Coffee	152,679	324,637	519,302	502,298	–3·3
Oil seeds	83,985	31,242	17,505	12,145	–30·0
Hides and skins	34,455	55,412	48,543	66,262	+36·5
Pulses	64,855	55,872	43,436	17,303	–60·2
Meat products	7,082	6,797	4,476	732	–83·6
Fruit and vegetables	7,579	7,721	7,639	3,383	–55·7
Sugar	1,489	17,880	2,036	—	—
Other	137,700	81,007	46,024	31,406	–31·8
Total	497,824	580,568	680,901	633,629	–0·08

Source: National Bank of Ethiopia, Annual Report, 1978.

decreases in the values of the major export crops. The most striking is in the area of meat production between 1975 and 1978. Oilseeds also declined in the same period by 30 per cent. The only noticeable increase was in the area of hides and skins, the effect of which is negated by the decrease in several other major export products. Thus, in general between 1976 and 1978, farm output has decreased by 800,000 tons. The USSR gave Ethiopia 6,000 tons of food aid which was equivalent to 4·7 million Ethiopian birr.

How well have the state farms done relatively to peasant holdings? It must be borne in mind that the government appears to have given greater priority to the development of state farms, as shown in Table 5.7 which gives estimates of hectarage and production. The table indicates that in 1975/6 the state farms were to have about 58 million hectares of land, decreasing in 1976/7 to about 53·5 million but increasing again in 1977/8 to 62·5 million hectares. Similarly, the output expected from the state farms was to be about 986,106 quintals in 1975/6, increasing to 1,371,441 quintals in the 1977/8 season. On the other hand, peasant holdings were estimated in 1975/6 at 52,526 hectares as against 46,881 hectares in 1977/8. Although no figures of estimated production were given for the peasant holdings it was intended that the state farms should gradually produce more than the peasant holdings. In the 1977/8 season the volume of production from state farms was 1·4 million quintals on an area of 62.5 million hectares. It has, however, exceeded that of 1976/7 by 0·4 million quintals. This increase can be attributed to an expansion of farms by 17 per cent or 9,000 hectares. The government had introduced new crops such as barley, finger millet, peanuts and vegetables on to the state farms, privileges which the peasant holdings had not enjoyed. Even though crop production from peasant holdings

Table 5.7 Ethiopia: Area and Production Estimates (areas in hectares, production in quintals)

| | 1975/6 A | | 1976/7 B | | 1977/8 B/A | | % change B/A | | % change C/B | |
	Area	Output	Area	Output	Area	Output	Area	Output	Area	Output
State farms	57,738	986,106	53,433	1,044,168	62,524	1,371,441	-7·5	5·9	17·0	31·3
Peasant holdings		52,566		48,993		46,881	-7·0		-4·3	

Sources: Ministry of Agriculture and Settlement, Results of the Agricultural Sample Survey 1972–8; State Farms Development Authority, Bulletin No. 1, 4 March 1978.

declined between 1976/7 and 1977/8 and there was also a decline in
hectarages, crop production from the state farms as against that of the
peasant sector was minimal. A report from the National Bank of
Ethiopia in 1978 claimed that crop production from the state farms
represented not more than 3 per cent of total output of major crops.
Therefore, in spite of the introduction and encouragement of state
farms, the peasant holdings still remain the bulwark of agricultural
production in Ethiopia.

Manufacturing and Industries

The overall level of output between 1976/7 and 1977/8 declined by 3·9
per cent; textiles alone had decreased by about 14 per cent. Table 5.8

Table 5.8   *Ethiopia: Indices of Manufacturing Sales (1972/3 = 100)*

	1974/5 A	1975/6 B	1976/7 C	1977/8 D	% change B/A	C/B	D/C
Industrial group	1967	1968	1969	1970			
Food processing	95·4	89·5	87·9	95·3	–6·2	–1·8	8·04
Textiles	95·2	97·9	92·8	79·8	2·8	–5·2	–14·0
Non-metallic mineral products	90·3	55·7	75·3	75·7	–38·3	31·6	05
Overall index	100·6	97·1	99·4	95·5	–3·5	2·4	–4·0

Source: National Bank of Ethiopia, Annual Report, 1978.

shows that production in the whole industrial sector went below the
figures for 1972/3. Food processing figures for 1974/5, which was the
first year of military rule, were equal to those of 1967. Overall there was
a decline of about 6·2 per cent in the index between 1974/5 and 1975/6.
Similarly, production and processing of textile materials in 1974/5 was
equal to that of 1967. The greatest decline was shown in 1975/6 in the
processing of non-metallic products; it fell to 75·7 on a base index of 100
for the year 1972/3. The overall index as revealed in the table shows that
there has been a decrease generally from 1974/5 until 1977/8. The
figure for 1977/8 was 95·5 against the base of 100 for 1972/3.

Trade

Imports have rocketed while exports have declined to an all-time low.
Table 5.6 showed a general decline in the major export crops and other
produce of Ethiopia. Table 5.9 reveals that between 1968 and 1978
imports have risen by 13·2 per cent in textile clothing and by 97·8 per
cent in chemicals. Two interesting sectors call for attention, the first

Table 5.9 *Ethiopia: Value of Selected Imports by Major Commodity Groups (in thousand birr)*

	1968	1976	1977	1978	%
Food and live animals	19,749	31,565	29,677	41,486	39·8
Chemicals	96,269	78,617	54,665	108,040	97·8
Textiles and clothing	46,556	77,216	119,102	134,313	13·2
Motor vehicles	75,513	90,104	96,184	171,857	78·7

Source: National Bank of Ethiopia, Annual Report, 1978.

being food and live animals which cost the nation less than 20 million birr in 1968 but about 41·5 million birr in 1978. In fact, between 1976 and 1978 the value of imported food and live animals has gone up by about 40 per cent. Another interesting area is the importation of motor vehicles. Between 1976 and 1978 there was a rise of almost 80 per cent in the importation of motor vehicles, and the importation of these vehicles doubled in the ten years between 1968 and 1978. We can relate these figures to those for Nigeria in Table 2.3 (p. 41) where the importation of motor vehicles also more than doubled in about the same number of years. It is probably safe to say then that military regimes in African countries have tended to increase imports over exports to a large extent. In general in the agricultural sector in Ethiopia in 1977, export earnings were about 690 million birr, but in 1978 they declined by 56·2 million birr to 633·8 million birr. Coffee revenue alone decreased from 519·3 million birr in 1977 to 502·3 million birr in 1978, and the export values of pulses and oil seeds also declined from 85,500 tonnes in 1977 to 23,700 tonnes in 1978, a drop of almost 73 per cent. One should not therefore be surprised to see a heavy deterioration in the balance of payments. In 1978 there was a deficit of 175·5 million birr compared with a deficit of 133·8 million birr in 1977. The National Bank of Ethiopia has attributed the upsurge in the value of imports to the war, to a decline in export earnings caused by lower agricultural production and finally to the fall in international coffee prices. In other words, the Ethiopian rulers themselves have realised that the decline in export earnings is a major contributory factor to the decline in the balance of payments.

We will now proceed to examine the direction of trade to see whether in fact there has been a major shift towards socialist countries in terms of trade. In 1978 goods valued at about 396·9 million birr were exported to capitalist countries while goods worth about 100 million birr were exported to socialist countries. The figure for socialist countries is high compared with the pre-revolution period, but it is clear that the bulk of exports still go to capitalist countries. Similarly, imports from capitalist countries in 1978 amounted to about 434·5 million birr whereas imports amounted to 240·9 million birr from socialist countries. We must bear in mind, however, the current problem of international inflation. The greater the level of importation into the country internationally, the greater the level of inflation. This might account for the large increase in the amount of money spent for imported articles. The value of imports is about 55 per cent from socialist countries which is equivalent to imports from capitalist countries. Can we infer then that materials imported from socialist countries may be carrying a higher inflationary value than those from capitalist countries? To make up for budgetary deficit, the Ethiopian military government has resorted to heavy domestic borrowing and also some borrowing from external sources, both capitalist and socialist. In 1978 a total amount of 131·3 million birr was borrowed. However, only 90·5 million of this was actually allocated. Of this last figure, transportation received about 30 million birr and agriculture about 19·36 million birr. It must be noted that the amount of allocation from loans to agriculture in 1976 was about 49 million birr. A comparison of these two years will show that there is a decrease in allocation to agriculture. One problem that contributed to the inflationary pressure was money supply. In 1976 money supply was about 810 million birr which increased to 985 million in 1977 and finally to over 1,200 million in 1978. It appears, therefore, that the government has itself contributed to the level of inflation by increasing the money supply on the market.

The government instituted a price control policy to combat inflation in 1975 but it appears that the price control has been effective only in the area of government concerns–a situation which limited profit heavily. Table 5.10 shows the retail price index for Addis Ababa excluding rent, using 1963 as the base. The increase in the general index between 1974 and 1978 was almost 100 per cent. Food alone showed an increase of almost 220 per cent, household items almost 200 per cent and clothing about 80 per cent. If the consumer prices in Addis Ababa are used as a base, the retail price index has been growing by about 15 per cent annually.

Table 5.10   *Retail Price Index for Addis Ababa Excluding Rent (1963 = 100)*

	1974	1975	1976	1977	1978
General index	159·7	170·1	218·7	255·1	291·6
Food	167·6	175·1	248·4	290·1	339·5
Household items	157·0	159·8	205·5	261·0	280·4
Clothing	175·2	190·6	205·9	223·7	245·2
Medical care	156·8	179·6	194·9	209·3	239·3

Source: Central Statistical Office, Addis Ababa.

The above figures, and general statistics in agriculture, manu-facturing, trade and price control policy, are evidence of poor performance. Can we, therefore, simply characterise the military as poor economic managers and stop at that? Certainly, we must now begin to see how the effect of socialist revolution has induced other social groups in the society to oppose military moves to achieve national consensus.

By 1976 the military had completed most steps aimed at dismantling the feudal aristocracy and redistributing economic and political power. The establishment of the Peasant Associations provided an institutional base for peasant control at the local level over land, tax collection and development projects. The abolition of rent due to the feudal nobility and of land tax and other forms of taxes to the nobility brought about a great redistribution of income for the peasants. All of these steps were calculated to reduce the power of the landlords. These developments were contrary to the expectations of the petty bourgeoisie who hoped to gain a great deal from the revolution. For example, by 1974 the petty bourgeoisie had expected to gain control of all of the nationalised enterprises. Secondly, the labour leaders had anticipated increases in wages and better condition of service. Thirdly, according to Bailey (1979), the radical group, the intelligentsia and the students supported these progressive tendencies precisely because they had hoped for a complete left turn in the political system of nation. Finally, the petty traders had hoped for an end to foreign domination and for gains in their own favour. But by 1976 the PMAC and its leaders had been perceived by the petty bourgeoisie as having established themselves as supporters of the peasantry at the expense of the petty bourgeoisie and urban groups (Bailey, 1979). The PMAC now had to face antagonism from the urban groups and the radical left who felt that they had been alienated from real power.

Even though power had shifted from the bourgeoisie, aristocratic élite and urban groups to the state apparatus it became increasingly evident that the bureaucrats had made a considerable gain of power. The situation resulted in the flight of expert personnel. Both foreign and indigenous private investment ceased because of nationalisation and other controls and there was very little new investment. In consequence, very little profit came into the government coffers. When the PMAC realised this, they attempted in 1975 to expand the role of the Peasant Associations. But even with this expansion the role of the Peasant Associations remained localised and they did not function well because the bureaucrats dominated their activities. In other words, according to Bailey (1979), the land reform which brought the Peasant Associations into existence did not specify the role of the associations in relation to other levels of government. Although the leaders of the revolution revised these measures they had previously disallowed the Peasant Associations from going beyond the local level. The failure to allow these mobilisation structures to grow beyond this level resulted in the failure of the Peasant Associations to improve agricultural production.

Another reason accounting for the failure to improve agricultural production has been the inability of the bureaucracy to change to the new ways of the revolution. In fact the revolution demanded that the bureaucracy be restructured and this was not done. Also, pressure emanated from urban centres and the bourgeoisie who hoped not only to keep food prices from rising but also to gain control of power. The landlords were prevented from performing the intermediate role of suppliers, therefore the market situation was interrupted and hoarding by private traders became the order of the day. Because of the greater purchasing power of the peasants, consumption on the farm itself increased. There were also poor handling facilities and aggravation of the situation from the war. Consequently, Ethiopia became an importer of food rather than an exporter. The failure radically to change the bureaucracy and to design strategies for carrying out its plans initially spelt the doom of the revolutionary programmes. I would argue that merely to use existing structures in order to carry out revolutionary programmes will not make the programmes of the military succeed.

Mengistu himself admitted failure on many counts. He said in 1979 that the present state of the national economy was weak, that a number of the economic structures had ceased to operate and that the national income was below expectation. He also said that the deficit in the budget was increasing and that the suffering of the people was increasing as well as the unemployment situation. He claimed that 90 per cent of the people were illiterate and a still higher percentage lacked clean water. He went on further to complain about the lack of mobilisation of available resources. Mengistu said that out of a total of 122 million hectares that were arable only 11 per cent were under cultivation. He also complained that the total land suitable for irrigation amounted to 3 million hectares and only about 100,000 hectares had been put to use. The water, animal and mineral resources had not been fully exploited. He said that in spite of riches available, poverty had prevailed in the country. His objective, he claimed, was to build a socialist economic system and to effect a radical change in the general economic structure.

While the military has shown a high spirit of nationalism, national consensus has not been achieved. Cohesion has also failed to help mobilise resources. For example, as outlined earlier, the military administration established Peasant Associations, Housing Associations and other institutions designed to mobilise resources. In addition, it engaged the students and the intelligentsia in a campaign designed to help educate the people towards development in order to mobilise resources. But we also saw that the élite groups, bourgeois class, student group, intelligentsia and particularly the bureaucrats have constituted themselves into antagonistic groups that either refused to support or directly sabotaged military efforts. The faults, however, have been largely those of the military who have failed to give the Peasant Associations the opportunity to operate beyond the local level and at the same time have failed to restructure the bureaucracy. In other words, new directions were needed to generate a national consensus and to mobilise natural resources. Later, in 1978, the PMAC established the Central Planning Supreme Council to perform the following functions: (1) to plan for the nation and formulate a development plan on the basis of democratic centralism; (2) to pull the nation out of its economic difficulties by issuing guidelines and development strategies; (3) to undertake literacy campaigns in the countryside. The Central Planning Supreme Council must note, it was emphasised, that the problems facing the nation included widespread shortages of consumer products as well as inefficient flow of goods and services to the nation. This council, known as the CPSC, is responsible to a congress whose membership includes all the sixteen standing members, all members of the Council of Ministers, provincial administrators, police and armed forces commanders and, significantly, the representatives of mass organisations. Mengistu is head of both the congress and the CPSC. The CPSC was given powers to mobilise all human, financial and material resources of the country for this campaign. This new institution was also empowered to ensure strict adherence to discipline in any organisation or association. It was recognised that lack of discipline must be severely punished because it slowed down production.

It appears that only now have the military recognised the need to give the Peasant Associations greater powers to operate beyond the local level. It has established the all-Ethiopian Peasant Associations to co-ordinate the services of co-operatives and co-operative farms on the guiding principles of self-reliance at the national level. It is hoped that the new National Association will work and co-operate with the CPSC in order to operate development and campaign programmes.

The CPSC has launched Operation Zemetcha, called the 'green revolution' and similar to the green revolution that the military has launched in both Nigeria and Ghana. In recognition of the need to improve infrastructure, particularly road communications, the military has injected a large amount of money into the reconstruction of the roads and has established the Ethiopian Highway Authority to reorganise and rebuild roads. In addition, the military has established co-ordinating corporations for export products. For example, it has established the coffee and tea marketing corporation whose duties are to purchase, store, process, transport and sell these products in a manner guaranteeing the national interest. Other institutions which have been established are the Ethiopian Sugar Corporation, with the government holding the majority share, and the Ethiopian Petroleum Corporation, whose duties are to co-ordinate the demand and supply of petroleum products to the nation.

Since these new institutions have been established so recently it is difficult to attain a proper perspective in assessing their effects on the society. However, as Mengistu himself has admitted, the introduction of the development campaign and these institutions may not result in any immediate significant improvement in the economy. In fact, with the earnings from coffee virtually stagnating and an import bill swollen by the recent sharp increase in the cost of oil, one should expect a further deterioration of the external sector and at the same time an increase in inflationary pressure. However, Mengistu claims that the importance of these campaigns is that by setting up an administration of the type which has already proved successful when dealing with the war effort, a measure of coherent economic management has been introduced.

The military also took steps in another direction and this concerned the revamping of the tax system. They amended the income tax law and placed the highest burden on those earning more than 1,500 birr; those earning 600 birr or less a year were exempted from any form of taxation. Tax for those earning between 2,000 and 2,400 was 10 per cent, graduated upwards to 59 per cent for those earning between 30,000 and 33,000, 79 per cent for those earning between 42,000 and 45,000, and 85 per cent for those earning above 45,000 birr. Each wage-earner had to pay an additional 6 per cent in educational tax and retirement fund. Business organisations, both state-owned and private, were also to pay 50 per cent tax on all taxable income, 25 per cent tax on dividends and 40 per cent tax on royalties. There were special incentives given to Peasant Association members. Co-operative members were to pay reduced land use tax, and they would not pay income tax on the first 600 birr. The retained profit of co-operatives was also exempted from corporate taxation.

It must be noted, however, that while the new taxation system placed a relatively heavy burden on the higher wage-earner, the lower end burden rose by about 50 per cent in absolute terms. This made it difficult for the urban population to live well because they were confronted with shortages of basic as well as luxury items. Apart from this rapid rise in taxation, there was rationing and a wage freeze. Thus in almost every aspect of their lives things have become more difficult. This situation tended to reduce the ability of the PAMC to gain support among the revolutionary urban classes and may be one reason for the failure to raise national consensus.

Finally, in considering the Ethiopian situation, I would like briefly to draw attention to government expenditure. Between 1977 and 1979 government general services expenditure increased by more than 250 per cent. In cash terms it increased between 1973/4 and the end of 1978 from 263 million birr to 906·5 million birr. Among general services is included security and military expenditure. But if these figures are compared to figures of the amount spent on economic development it will be discovered that while economic development rose by slightly over 100 per cent in the seven years between 1973 and 1978, general services expenditure, which is composed largely of security, increased by more than 300 per cent. In other words, although it must be borne in mind that the military was pursuing a war, much more money than would ordinarily have been the case had been spent on the military and defence while correspondingly little had been spent on economic development.

We will now turn attention to the other model, state-directed capitalist development.

State-Directed Capitalist Development in Nigeria

The Nigerian economy prior to the discovery of oil was dominated mainly by agriculture and agricultural products. However, since the discovery of oil, particularly from 1973, there has been a shift away from agriculture to oil, making oil now the dominant contributor of national revenue. Simultaneously agricultural production has declined massively. Today Nigeria is heavily dependent on oil for the development of her whole economy. Such an orientation has encouraged great ambitions but has not encouraged, and indeed has threatened, productivity in the non-oil sector. It has been said that oil is the locomotive for impelling the vigorous growth of the other sectors in Nigeria. It would have been a wise strategy to take the oil industry's primary potential as a base to achieve a self-sustaining take-off. However, it will be demonstrated that Nigeria's dependence on oil has been vigorously reduced. The national economy started to deteriorate in the 1976 to 1978 period because of the reduction in the production of oil. For example, in 1978 oil production and revenue fell by 10 per cent. The result was that the Gross Domestic Product rose by only 4·5 per cent as compared with a 13 per cent growth in 1977.

Agriculture

Table 5.11 compares Ghana, Ethiopia and Nigeria in terms of total agricultural production between 1974 and 1978. The average of the years 1969 to 1971 were used as the base and equal to 100 units. In 1974

Table 5.11   *Index Numbers of Agricultural Production of Food
(1969–71 = 100)*

	1974	1975	1976	1977	1978
Ghana	115	104	99	96	101
Ethiopia	100	97	100	97	96
Nigeria	103	106	110	110	113
Libya	177	185	209	181	209
Kenya	102	103	110	114	117

Source: United Nations 1978 Statistical Yearbook, p. 98.

the index for Nigeria was slightly above that of the base period and rose only gradually to 113 in 1978. The figures for Ghana are rather interesting because production rose briefly in 1974 to 115, the highest figure for any of the three countries. However, in Ghana a decline set in between 1975 and 1977 and production only picked up slightly in 1978. The figures reveal a general decline in Ethiopia more severe than the situation in either of the other two countries.

Leaving general comparisons till later, let us briefly look at what has been done in Nigeria. To mobilise human resources the federal military government launched a programme called 'Operation Feed the Nation' in 1976. This programme was designed to embrace not only all the peasants but also students who were engaged in the campaign initially. In addition, the military enlisted the support of the bureaucracy by asking them to organise the importation of materials such as fertilisers and tractors that would be necessary for the operation of the programme, and the business group was alerted to undertake the importation of these products. In other words, the Nigerian military had, in the process of achieving a national consensus, given each of the various groups certain duties to perform. However, the campaign by students did not succeed as intended and virtually died out after the first two years. The bureaucrats and the business élites engaged in a mild conflict over the importation of the material resources necessary for the operation. With respect to the peasantry, the military government had included the following features: (1) farm prices were guaranteed; (2) there were attempts to reorganise the marketing board systems, while the existing ones were disbanded by March 1977. Agricultural credit schemes were launched and several commodities boards which guaranteed local prices to farmers were empowered to sell direct to local processors and consumers. While Nigeria became a net importer of food like Ethiopia, the decline in agricultural production in Nigeria has not been as severe as that in Ethiopia.

What, we may ask, is responsible for this difference? If we examine the two models of development, we will observe that the role given to the businessmen, bureaucrats and entrepreneurs in Nigeria augurs more favourably for production than the situation in Ethiopia where the military depended on a bureaucracy it did not trust at all. The reorganisation of the marketing boards altered matters so as to give the farmers more help than before. But although the farmers were guaranteed local prices and empowered to sell directly to local processors, middle-men stepped in and took the profits from the farmers. It is probably true to say that because the private sectors were given a considerable role to play in the economy, they have not completely sabotaged the economy as has happened in Ethiopia. Thus it appears that the first step in the movement towards reaching the national consensus has not been as difficult to achieve in Nigeria as it has been in Ethiopia. If Mengistu was to succeed, he probably would have had to destroy not only the feudal structure but the bureaucratic structure as well. He may still have to take that step, but such a measure seems not only extremely difficult but full of hazards as well. It is the bureaucracy in African nations that represents the oldest, if not the most abundant, pool of skill and manpower resources. To build an alternative would require a new kind of consensus as a precondition. The agricultural credit schemes set up to aid the farmers have also not worked out in a manner highly favourable to the farmers. Many of the élite groups who were not in fact going to farm managed in one way or another to obtain loans intended for farmers. And in cases where farmers have been fortunate enough to obtain the loans, petty low-level bureaucrats have gained from the farmers by demanding bribes from them. Thus, in all three countries sabotage by social and economic structures has prevented the military in Ethiopia, Ghana and Nigeria from achieving national consensus. The sabotage has been of the same kind but of different degrees.

Manufacturing and Industries

In harmony with its orientation to develop the powers of the state, the military governments in Nigeria between 1972 and 1977 set out to expand the state sector expenditure through indigenisation proposals for several manufacturing industries. A group of industries were indigenised in 1972 and another group were indigenised in 1977. Indigenisation is a major step towards nationalisation though the two are different.

The areas put under indigenisation proposals in 1977 included refineries, liquid natural gas, pipelines, rails, roads and oil tankers. Extensive state involvement in oil became the order of the day: for example, 55 per cent stakes in oil-producing companies were requested by the federal government, and the government also began to own outright all new refineries and to own 80 per cent shares in two natural gas industries and a holding interest in a network of pipelines. In July 1979 a new corporation, the Nigerian National Petroleum Company (NNPC), raised its participation in the oil companies from 55 per cent to 60 per cent; and after nationalising British Petroleum, which later became African Petroleum, it began to implement a policy of selling its oil through state deals. Earlier, the government had taken between 40 and 50 per cent shares in leading commercial banks and insurance companies. All these steps were taken in the spirit of economic nationalism designed to control the commanding heights of the Nigerian economy. It must be noted, however, that in addition to these measures of nationalisation, by 1975 there were massive new investments in the private sector. In fact, in 1975 manufacturing firms reported an increase of 34 per cent in their production and private trading firms had a 53 per cent turnover in the same period.

There have been certain constraints that must be noted as obstructing development in the manufacturing sector. Nigeria today still fails to develop an integrated industrial sector which can service the national domestic economy, the obstacles being unreliable power, water supply, and obstructive bureaucracy and traits of industrial unrest. In addition, it must be noted that there are shortages of manpower and a decline in earlier standards. In 1977 a super-permanent secretary said that standards had fallen in the banks, in stores and in the distributive sectors. This, he said, was due to the recent expansion of economic activities which had led to excessive expansion and creation of new institutions in the government and private sectors which were difficult to manage. As secretary to the federal military government, he said in 1975/6 that Nigerian wealth was difficult to manage and as a result a crisis situation existed in the way the economy was being run (*ARB*, December–January 1977, p. 4127). It is clear, therefore, that the military government, in view of increased wealth, had tried to develop on too many fronts at the same time. Before we examine what changes were made by the Obasanjo regime, let us take a brief look at the index of manufacturing and industrial production in Nigeria.

Table 5.12 on the index of industrial production, with 1972 as the base period, shows a general increase overall, particularly in manufacturing, rising from 123 units in 1973 to 220 units in 1978. Similar increases are recorded in the mining sector; however, there was a sharp decline here below the base figure in 1975, and also a slight decline in 1978 to 102·5. In general, total industrial production rose to 143, a rise of 43 per cent. But a higher goal could have been reached. I certainly believe that it could have been higher if other national social groups in the society had made a strong contribution to the progress towards reaching a national consensus.

Table 5.12   *Nigeria: Index of Industrial Production (1972 = 100)*

	Manufacturing	Mining	Utility	Total average
1971	92·8	85·6	87·9	87·9
1972	100·0	100·0	100·0	100·0
1973	123·0	112·6	117·5	116·2
1974	119·5	123·4	130·3	122·3
1975	147·7	97·4	153·8	115·1
1976	182·2	113·4	184·5	137·1
1977	194·5	114·6	213·7	142·5
1978	220·2	102·5	203·9	143·6

Source: Central Bank of Nigeria, Annual Report and Statement of Accounts, December 1978, p. 12.

The ideal of subversion here does not imply that social groups in the society cannot protest or that they must always go along with the military progress towards consensus. It is simply that many of the social and economic groups in the society will, in the effort to preserve their own interest and gains, behave in such a manner as to thwart real movement towards national goals. For example, following the Udoji salary review in Nigeria in 1975, a spate of industrial unrest ensued. Several employers refused to pay or negotiate wage increases for their workers. Three big private sector employers–the Nigerian Employers' Consultative Association, the Manufacturers' Association of Nigeria and the Nigerian Association of Chambers of Commerce and Industries–were not prepared to negotiate wage increases for their workers because they argued that the government was awarding increases not because of improved efficiency but because of oil. They asked that the government should give them an oil subsidy to pay these wage increases. I am not arguing about the rights and wrongs of the wage increases recommended by the Udoji salary review, but simply that many private sector employers composed of the national bourgeoisie became recalcitrant in negotiations and constituted blocks in the way of reaching the national goal.

Besides such problems as industrial unrest, another major stumbling block has been the problem of hoarding by the business group, particularly by the distribution network. Hoarding has added to the inflationary pressure and raised consumer prices all over the different areas of the economy. For example, if we take a look at Table 5.13 showing the composite·consumer price indices in all Nigerian cities, we see that using 1960 as a base, the consumer price index went up by 79 per cent in 1972. That is, over a period of twelve years the price index increased by less than 100 per cent; but between 1972 and 1977, a short period of five years, this index went up by more than 200 per cent. While

Table 5.13   *Nigeria: All Cities Composite Consumer Price Indices
(1960 = 100)*

1972	179·6
1973	184·3
1974	214·7
1975	287·4
1976	348·2
1977	401·0 (estimated)

Source: Central Bank of Nigeria, Economic and Financial Review, 1977.

we take account of the international inflationary pressure and of the rise in wealth at home, we will observe that the real purchasing power of the masses of the people has declined considerably. Orientation towards importation between 1973 and 1975 went up. The non-oil sector imports rose by over 40 per cent in 1974, resulting in a total deficit of 1·2 billion naira. Price inflation accelerated and the governor of the Central Bank at that time wondered whether the reduction in import duties announced in the last federal budget in 1974 were really worth it. He also suggested the reorganisation of the institution of the Nigerian National Supply Company and the abolition of the Price Control Board. The Commissioner for Petroleum at that time, Colonel Buhari, said that the most obvious problem that oil had brought to Nigeria was that it had given Nigerians an almost embarrassing boost to their capacity to consume foreign goods and it had provided the means to satisfy the appetite to consume. He claimed that it had not improved Nigerians' ability to repair or maintain essential services. It had not improved the capacity of Nigerians for hard work and had also stifled the ingenuity of the Nigerians to adapt (*ARB*, October 1975).

A new kind of mobilisation had therefore become necessary because of the trend towards unnecessary consumption. In the 1975/6 budget General Obasanjo announced that money liquidity would be reduced in an attempt to control inflation. Secondly, subsidies would be given to individuals or organisations in the society who were engaged in developing housing estates or such other concrete development projects. Certain imported items remained banned and those materials that could aid the building industry as well as the construction industry no longer earned import duties. In 1977 the government changed its credit policy in an attempt further to reduce money liquidity on the market. In another direction, the military government refused to review wages because it felt satisfied with the Udoji salary review of 1975. It must be pointed out that as soon as the civilian government came into power in 1979, the salary of certain grades of workers in the lower category were revised upwards.

The argument that I have put forward here is that the Nigerian military government between 1975 and 1979 attempted to hold the inflation-fired economy in check by restrictive measures which in the end became successful. It has been said that by the time the military handed over power in 1979, the economy had reached a peak: annual revenue had reached between $11 and 15 billion.

Defence Expenditure and Military Budget

We have seen in the Ghanaian and Ethiopian examples defence budgets going up rapidly under military rule. Table 5.14 showing current

Table 5.14   *Nigeria: Current Expenditure of Federal Government (in million naira)*

	1972	1973	1974	1975	1976	1977
General admini-stration and internal security	498·3	434·3	555·4	1,055·4	1,010·2	448·8
Agriculture	12·4	13·4	24·6	38·8.	18·5	16·7
Education	7·3	10·4	62·5	218·9	522·0	226·8

Source: Central Bank of Nigeria, Economic and Financial Review, 1977.

expenditure in Nigeria reveals the same trend. Recurrent expenditure on general administration and internal security increased from about 500 million naira in 1972 to about 555 million naira in 1974, a period that represented rapid national reconstruction after the civil war. However, there was a massive leap to over 1,000 million naira in both 1975 and 1976. This was the period of euphoric spending by the Gowon regime in Nigeria. There were no new armies being established and one wonders what the money was spent on. The total recurrent amount spent on agriculture between 1972 and 1976 was less than 110 million naira, equal to about 25 per cent of the recurrent expenditure on defence in any one year during that period. Spending was reduced drastically in 1977 to below the 1972 figure. Turning to capital expenditure, we can discern a similar trend with the greatest increases in the 1975-7 period. Capital expenditure on agriculture and education combined was less than half that on defence alone in 1972, and again in 1973. 1974 to 1977 saw some measure of improvement in allocations to agriculture and education. In the 1978/9 budget period, defence took the lion's share of the budget.

Table 5.15 reveals capital expenditure on agriculture as less than one-ninth that of defence–a situation expressive of wrong priorities since agricultural production was declining. Defence expenditure seems

Table 5.15   *Nigeria: Capital Expenditure of Federal Government (in million naira)*

	1972	1973	1974	1975	1976	1977
General admini- stration and internal security	108·8	133·8	268·3	747·8	795·4	415·8
Agriculture	20·7	35·4	87·4	261·2	129·2	42·5
Education	21·3	16·3	134·4	631·1	529·2	220·0

Source: Central Bank of Nigeria, Economic and Financial Review, 1977.

unjustified in the face of the crying need for improvement in other sectors. There can be no doubt that military defence spending does harm to the national economy.

Perhaps we can partially explain this by saying that the exercise of building state power demands the strengthening of the apparatus of coercion. But this agrument breaks down when we realise that the military can achieve legitimacy by making adequate provisions for the livelihood of the people.

State-Directed Capitalist Development in Ghana

The economic situation in Ghana, a country which has not faced internal or external wars, has in fact been the poorest. In 1965 Ghana had a per capita income of $229. This was the third highest in Africa, and it was three times the average for the whole developing world and far above the projected growth rate for 1985. At that time the growth rate in Ghana and its projected growth rate was the best in Africa (FAO, *World Report*, 1968, pp. 13–14). In addition, in 1965 about 40 per cent of Ghana's population aged under 40 were literate. The members of the society were consuming an average of 2,000 calories daily, and about 24 per cent of Ghana's population were urban dwellers. These figures were high in comparison with other African societies. Ghana also had a rapidly expanding group of professionals, lawyers, secondary and university teachers, civil servants and managers comprising a new middle class. It will be recalled that the first military coup in Ghana occurred in 1966. Further comparisons will show the fairly buoyant state of the Ghanaian economic and social situation prior to the military take-over. In 1959 Ghana had less than one-third of Ethiopia's population but had more secondary-level students than Ethiopia had primary-school children. The per capita consumption of electric power in Ghana at that time was one-third that of Kenya and one-quarter that of Nigeria. It was reported (*ARB*, December 1979, p. 4882) that by the end of four months of violence after Rawlings, Ghana had been left in an abysmal state of economic chaos. For example, petrol was rationed, factories were producing at less than 30 per cent of their capacity, there were no spare parts and no raw materials, and the professional middle class were fleeing the country. In the interim period between 1966 and 1979 we had a succession of military coups in Ghana when power was held by General Ankrah, General Acheampong and General Akuffo; Flight Lieutenant Rawlings ruled briefly for about four months in 1979, and there was a short period of civilian rule when President Busia was in power. We may now ask the question, what has happened in the periods when the military were in power? It is true that we have had a greater succession of military coups than either of the other two nations we are comparing. We will now briefly attempt to see what these army rulers have done and why they have failed in Ghana.

When Acheampong came to power, he gave a series of economic development guidelines which appeared very impressive and utopian. One of the guidelines he issued was to expand the production base of the economy commensurate with the need to raise the living standards of the Ghanaian people as fast as resources would permit. Secondly, he aimed at promoting full and efficient use of all resources, human and material, and determined to eliminate the great differences in the distribution of income and wealth. He promised to promote national economic independence especially in food production and in investment, and to maintain a reasonable external balance of trade. He also promised to maintain reasonable price stability and to avoid sustained and rapid increases in the general price level. Rather impressively, he attempted to give priority to the need to relate production to social-psychological and biological variables such as nutrition requirement, raw material requirement, and so on, and he promised to give priority to the neglected small producers in both agriculture and fishing. This emphasises the need for private investment, however small. Acheampong also promised to revamp the state of agricultural statistics in the nation and to reorganise the state of land tenure practices. He further determined to apply all financial resources to the productive sector of the economy in areas of priority such as agriculture in a manner which would make Ghana more self-reliant. There is a tremendous gap between military rhetoric and ability to achieve results.

In 1974/5 the National Redemption Council headed by Acheampong was spending about 555,000 million cedis on the national economy and this represented the largest sum ever voted by a government of Ghana for development. We can now begin to see mistakes of management. Acheampong had hoped that injecting so much money into the economy would improve the state of the economy. The chairman of Ghana Commercial Bank commented in 1975 that in spite of the injection of this amount, Ghana was yet to achieve a major breakthrough in agriculture. Indeed, cocoa production was declining and cocoa had been the mainstay of the Ghanaian economy for decades. In the 1961–5 production period an average of 454,000 tonnes were produced annually; by 1974 this had declined to 381,600 tonnes.

Upon assumption of power General William Akuffo accused General Acheampong of a series of offences including: (1) interference in the Central Bank operations by causing overprinting and issuing of cedis currency; (2) the affecting of dubious foreign loans to the detriment of Ghana; (3) personally granting undeserved concessions to his favourite businessmen; and finally (4) that General Acheampong had brought the armed forces to the brink of disintegration and had contributed to the breakdown of armed forces discipline by showering favour on his close friends. It was obvious that during Acheampong's rule the Ghanaian economy had been plundered by both the army and the civilian businessmen and that his rule represented a textbook case of mismanagement. Between 1975 and 1978 the trade deficit had increased, money supply was completely out of control, inflation between 1976 and 1977 reached triple figures. The productive sector of the economy had been starved of foreign exchange, and of spare parts and raw materials; and cocoa had been neglected. The Gross Domestic Product had shrunk by 5 per cent between 1975 and 1977, and by the end of 1978 Ghana had an estimated current account of only £40·4 million. During 1976/7 the money supply had risen by 45 per cent, and by 65 per cent in 1977/8. Such budgets were financed largely by printing money. When Akuffo came to power he reduced the development programme to almost nothing, but his regime still failed to keep within its target for controlling a budget deficit.

While the case of Ghana seems to be a classical example of mismanagement of the economy, it must be pointed out that natural resources in Ghana were generally meagre compared with Nigeria. Cocoa had been depended upon for far too long as the mainstay of the economy, and the economy had thus not been sufficiently diversified to take account of modern development. However, as we said earlier, where resources are meagre new crises tend to arise. The Ghanaian crises have been reflected in the massive flight of the emerging middle class of businessmen and professionals to neighbouring West African countries, particularly Nigeria, and also to Europe and the United States. This flight has reduced investment in the private sector as well as the supply of manpower to run the national economy. Thus, while successive military regimes in Ghana have either plundered or run the economy poorly, it is also obvious that several social groups have related to the economy in a way that has not augured well for development.

In concluding this chapter, I have demonstrated that where the military has ruled in Africa it has attempted to espouse its values of coercion as well as military nationalism but it has had to contend with competing social and economic groups and structures in the society some of which are antagonistic, some of which are relatively ambivalent and some of which agree to be incorporated into the system. The greatest problem lies with rising business groups and the bureaucracy. The military has failed to restructure and reorganise the bureaucracy in line with the new orientation which it is attempting to bring to the society. If this had been done, the military might have been more successful. We have also seen that the structure of the society and the relationship among the various groups have implications for the ability of the military to rule. One important final feature of this mode of development is the eventual alignment of the national bourgeoisie with external financial capital which in the final analysis may begin to stifle development. This is simply because production will stagnate as the importation and distribution of goods increase. Such a factor may lead to instability.

6
Military Regimes and Political Change

The first section of this chapter will be devoted to a theoretical consideration of the issues of political integration and development under the military. The second section will deal with empirical evidence of political institution-building, political participation, recruitment, military disengagement from powers and political action of the military as each relates to the political process. The final section will consider military rule and the balance of power.

The Military: Problems of Political Integration and Political Development

One of the major problems facing political development in Third World nations (especially in Africa and Asia) is the lack of national integration. Ethnic rivalry, primordial sentiments and regional parochialism are significant deterrents against the development of nationhood (Geertz, 1963). Because of its organisational characteristics of cohesion and its ideology of nationalism, the military is considered as a melting-pot 'in which various heterogeneous elements are united' (Pye, 1962). It is also regarded as an organisation which can draw 'recruits from all tribes and regions in the state and give them the same training and experience' (Jordan, 1962), and where 'troops of diverse origin commingle into an arbitrary social group in which position and relations are determined by criteria of military rank and proficiency rather than pre-service status' (Walterhouse, 1964, p. 22). How applicable to African militaries are these characteristics?

It cannot be assumed that membership in a heterogeneous army necessarily fosters a 'national outlook'. Evidence shows that recruitment to African armies is so skewed, that it becomes difficult to see the military as diminishing ethnic rivalry. For instance, the Kamba and Kalenjin of Kenya, while representing 9–11 per cent of the total population, provided 34 per cent of the army in 1961 (Rosberg and Nottingham, 1966, p. 26). In Ghana, 62 per cent of the 'other' rank came from the far north. In Nigeria in 1961, of 81 officers, 60 were Ibos. It was a deliberate policy of the British government to recruit the 'other' ranks from the minority groups which were thought to be suspicious of nationalist movements (sponsored mainly by major ethnic groups). In this way a constant division was ensured among the groups (McWilliams, 1967). Lee (1969) commented that the African military has broken down exactly at those points at which the rest of society show signs of stress (for instance, the second military uprising in Nigeria reflected the internal ethnic divisions of the country). The sensitivity of military institutions to political and class (let me add, 'ethnic') cleavages makes them as much part of the problem as the solution. I will hasten to add, however, that the example of the Nigerian first coup seems both exaggerated and used out of context. The first military uprising saw an Ibo officer commanding Hausa soldiers who killed the country's Prime Minister (Hausa), and the Northern Nigerian Premier and spiritual leader (Hausa); another Ibo officer commanding Yoruba soldiers killed the Western Nigerian Premier (Yoruba), and top-ranking Yoruba and Hausa military officers. Thus, the internal cohesion of the military broke down only after the first coup following upon what are now considered to be partisan policy and planning on the part of the General (himself an Ibo) who took over power. This underlines the significance of analysing the internal dynamics of coups in the effort to make for better theory-building.

On balance, however, the very fact that the military broke down in many African countries exactly at the same ethnic line as the rest of the society reveals that the military organisation is not exempt from tribal influences. At a conceptual level other than the ethnic, the military has often intervened as arbiters between two warring élite sectors: the 'politicians' and the 'bureaucrats'. It has, however, more often leaned in support of the bureaucrats. But by whatever mechanism it has established order, its role in communication (and therefore institutional building) at the political level seems inevitable. The fact of its involvement in the maintenance of the social structure is clear, especially bearing in mind that stability was difficult for civilian politicians to maintain in Nigeria.

Military rule, it is claimed, is one of several practicable and apparently stable alternatives when parliamentary democracy falters (Shils, 1962). It is also maintained that the 'political regimes–the civilian-based political regimes–tend to be much less stable than the military regimes and in many of these nations there are coups within the coup, that is, inner coups within the military structure that function to make civilian rule superfluous' (Possony, 1961, p. 239). Jordan (1962) contends that the ineffectiveness of civilian governments contrasts forcibly with the comparative efficiency of their armies in matters of planning, organising and accomplishing. His position has derived from the organisational characteristics of centralised command, hierarchy, internal discipline, efficient means of intercommunication and *esprit de corps.*

The issues raised are quite clear: Is the military an evidence of authority rather than of sheer power? To what extent is the military capable of harmonising varied interests in the society? Can its shared organisational characteristics enable it to reach down to the grass roots to mobilise people and to direct social and economic change? These are ideas of political development that stress the role of the party rather than the military.

It will be emphasised that those who hold the view that the military can establish stability are cautious to stress that in the long run the party appears to be the institution that can fulfil this role and that the military can only establish the preconditions for stability. Halpern (1963), who had himself earlier stressed the relative modernity of the military and their special political virtues in the Middle East, argued that only parties were capable of instilling a sense of citizenship and organising public participation in political decisions in the Middle East. He maintained that it was only a party that could be in daily contact with the constituency to adapt new ideas and policies in the Middle East. Only a party could stimulate involvement and gather new talents and thus regularise recruitment into the New Elite–'only parties can link leaders and masses in almost daily contact–only parties can organise enthusiasm on the basis of solidarity with citizens outside the country' (pp. 283–5). Horowitz (1966, p. 368) stresses that the military role in political development is enhanced by political or bureaucratic consensus but that the military may 'also become a mark of sectional and regional cleavage when there is an absence of consensus'. Bell (1965) was rather ambivalent and pessimistic, and believed that the military can provide only 'something' of a guarantee against the kind of chaos which would make development, hard as it is now, almost impossible.

We must bear in mind that military oligarchies may have no definite conception of the kind of regime towards which they wish to move. This remark is well illustrated by Price's (1971b) analysis of Ghanaian political development during the military regime. He established that the Ghanaian National Liberation Movement bungled every political move it made at institution-building and showed that it lacked any clear programme of development for the nation. While Janowitz (1964) acknowledged the organisational characteristics of the military (his analysis is essentially on an organisational model), he commented that it is easier for the military to accumulate power than to govern as a ruling group.

There are those who posit that these same organisational characteristics are real weaknesses or disadvantages in the process of political development. First, the characteristics of authority and centralisation do not allow for full participation and mobilisation, a phenomenon which may be perceived by the military as inducing disorder. It has been suggested that the military has not been conspicuously successful in social history in long-run administration conducted in terms of armed force organisations, because pre-occupations with the rational application of force and high levels of coercion tend to preclude consideration of other measure-'and in the context of all viable armed force systems there is an emphasis on command which is never easily identifiable with an emphasis on governing in general' (Levy, 1966). Bienen (1968), McWilliams (1964) and Janowitz (1964) all agree that the armed forces can be more concerned with control than with modernisation, because the passion for control, organisation and routine can replace politics. Hopkins (1966), evaluating the major postwar writing on military coups in non-industrial states, expresses preference for cautious generalisations and concludes that the very supremacy of military power prevents the growth of other mechanisms of tension management and limits further growth. This position has also been well documented by Horowitz (1966) who expressed doubts about military capability to maintain social order over a long time. Huntington (1962) came out with an outright denial of the role of the military in political development. To Huntington political development simply means institutional building. This he contrasted with political modernisation, as we noted in Chapter 1 (that is, mobilisation and participation), which, he contended, other analysts have used. The military is, in his view, hostile to the needs of political institution-building since they can eliminate from politics individual civilian politicians, and are still prepared to make fundamental changes in political processes and institutions.

The situation of political change varies from one Third World country to another. In Brazil and in Ghana (before 1972) the military was unwilling to make such changes. But in Nigeria since 1970 it has been the military that instituted far-reaching changes like dividing the country into states to ensure the participation of minority ethnic groups-a goal the parties found impossible to achieve before that time. The military in Ethiopia built viable if not highly successful political institutions. For Huntington it is the political party and not the military which can be effectively institutionalised as a ruling force. The importance of the political party, in providing legitimacy and stability in a modernising political system, varies inversely with the constitutional society. Military coups and military juntas may spur modernisation, but they cannot produce a stable political order, Huntington (1962) finally maintained. But indeed the military *has* produced order and stability, if only in a transitional holding role, especially in countries like Nigeria hopelessly torn by ethnic rivalry and political cleavages. The question of legitimacy and authority that this issue raises opens a whole new area which I shall not deal with extensively here since I have done so elsewhere (Odetola, 1978). Suffice it to say that the contents of the national political system become stabilised at that point in time when basic socio-economic needs are satisfied; there is in fact no mass mobilisation beyond such a point. If socio-economic needs are satisfied within a socialist regime then that system is stabilised; 'if they become satisfied during the military era–then the military dictatorship becomes normative and durable. Satisfaction of basic social services and economic wants is a crucial factor beyond which masses do not carry on active political struggle' (Horowitz, 1966; Odetola, 1978). The significance of this theoretical position is that it allows us room to manoeuvre and enough flexibility to assess the performance of each political system on its own merit. Such a monolithic position as that taken by Huntington renders comparative and historical political analysis irrelevant *ab initio*. This critique reinforces the idea that under certain conditions the military, far from being a threat to democratic institutions, may serve as a force to uphold and safeguard them. The military has intervened in some cases to remove another military regime which has usurped democratic power, as happened in Sierra Leone during the short tussle involving Lamisana, Stevens and others. Huntington's position would make it theoretically and empirically impossible to determine what those conditions may be.

Political Institution-Building

The question to which I shall be seeking answers in this section is not whether the military can build political institutions. This question has already been asked in the body of the literature. But I am of the opinion that the military can build political institutions if the need arises and if it has clearly defined goals for the nation. In other words, I shall be examining why certain political institutions have been built by certain military rulers and not others. Also, I shall be trying to seek answers to the question, what uses have been made of the institutions that were established by the military? From these answers, it will be apparent what the goals or aims of the military have been in the different African states as well as the extent to which they have made use of the institutions which they have built.

The uses to which they have put these institutions will also help to categorise types of institutions built by them. My emphasis will be largely on two types of institutions: the mass political institutions such as the Peasant Associations and the Urban Dwellers' Associations called Kebeles in Ethiopia; and secondly, what I have called administrative institutions such as the National Youth Service Corps in Nigeria, Ghana, Mali and Benin. We will then be able to examine the performance of these institutions and see whether they have succeeded in making any structural political change in their societies as well as whether they are likely to last. While discussing mass political institutions, I will also attempt to examine the efforts of military rulers to build political parties.

The military rulers who have socialist goals for their nations have attempted to build mass political institutions more effectively than those military governments that do not have socialist goals for their nations. In other words Ethiopia, for example, has built institutions which appear to be geared towards the achievement of their aims more than have Ghana or Nigeria. Attention will now be turned to the kinds of institution built by Ethiopia. We will then consider what institutions the other nations have built.

Ethiopia established the Peasant Associations and Urban Dwellers' Associations as mass political mobilisation agencies. The Peasant Associations, as noted earlier in this book, had various duties to perform. Among these were: (1) villagisation; (2) land distribution; and (3) the adjudication of land disputes. Other functions that the Peasant Associations were to perform included the establishment of service co-operatives as well as the distribution of market and farm products. In other words, the activities of the Peasant Associations ramified the total life of the rural people. The adjudication functions of these associations could not go to the local courts. Also, the bureaucracy and the local landlords were not allowed to be members of the associations. These steps ensured that these two latter groups could not interfere in the administration of the land reform. By the middle of 1975 there were about 18,000 Peasant Associations and in March 1978 the number had increased to 25,000.

The achievements of the Peasant Associations ranged from minimal to moderate, as noted in Chapter 5. There were a number of problems facing the operations and activities of the Peasant Associations. First, the associations were established only at the sub-district (Woreda) and district (Awraja) levels, not at provincial or national levels. This failure did not allow the Peasant Associations any structural relationships at the national level and therefore limited their performances to the district level. In other words, the role of the Peasant Associations was not clearly outlined initially in relation to other levels of government (Bailey, 1979). This nebulous situation did not give the precision necessary to the movement of the Peasant Associations. The associations faced opposition from different social groups. For example, the trade union called the Central Ethiopian Labour Union

(CELU) saw no gain for labour and therefore did not give any support to the Peasant Associations. In fact they perceived the adjudication role of the Peasant Associations to be in conflict with some of their own roles in settling quarrels among their own members. Also, the roles defined for the Peasant Associations did not satisfy the aspirations of students and other leftists who wanted the Peasant Associations to be armed. These groups perceived the establishment of the Peasant Associations as an opportunity to increase political consciousness and class struggle. Of course, other students saw it in a different light. They perceived this institution as an attempt to remove them from Addis Ababa which was the focus of action. Similarly, the nobility became extremely nervous and the bureaucracy and the national bourgeoisie saw that they were going to lose power. In recognition of these problems and failures, the military expanded the role of the Peasant Associations. Even with this step the activities of the associations remained localised, with serious implications at the national level. Therefore the military took the further step of establishing the New Revolutionary and Development Committees comprising students and peasant campaigners. Again these new committees did not function well because they were dominated by appointed officials.

In April 1978 the military took the much more logical step of establishing the All Ethiopian Peasant Association. This was to serve as a co-ordinator over all organisations for the activities of the local Peasant Associations. Also established was a Peasant Leadership Training Centre to produce leaders for the associations; and members of the PMAC, that is, the ruling military council, were appointed as regional administrators and campaigns began at the national level in 1979. In addition, 1,000 newly and hastily trained production leaders were introduced into the rural areas to intensify class struggle as well as to increase production and to help farm collection (Bailey, 1979).

It will be observed that the military had taken half-halting steps in the establishment and definition of the activities of the Peasant Associations. We can infer, therefore, that the initial goals of the military itself were not clearly defined, and that it took pragmatic steps as problems arose in order to take care of problems and build in new strategies to counter the activities of the opposition. We can argue in two different ways. First, we can say that these half-haphazard steps would not establish a sound basis for the operation and continued existence of the institutions. On the other hand, we can suggest that the ability to reflect at every turn and be pragmatic could only strengthen these institutions.

The military in Ethiopia has succeeded permanently in redistributing political power by establishing local control over tax collection, land distribution and village organisation throughout the country. If these particular institutions are eventually dismantled, the results they have achieved so far will certainly have a permanent effect on the structure of society and relations within it. The land reform, the resultant income and power redistribution, and the Peasant Associations have given the peasantry as a group an identification and a power which have strengthened their support of the PMAC. In other words, the PMAC have established a viable base of support for themselves. The Urban Dwellers' Associations represented the Ethiopian military regime's principal political structural innovations in the urban centres to complement the activities of the Peasant Associations in the rural areas. The Kebeles were a low-level organisation comprising 300 households. Next in the hierarchy were the Kiftegras or higher Kebeles, the next level was the Central Committee, and finally there was an Executive Committee of State among whom the mayor of the city served. The members of the Kebeles were elected democratically by universal adult suffrage. Former landlords were excluded for one year from becoming members: thus their power was curtailed and thereby a little time was given for this new political institution to consolidate itself. The Kebeles were administratively linked to the Ministry of the Interior. Not until October 1976 were the roles and activities of the Kebeles clearly formulated and expanded. These included the administration of houses rented for 100 birr or below.

Other duties included the adjudication of low-level criminal cases, the administration of schools and local government, and also the formulation of defence squads and the organisation of Women's and Youth Associations. These activities, which ranged from the organisation of voluntary associations to the adjudication of criminal cases, give wide-ranging power to the Kebeles. However, their achievement was again below expectation. They helped to improve and expand educational facilities, and also helped with development projects and to some extent controlled urban crime through the activities of the defence squad. Thus they have performed useful functions in local governments but they have not developed as a political structure. The PMAC used the Urban Dwellers' Association as an instrument to combat opposition to itself. For example, in 1976 when the opposition from the Ethiopian People's Revolutionary Party became evident the Kebeles became the political instrument of the government. Government supporters infiltrated or were directly elected into the associations. They were armed and they stormed Addis Ababa in search of EPRP members. The violence which followed harmed the image of the Kebeles as a voluntary group aiming at national consensus. The image of a violent coercive group drives away many members of the community. The emerging élite groups avoided the associations because these élites were not initially members and were even subject to suspicion of all kinds. Comparing the Kebeles to Peasant Associations, it will be seen that the land distribution function given to the Peasant Associations endowed them with a great power which was not available to the Kebeles. The distribution of land defined economic relations in the society since 95 per cent of the people were farmers. However, control of house rent did not. For example, the petty bourgeoisie rented houses worth more than 100 birr and therefore owed no allegiance to the Kebeles. In fact, as noted earlier, the petty bourgeoisie snobbed the associations by moving from houses rented for less than 100 birr. The disparate collection of members ranging from artisans to low-salaried workers did not make for the homogeneity of interest necessary for the establishment of cohesion. The activities of the Kebeles were therefore not highly central to the daily life of the people as were the activities of the Peasant Associations. Therefore, the Kebeles did not provide a national focus of political activity.

This limited success of the military in political institution-building is even greater than the success of the militaries of other African nations. In fact, what most African military rulers appear to have done is at one time or another to have organised movements aimed at achieving national consensus and mobilisation. These movements have been managed by the bureaucracy largely in Nigeria and Ghana, the Republic of Benin, Niger and Upper Volta. They have not been in any way organised or structured to relate to other political structures in the society, and thus have served more or less administrative functions. For example, in Nigeria a National Youth Service Corps was organised and comprised university and college of education students. Its aims were to train farmers in the movement towards the increase of national production. A similar organisation was established in Ghana, also aimed at increasing national production. However, since its administration was carried out largely by bureaucrats it has had very little political impact. In fact its original aim of campaigning in the rural areas has been discontinued and most of the members are deployed largely to teach and perform other such functions in the urban centres. Members had also become increasingly unwilling to go into the rural areas and the original aims and goals of the movement had been dissipated. In the Upper Volta, Lamizana in 1975 announced the formation of a National Movement for Renovation, to provide a single framework for all economic, social, cultural and political activities, and to awaken national consciousness in order to achieve national unity. Other aims were to mobilise and organise the masses for development, to work for the social, political and cultural emancipation of the people and to work for lasting economic development for the country. In 1975 in the Republic of Benin the military organised all students who had completed their studies into a twelve-month course and work programme characterised as patriotic, ideological and civic service which would provide them with military and ideological training. The completion of this programme is, as in the Nigerian example, a prerequisite to employment. In the Niger Republic, the Supreme Military Council said that it did not intend to establish institutions such as political parties because it believed that the absence of such institutions hitherto had not prevented the state from functioning. However, the army did decide to restore the Samarias. These are traditional village and regional groups which comprise the youth, the women and the elders. The army intended these groups to form the basis for future national political structure.

It is obvious from the above that the grandiose aim of the military to alter the political structure of the society has not been matched with a corresponding effort to build the institutions that are designed to achieve those aims. The only exception we have analysed is that of Ethiopia which has proceeded to alter the political structure of its society.

Perhaps the establishment of political institutions would necessitate also the building of another mass organisation to embrace the minor political institutions. Such organisations can be a political party. The Ethiopian military government announced in July 1975 the formation of a new political party to be guided by the aims of Ethiopian socialism. If this had taken off, it would have been the first political party in modern Ethiopian history, the emperor having banned all political parties for the forty-four years of his reign. It was only in 1979 that the military rulers finally decided to move forward with the establishment of a political party. A Communist Party Centre headed by Mengistu himself was inaugurated in December 1979. He also created a commission to work towards the establishment of a political party at the same time. The Kebeles had organised rallies and support movements in Addis Ababa as a response to a call by Mengistu for popular backing for a commission he was organising to oversee the party organisation. It must be immediately pointed out, however, that the Urban Dwellers' Associations or Kebeles had always been successful in organising parades and support rallies but the extent to which they can be used as a base for the establishment of a political party is yet to be seen. Perhaps the longer the military stays in power, the lower is the potential for a political party to be formed. For example, the ten years of military rule in Mali by Traore had left little room for the potential development of a party. Traore had constituted the military Commission for National Freedom (CMLN) in order to establish the Mali People's Democratic Union. He had said that the military would never return to the barracks but would govern with the civilians. Similar steps are being taken in the Republic of Benin and there is evidence of this in the Niger Republic.

Perhaps again it is only in Nigeria and Ghana that this had not taken place. I am arguing that the military, particularly those who have a socialist orientation, attempt to fuse the party and the state together by incorporating the military completely into the government, as the example of Guinea shows. In Guinea the army has been completely integrated into civilian administrative structures. The army is to train and to develop the society and it now has production brigades and was expected to contribute its own visible support by 1976. Local government in Guinea is carried on by 2,000 Local Revolutionary Parties (LRP) and run by a committee which is a committee of the local section of the National Political Party (PDG). It is also the holder of all administrative power. In Guinea the local government is responsible for defence, whereas the (PRL) militia company forms the mainstay of national defence. All the Local Revolutionary Parties own shops, tractors and village co-operatives. Between the PRL and central government are the Regional Revolutionary Councils controlled by political commissars. At the central level the fusion is personified by Toure who is the General Secretary and President and is subject to re-election after seven years (*ARB*, September 1975, p. 5756). It is evident that in Africa where the orientation of the ruling military or group is towards socialism, the army has tended to be integrated into the party system in an effort to form a strong state apparatus. While the efforts of Mengistu to form a mass political party have been rather haphazard, we may predict that in the end he will follow the footsteps of Mobutu in Zaire or Sadat in Egypt.

Political Participation

I will make the hypothesis in this section that the level of participation encouraged by military governments in many African states is higher than anticipated and broader in scope than the literature would allow for. For example, civilians have been allowed to participate in the top decision-making levels of most military-run governments in Africa. In Nigeria the number of civilians in the federal Cabinet throughout the Muhammed and Obasanjo regimes was about equal to the number of military personnel in government. This is also true of state governments throughout Nigeria and examples can be found in Ghana and Mali. Even in Ethiopia the establishment of political institutions has broadened the scope of participation by civilians in government operations and in decision-making. The difference between the situation in Ethiopia and that of Nigeria and Ghana is that the scope of participation in Ethiopia at the lower levels is much higher than the scope of participation in Ghana.

During the Gowon era in Nigeria state-appointed commissioners were the people who operated local government, whereas in Ethiopia, as we have seen, local government was run by Peasant Associations and the Urban Dwellers' Associations. The Muhammed–Obasanjo regime in Nigeria introduced local government reforms to improve participation in government at the grass-roots level. That is, in the time of Obasanjo and Muhammed there were direct universal adult suffrage elections into local government councils similar to the universal elections into Peasant Associations and Kebeles in Ethiopia. The local government reforms in Nigeria were, however, limited in scope. For example, the local government councils held office through the goodwill of state governments. In other words, the pattern of relationship among the lower, middle and higher levels of government were not basically altered in Nigeria when compared with what was done in Ethiopia. We can safely say, therefore, that political awareness was raised in the Ethiopian case to a much higher level than had been the case in the Nigerian and Ghanaian experiences.

Another important issue to be dealt with here is the level of consultation that the military makes with the civil society since there is no direct participation of the mass of the people in government. An empirical study which I made revealed that military governments make extensive consultations with the civil society when important decisions have to be made (Odetola, 1980). General Obasanjo, in an interview I had with him, said that he had instructed members of the military in his Cabinet to take over certain areas of the nation as if those areas represented their constituencies. Such men had to have a good knowledge of the areas they supposedly 'represented' and they were to conduct informally any investigations necessary when important issues arose in order to put out the fire when problems were about to arise. Some of these men had taken part in what is regarded as pacification efforts. Therefore, in a non-legal sense, these men had their own constituencies which they had to oversee from time to time. Also, General Obasanjo and his successor head of state made informal contacts with the rest of the society by keeping close touch with their personal friends. Some of these friends later became commissioners in the Cabinet. Such friends also usually made contact with other friends and local leaders and there was regular feedback into the executive or Supreme Military Council about what went on in the society. This network of consultations became very important.

Major General Jemibewon, as governor of Oyo state, made extensive use of these informal channels of communication. So also did his predecessors, Brigadier Rotimi and Major General Adebayo. Jemibewon (1978) said that he built up his own unofficial sources of intelligence so as to know and anticipate events not only in the state capital but in every part of the state. He stated that these sources were often private and sometimes personal. He admitted that aside from the conventional means of communication and in the absence of a political apparatus to fulfil the need of constant communication with the people, he had devised these unofficial sources of intelligence. He said that he had not found the absence of political participation or political activities to be any serious handicap to the working of government especially in the area of decision-making.

This statement is similar to that made earlier by General Kountche of the Republic of Niger who also said that he did not find the absence of direct political participation harmful to the running of the government. Jemibewon said that whenever he needed advice, the absence of political involvement of the mass of the people appeared to be a distinct advantage. For example, he found it easier to consult all shades of opinion whenever he needed advice. The result was that he had at his disposal advice and comment from all possible and available quarters. This had aided him in arriving at balanced opinions. He argued that this is not the case in a normal civilian government in which the head of government consults only his lieutenants and political party supporters and can sometimes be indifferent to the opinions of the opposition. Jemibewon further claimed that this kind of consultation represent the hallmark of government identification with the people He said: 'in the face of all of these it will certainly be an overstatement for any one to suggest that lack of political participation and therefore consultations in a military regime produces a gap in communication between the government and the governed and reduces the quality of decision-making' (1978, p. 184). General Obasanjo himself said that the federal military government had had to send emissaries to Obas and Chiefs and Emirs in an attempt to find out their opinions on specific issues. This supports the position that the military makes use of patrimonialism in their effort to rule the nation (Odetola, 1978).

The character of participation described above is of course very different from direct access to decision-making at the local level by the mass of the people in their local government councils under civilian regimes. In fact, the nature of consultations described above will be limited to the elite in the society whose opinion will be respected. Therefore, the kind of participation in Ethiopia appears to be more broadly mass-oriented than is the kind of participation described in the Nigerian situation. Jemibewon himself does not pretend that government can be carried on at all times in this way. In fact, his assertion merely emphasises the transitory nature of military rule.

If the military consults with the civil society both during normal peacetime and during crises, what, we may ask, is the nature of the military response to civilian demands to exercise their civil rights? Such rights are freedom of assembly, press freedom, and so on. How does the military respond to an open confrontation mounted by the civilian population? Does the military respond by crushing the rebellion with force or by conciliation? I would argue that from the evidence I am about to provide the military attempt first to conciliate by inviting the leaders of demonstrating groups for deliberations, but follow that up with a hard line; they may again come back to conciliate, and in the final analysis if the situation is not solved may resort to repressive measures. 'Hard line' as used here may mean arrest, detention, imprisonment, or, finally, the execution of demonstrators. The particular steps to be adopted and the variations of adoption of these steps depend on several factors such as the significance of the issue on demand and the severity of the demonstrations, and also upon the social milieu currently existing in the society. This factor will make for variations of response from nation to nation and also within a particular nation between successive military governments if there has been more than one.

In Ethiopia in 1974 the labour workers, teachers and others demonstrated against the PMAC for prohibiting their right to assemble publicly as well as protesting against control of press freedom. The military responded by arresting three leaders of the trade union. It then instituted a Civilian Advisory Commission to investigate the demands of the demonstrators. It will be seen that the pattern runs here from hard line to conciliation. The military had earlier enshrined into the proclamations of socialism the right for the anti-imperialist and anti-feudal masses to form associations, to hold meetings, to demonstrate or to strike and the right to freedom of written and spoken expression. Of course, it will be noted that it is the military alone that is in a position to decide what is anti-imperialist and anti-feudal. In September 1975 Addis Ababa was partially paralysed by strikes. On 25 September 1975 four people were killed and about thirty injured near the airport. Most of those injured were Ethiopian airline employees who were distributing leaflets in support of their demands (*A RB*, September 1975). When the agitations could not be resolved, the government proceeded to increase repressive measures. Universities were closed down and the students were drafted into the countryside to educate the farmers rather than demonstrate in the cities. The military declared a state of emergency on 30 September having already executed more than 200 people, some for opposing the land reform. Some people were executed because they were killing farmers who were loyal to the government. It will, of course, be seen that the military government resorted to massive use of force when it discovered that important economic units such as the Trade Union Federation (TUC) were delivering ultimatums to it requiring it to increase democratic freedom, freedom of the press and other civil rights. The Trade Union Federation resolved that it wanted the establishment of several political parties and disagreed with the single-party system. It had threatened the government earlier that if these steps were not taken, then the TUC would take appropriate measures. Perhaps even a civilian government would react by introducing repressive measures when faced with this kind of ultimatum. We must remember that during the reign of Nkrumah in Ghana several people were incarcerated in prison without trial and that several of them died in prison. The comparison being made is not designed to justify the repressive measures of the military but to call to mind the fact that civilian governments are themselves not immune from this kind of response.

Turning to Nigeria, several people were arrested during the Gowon regime for varying types of offences. For example, four men were arrested in February 1975 for attempting to stir up disturbances aimed at overthrowing the Nigerian military government by circulating new salary scales for the armed forces so as to discredit the government. They were also charged with being in league with the students who were allegedly planning to overthrow the government. Some newspaper journalists were arrested and one of them was subjected to the indignity of having his hair shaved off on the orders of a state military governor.

In the Sudan Republic General Nimiery proceeded to take a series of highly repressive measures. These measures were in response to the very deep cleavages which had threatened to tear the society apart. There was an attempted coup led by Lieutenant Colonel Osman who alleged that repression in the Sudan was reaching unacceptable proportions. Osman said that persecution, torture, destruction of the freedom of the press, closure of the Islamic University and the curtailing of the freedom of Khartoum University were no longer tolerable to the people. He was sentenced to death. In September 1975 Nimiery instituted certain constitutional amendments which enabled the President to take any measures and decisions he deemed suitable against 'saboteurs'. The legislative authorities were to be able to define the bases in which people could be detained, when their residences could be assigned to other persons and when their movements could be restricted for reasons connected with state security, safety and public order. Examples of these repressive measures abound in most African nations. In Mali in April 1975 certain people were jailed for publishing tracts which had urged people to vote 'no' in the June 1974 referendum on the new Mali constitution. At the same time, 267 people had been drafted to the army in Mali for rioting in 1979. It appears that in Mali Traore had not even given people the opportunity to vote 'no' in the referendum.

Another dimension that we will turn to finally in these considerations of political participation is the degree of press freedom which I have referred to earlier. Many military governments have always claimed that they would guarantee freedom of the press and be close to the people and be responsive to their yearnings and their aspirations (Obasanjo, 1980; Ocran, 1977). The press is regarded as one of those agencies which help to project the aspirations of the people and to bring out weaknesses in the government. The relationship between the press and the government even during the civilian era had always been at best an ambivalent one and at the worst a very hostile one. In considering African military governments, it is fair to say that this relationship ranges in general from fair to ambivalent. Of course, this includes those nations where the relationship has been markedly bad and hostile. In the Nigerian situation, which we will consider at length, the relationship between the government and the press has been ambivalent and sometimes hostile. Generally, however, only occasional hostility has been expressed and when this happens the government comes out to take what it considers to be corrective measures.

In Nigeria in 1975 the relationship between the press and the government was going from fair to bad. The Chief of Staff of the army at that time, General Ejoor, declared in a press conference in Lagos that Nigerian journalists were corrupt and that this corruption did not only involve money but also extended to the handling of political issues. General Gowon, the head of state at that time, also supported this allegation. The *Nigerian Daily Times* of 9 April 1975 viewed this with apprehension. In an editorial it called on the government to reiterate its commitment to the freedom of the press which the *Daily Times* regarded as the freedom of the citizen to have a say in the affairs of his own country. Similarly, the Nigerian Guild of Editors challenged the Army Chief of Staff to expose all corrupt journalists known to him. The statement appeared quite shocking to the association of journalists who had wanted the head of state to make a policy statement on press freedom. They had asked the Gowon government to guarantee press freedom because, they said, the army could not govern Nigeria, the biggest black race in Africa, without a strong press. From then on the furore gathered momentum in the newspapers and the mass media generally.

The Nigerian Union of Journalists defined press freedom as the absence of unnecessary control, freedom to report and freedom from excessive laws. An examination of this definition will show that it is not clear what the terms 'unnecessary control', 'excessive laws' represent. The Nigerian press became quite agitated about ensuring freedom of the press in the constitution. It complained that press censorship was being introduced by the military governors of certain states, for example, the Bendel, Ogun and Oyo states, and that this control required that all news and features articles meant for publication should be censored. At this time most national newspapers cried out in their editorial opinions against this alleged control. In a swift reaction of reassurance the next day, the federal military government claimed that the Nigerian press remained as free as ever. It said that neither the federal nor state governments had planned any censorship. The Commissioner for Information claimed that the fear of control emanated from talks he had recently had with top journalists and newspaper executives on the need for restraints and caution in their publications (*Daily Sketch*, 10 May 1978). The Nigerian press organisations also reacted swiftly by assuring the nation of adequate performance at all times and welcomed the federal government's assurance of freedom. In a statement the leader of one of the organisations said that he saw this assurance as an indication of good faith by the present administration in pursuance of its declared objectives of open, responsive and democratic government. These exchanges underlined the ambivalence of relationships.

Meanwhile, in 1979 the federal military government established a Press Council for Nigeria (*Africa Report,* May 1979). The Guild of Editors questioned the composition and the powers of this council. The council was made up of fourteen members, eleven of whom were to be appointed by the government, and it was to be chaired by the Commissioner for Information. The duties of the council included registration of journalists and the setting of regulations and requirements for the registration, as well as taking disciplinary steps against erring journalists. It also had the power to remove journalists from the register. Although this was meant to set standards, it is fair to say that it was also designed to control the press to some extent. Some of the criticism aimed at it questioned the ability of the council to judge journalistic standards and training. Meanwhile, the Constituent Assembly set up by the military had refused to insert a clause in the new constitution guaranteeing press freedom.

The federal military government had itself become the major shareholder of the important national newspaper, the *Daily Times*, and the state governments more or less owned the most important local newspapers. The federal government had also come to control the radio and the television. This effort by the military to control the press, as it were, is in line with its orientation of centralising power in the state. The activities of the military have not differed from those engaged in by previous civilian governments. For example, the civilian administration preceding the military coup had passed the Newspaper Act. This made provision to control or have the means of checking publications in the press. The relationship between the civilian politicians and the press had thus been ambivalent. Therefore, the character of the relationship between the press and the government, whether civilian or military, had not shifted. In the Nigerian situation we can say that the press were as free under the military government as it had been under the civilian government.

Political Recruitment

How has the military government recruited into political office? From what categories have they recruited and with what consequences? How have recruitments into political office during the military era been different from those of the civilian era? The kind of recruitment made varies from nation to nation, and also with the goals of the military. In the Nigerian situation, the military government has selected most of the political office-holders from among university professors and lecturers as well as from other professional groups distributed among relevant geographical areas from state to state in the nation. In the process of selection, the military government of each area has held consultations locally with former politicians to find out who were most suitable. Now this process underscores the fact that the military itself was aware that some underground politics was still going on even during military rule. While the military occasionally made noises about such activities, it dared not clamp down on them with any direct force. The old political basis, therefore, provided the communication channels with the rest of the community. Some of the state Cabinets were about 75–90 per cent composed of university lecturers and professionals. In other words, we have on many occasions a Cabinet of experts. This had the effect of increasing the élite–mass gap both in communication and in practical politics, although it cannot be denied that this gave the military an opportunity to test the ability of other élite groups in the societies. Again, the process of recruitment underscores the kind of alliance that the military makes with the bureaucracy and also, to a limited extent, with the intelligentsia. Even in Ethiopia, where there are mass political institutions built by the military, most of these institutions were controlled at first by bureaucratic élite members. The pattern of recruitment into political office before the first military coup in Nigeria was only slightly different from that during the military era. The point here is that elections in Nigeria brought to office many members of the élite class. For example, a fair number of those who were in the legislature prior to the first military coup in 1966 were teachers in secondary schools, university lecturers, or lawyers and other professionals. This did not of course mean that people of lower education and skill were not elected into the National Assembly. The presidential system adopted since the civilian politicians have regained power allows some scope for state governors as well as the President of the nation to constitute their own Cabinets and make appointments to other political officers. The legacy of military era is continued by some of the states. For example, in Ondo state a high proportion of Cabinet members have been of the highly educated cadre. In the River state of Nigeria and in some northern states a high proportion of members of the

Cabinet have been university teachers and highly qualified professionals.

To illustrate the points made above, I will now proceed to examine the way in which Brigadier Jemibewon, the former governor of Western Nigeria and Oyo state, selected his commissioners. The governor said that he was guided by five principles. These principles were, first, to select those who were endowed with understanding and a breadth of knowledge such that their ability could not be questioned. This accords with the idea that those who were selected were people of high academic or professional qualification. Indeed, out of a Cabinet of fourteen people, seven were people with doctorates; one was a tutor and acting principal of a high institution, four were lawyers, one was a journalist regarded as a member of the national intelligentsia, and only one was a business woman. In fact, this business woman had a nursing degree. The second principle was to select equitably from among various geographical divisions in the state, the third was to avoid choosing those who had served before, and the fourth, to avoid anybody who was actively engaged in partisan politics. The final principle was to ensure that he had selected people holding good jobs which commanded a remuneration not far below that of a civil commissioner.

We will see that the second criterion agrees with our basic idea stated earlier that there was some consideration for geographical distribution. He also took special care to select from among those divisions not previously represented in the Cabinet, as well as to take care of minority sub-ethnic interest in the selection. Finally, he selected from various special interests, for example, from among women. It has been alleged, of course, that some of the commissioners must have been close personal friends of some of the military governors. While there is no direct evidence of this, one cannot rule out the likelihood that the military governors themselves, being human, would want to choose those they trust and can regard as loyal to them. Some of the principles used by Brigadier Jemibewon have been similar to those used by the President of the Federation itself. For example, the principle of taking care of geographical distribution, ethnic and special interests are obvious in the selection of the present federal civilian Cabinet. Of course, it must be noted that the present Cabinet of Oyo state headed by Governor Bola Ige has practically no university lecturers on it. In fact it is a Cabinet that represents the so-called uneducated class far more than the Cabinet of Brigadier Jemibewon. It must be emphasised, though, that the Oyo state Cabinet is not typical of the Cabinets in the rest of the nation.

The Nature of Military Action in the Political Process

The question I want to ask here is, can we identify a set of political issues whose handling by the military may be very distinctive from the way civilian politicians deal with them? Such issues include the handling of censuses, land reform, education, taxation, and so on. I would also like to examine what the consequences of military actions are for the general political system. Military sociology has identified certain characteristics of military organisations. These are that the military is prompt where the general society is tardy and is swift in action where the general society takes too long to make decisions (Horowitz, 1966). We have demonstrated that while the military may be prompt in making its decisions, it does deliberate and takes time to arrive at conclusions. If the military makes hasty decisions, this has adverse effects on the acceptance of its authority and on the general political system. Such effects include the fact that many problems are left unsolved and leave the nation as unstable as it was before the military came into power. We will now consider some specific issues which the military has handled in Nigeria, Ghana, or Ethiopia. The first of these is land reform.

The Ethiopian military government after nationalising the land in Ethiopia promptly declared all litigation that was likely to arise from the land decree null and void. Thus they built into the proclamations solutions to the problems which might arise at the interpersonal level over the exchange of land. In the Nigerian case, the situation was not so clearcut. In fact the Nigerian land decree has had much less obvious effects and has been carried out much less skilfully than that of Ethiopia. While both societies had one common problem over the administration of the land reform, that is, there were no adequate survey data of the total land available, it appears that the Ethiopian government has made further progress than Nigeria.

The explanation for this difference lies in the fact that the socialist goals of the Ethiopian government were much more clearly defined compared with the mixed public and private sector orientation of the Nigerian military. This mixed public and private orientation allowed for a large sector of the élite to own large acreages of land which were already nationalised, mainly from peasant holdings. The Ethiopian government also sent students to campaign in the rural areas, thus incorporating a strategy to make these reforms politically acceptable to the countryside. In any case, whatever the differences between the Nigerian and Ethiopian approaches to land reform, it is obvious that on both occasions the military handled a very delicate matter quite promptly, as against the vacillations which would have attended this situation if it had been handled by civilians. The military had the opportunity to do this simply because they do not have constituencies to which they have to explain their actions. We have heard that when preliminary investigations were being made by a committee into the land reform situation in Nigeria, only a minority of the group recommended nationalisation of all land. The military went ahead anyway and instituted the land reform because it believed such a step was absolutely necessary for development.

Another situation that was handled with speed by the military in Nigeria was the creation of states. The civilian government which preceded the first military coup had vacillated over the creation of states. The issue of the creation of states had centred around the demands by the various ethnic groups in Nigeria for increased political participation. I have argued elsewhere (Odetola, 1978) that civilian politicians at that time bargained tacitly among themselves over the problems of minority groups in the areas which their respective political parties controlled. In other words, they were not genuinely motivated to create states. The creation of Mid-West state of Nigeria came about in part because of a fratricidal division within the Action Group Party of Nigeria at that time, and the opportunity which the alliance between the Northern People's Congress and the National Council of Nigerian Citizens at the federal centre perceived to break further the strength of the Action Group of Nigeria.

The military created first twelve states in 1967 and then an additional seven states in 1979. Thus, it had once and for all laid the basis for the permanent solution of Nigeria's ethnic minority problems. Although the present civilian government have also been considering the creation of more states, the basis and the orientations for this were laid down by provisions that were written into the Nigerian constitution during the military era. Of course there is the general feeling that the military believed that all the states necessary to be created had been created, and in fact the provisions in the constitution written during the military era made it difficult for any new state to be created. My argument here is that if the military had not come to power, it would have been a near-impossible task for states to be created. Civilian governments perceived the creation of states as a means of dividing their base of power and thus as an attempt to undermine their political power and authority. However, once nineteen states had been created, the military were not ready to create any more. The creation of states in Nigeria brought the opportunity to generate crosscutting divisions across groups that probably would never have thought of coming together otherwise. In other words, the base of a new type of stability had been created in Nigeria (Odetola, 1978). The division of the nation into much smaller units than before would now enhance the prestige of the larger centre which can make claims to the loyalty of several smaller units.

Another issue to which I would like to turn attention is the handling of censuses in Nigeria. The census issue has been a highly problematic one. The results of the 1962 census were cancelled but those of 1963, which immediately followed, were accepted. Similarly, the results of another census in 1973 were cancelled. The reason for these cancellations was that the numbers game in which all the ethnic groups had engaged had created situations where mutual suspicion predominated, and each ethnic group feared it would not be safe and that its interests would not be catered for. The 1973 census threatened to divide the nation because the political, economic and social consciousness of the Nigerians were heightened at that time. Members of the population at large and particularly their leaders saw the numbers game as a basis for the division of the national resources. Indeed it also threatened to disintegrate the army itself. General Muhammed moved promptly to cancel the census results and thereby allay the fears of most Nigerians. However, the cancellation did not solve the problem but merely postponed it (Campbell, 1976). In any case, however, it had the effect of making this immediate problem loom less large than it would otherwise have done. It also allowed time to elapse until more stable conditions might arise for carrying out a new census.

It appears that on particular issues when national cohesion is threatened and where the civilian politicians have vacillated, the military's prompt actions have saved the society from immediate collapse. This we can explain by the orientation of the military to build national unity and cohesion through strengthening state power.

Military Disengagement

What is the significance of the withdrawal of the military from the political scene? What factors can make them withdraw? What is the general pattern of their withdrawal and how does it influence the general political development of the society? In general, withdrawal of the military may strengthen the belief of the members of the political community in succession and that a permanent political dictatorship is to be avoided. That is, it is possible for one group to succeed another albeit illegitimately at times. It therefore provides an opportunity for the political community to grow by expecting that certain changes will be made.

Several factors may be responsible for the withdrawal of the military from politics. The first of these is the general populace's disenchantment with the results they are getting from the government. One way that the political community can begin to give expression to this is by demanding the withdrawal of the military from power. Continued demonstrations and demands by the people may sometimes force the military seriously to consider leaving office. When the general populace also perceives that the military does not want to leave office, their demands and pressure on the military increase. Gowon said he did not intend to rule for long and that his ambition as a man was merely to be a brigade commander and possible commander of the entire army. However, what followed was that the Gowon regime proceeded to entrench itself in power and to insist that it was not prepared to leave government at that time. The new Gowon Cabinet of January 1975 which was made up preponderantly of military men was perceived as the beginning of the entrenchment of the army and the police permanently in power. Proclamations by military regimes of their intention to hang on to power are a function and consequence of their perception of the weakness of the polity–a situation to which the polity responds by demanding their withdrawal. Therefore, such relationships often generate instability for the society. In Uganda Amin said that if he handed over the government the civilians would again plunge the country into chaos. In other words, he did not believe that the civilian politicians could rule the nation. In March 1975 the PMAC in Ethiopia said that it intended to stay in power until a sufficiently large number of people were politically ready for civilian rule. This was a means of paving the way to hand over power to the masses because it did not believe that Ethiopia's few politically conscious élites were the sole representatives of the people. These aims were realised in the formation of a national party in Ethiopia between 1978 and 1979. Of course, it was like a delaying action to allow the military itself to build a sufficient base of power in the effort to launch its own party. It built this base of power so that the political institution it had established earlier in the Peasant Associations and the Urban Dwellers' Associations would survive. We have also seen a similar example in the case of Mali where Traore stayed in power until he believed there was sufficient opportunity for him to launch his own political party.

Another reason that the military may leave office is, in part, as a consequence of rift and disintegration within the military itself. Muhammed claimed that there was disillusion among the members of the armed forces whose administration was neglected and who had previously thought there would be a change in their own condition and the condition of the entire nation. In the Nigerian army Campbell (1976) identified a few opposing groups. The first of these were the members of the armed forces who opposed the return to civil rule. Secondly, there were those recruited from the middle belt provinces of Nigeria who constituted two-thirds of the postwar army and who expected the first civil rule to consolidate their position. Another group, mostly Hausas and Yorubas, remained in the margin of power in the army and some of them could be said to command more support among politicians and greater loyalty from large sections of civilian population than from their own military colleagues. Thus, the internal divisions within the army, while paving the way for another group to take over power, also laid the basis for the final return of the military to the barracks. Immediately on assumption of power the Muhammed regime promised to clean up the image of the military. One way, of course, that it could have done this was to fulfil its promise of leaving the political scene and returning to the barracks. It proceeded immediately, therefore, to take steps that would eventually return the politicians to politics. Therefore, the withdrawal of the military from politics had implications for the political processes that would follow. In fact, one of the important steps taken by the Obasanjo regime was to ensure the writing of a constitution and the organisation of civilian elections before it left office.

In Mali by 1979 internal disintegration within the military had reduced the ability of the military to govern. Many of the members of the ruling junta which came to power in 1968 had left. Many of them had been eliminated on charges of corruption. Traore himself was getting very tired of the situation and his preoccupation, even obsession, was to return the nation to a normal constitutional life and the development of the institutions which were sufficiently stable to be credible. So why did he not dissolve the military junta? He said that if he did he would find himself alone in power with no one to criticise him and with no balancing structure (*ARB*, February 1978, p. 5160).

If the military are forced out, as is so often the case, we may have a pattern of coups and counter-coups with resultant instability. If they leave voluntarily, as has happened in Ghana and Nigeria, it is quite possible that at least a measure of opportunity will be given for civilian trial at the political process before the military may again in the long or short run consider leaving the barracks to rule the larger society. It must be stated that there are other factors such as economic development which may determine the level of stability of successor governments. The argument is that if the military are forced out and a civilian government succeeds them, elements of the military that are loyal to the ousted military government may still remain in the wings expecting some day to be regrouped to come back to power. There has been evidence of this in the recent attack by forces loyal to Idi Amin of Uganda to restore their leader who was forced out. On the other hand, there is a slightly greater level of stability in the Ghanaian and Nigerian situations where the present military governments are not anxiously looking over their shoulders expecting the forced-out regime to make an attempt to come back.

Centralisation of Power

In theory and in practice the military has always tended to centralise decision-making and power. This tendency derives from the need to build a strong state through increasing co-ordination of activities of sub-units of state apparatus. It is enhanced by the military organisational characteristics of centralisation, and it becomes necessary due to the arbitration functions of the military among competing élite groups. Western scholars have agreed that this tendency to centralise power in the military makes it a modernising agency. Welch (1970, pp. 36–40) believes that it is precisely this important feature of centralisation which makes the military the paragon of a modernised political system in developing societies. It cannot be denied, of course, that a strong measure of centralisation of power is required to achieve political modernisation (Huntington, 1966, p. 328). The military government at the federal centre in a society like Nigeria as well as in Ghana have increasingly taken over the activities and functions of other sub-units of national government such as state governments. The state governments have in turn increasingly assumed the powers of the local governments. Consequently, it appears that the state governments under military rule had a more subordinate position in the federal system than did the regional governments in Nigeria during the civilian era. This position under the military government has tended seriously to undermine the true federal character of government. One of the first steps taken by the civilians when they returned to power in Nigeria was to enforce the provisions of the new constitution which guaranteed much greater power to the states.

It must be emphasised, of course, that in the Nigerian example the federal military government, particularly under Muhammed–Obasanjo, was anxious that more power be given to local governments who were operating at the grass-roots level. The military government at that time stated that local governments over the years had suffered from the continuous whittling down of their power. This military government accused the state governments of encroaching upon what was normally regarded as the exclusive preserve of local governments (Federal Government Guidelines on Local Government Reforms, 1976). The federal military government lamented the fact that lack of sufficient funds and appropriate institutions had made local governments ineffective, and therefore decided to write new guidelines for the operation of local governments which were designed to increase the power of these governments. But what actually followed was that the state governments did not give enough opportunities for local governments to operate when interpreting the federal guidelines. There appears to have been some kind of contradiction in the effort of the federal military government to take over more powers of the state without anticipating that the states themselves would almost naturally move over to acquire some powers of the local governments. However, this may be explained by the peculiar interest that the Muhammed–Obasanjo regime had in encouraging local participation in government. We can see a similar example in Ethiopia where the Mengistu regime attempted to encourage voluntary associations in the rural and urban areas to take over local government without properly structuring the activities of the intermediate sectors. One may suggest, therefore, that in Africa military governments have tended to bypass the intermediate level of government and go on to encouraging local and mass participation, thereby neglecting the proper mechanisms of communication between the grass-root level and the top decision-making level. Not only has this resulted in a great deal of confusion and failure, it has also hampered the military effort to move in specific directions and has been responsible in part for the half-haphazard and halting steps that government takes in several areas of operation. The intermediate strata who normally are the people controlling the intermediate level of government often view this apparent neglect of their duties as a slap in the face and consequently sabotage the efforts of the military government.

One way in which this has been amply demonstrated in the Nigerian example is that the state governments have continually taken away or decreased the base of financial resources which the local governments were supposed to use to perform their activities. Resources have become inadequate for the local governments, and since the federal government has taken over many of the resources of the states, the states themselves have had an increasingly inadequate tax base to acquire money to perform their duties. A good case in point is the situation in the capital city of Oyo state of Nigeria. The Ibadan municipal government were responsible for collecting refuse and cleaning the town, but the tax base for doing so was absent. Meanwhile, the federal government had paid an amount of money into the treasury of the state government for transmission to the municipal government. Since the state government was itself somewhat indigent, the money was not swiftly transmitted to the end for which it was initially designed. The city streets gradually became a refuse centre, thereby increasing health hazards for the people. But since the federal government could not transmit money directly to the local-level government a great deal of confusion arose and the goals of the federal military government to increase power at the grass-roots level were incapable of achievement. This situation has been rectified in the new civilian constitution where the federal government can transmit money designed for local treasuries directly to them. In other words, where a redistribution of functions has been made to decentralise power, not enough resources have been forthcoming to carry out the duties of the new sub-structures properly.

The volume of functions that were taken over by the federal military government from state governments reflected the federal government's intention to co-ordinate more effectively larger and larger areas of national development. Also the nature, ramifications and implications of the particular areas of duty taken over by the federal government reflected the changing balance of power and relationship between the federal centre and the states. In other words, while the volume of functions taken over by the federal government was increasing, so was the character and importance of the areas taken over becoming more significant for national development. One obvious direction of the shift has been that the areas where both the federal and state governments had powers had now completely, before the military moved out of government, become federal areas of concern. A military government does not want several divergent policy decisions on specific areas of national development and consequently it immediately takes such areas over. A specific example is higher education in the nation. Higher education has policy implications for manpower development and therefore is a very important area of national development; it was therefore taken over. Also, policy on utilities like electricity, water and energy production, which have implications for national productivity, and which hang on the operation of one central power unit at Kanji Dam in Nigeria, needed to be co-ordinated for development. Similarly, in such areas as labour and industrial relations, the federal military government in Nigeria and elsewhere moved to centralise decision-making. Labour and industrial relations represent the sensitive external policy area for developing nations. This is because the area is an area of ideological conflict in the Third World nations and therefore needs to be approached from a position of nationalism. The Nigerian federal military government demanded that the varying and warring labour unions must form a central labour organisation. The government induced these labour unions to do so by promising them money to organise their activities. Eventually, the labour unions came together under one umbrella. A similar process has taken place in Ethiopia but the labour unions were organised in a more coercive manner than happened in Nigeria. For example, the Federation of Trade Unions was disbanded and the All Ethiopia Federation of Trade Unions was formed to take care of the activities of this dismantled organisation. Another reason the military interferes in the organisation of labour unions is that the relationship between the control of labour force and level of productivity demands that policy be highly co-ordinated in this area if planning is to be guided.

7
Military Regimes, Social Policy and Planning

One specific reason I have decided to deal with social policy under military regime is that virtually all the military rulers who come to power make very fine proclamations about how they intend to change the social life of the community. They promise a better life for the citizens in the areas of housing, education, health and general welfare to be carried out within the framework of egalitarianism. In other words, a proper redistribution of power and income appears to be the goal of social policy and planning by most African military rulers. We need not cite too many examples here but the proclamations of Mengistu, Gowon, Ankrah, Akuffo, Rawlings, Muhammed and Obasanjo are all in this general vein. But it must be noted that there is always a gap between the military proclamations and the result which they produce in the end. One way of finding out how wide these gaps are, that is, the distance between the policy marked out and the way the policy has been carried out, is through an analysis of policy design and policy implementation in these societies.

First, I would like to examine some theoretical positions concerning social policy with particular reference to such structural variables of distribution as inequality, need and ability to pay. The theoretical framework thus examined will be the basis for analysing the success or failure of the military and also will give the opportunity of comparing them across nations.

The main focus of social policy has always been the public administration of welfare; and under this rubric the specific areas that are to be taken into account are the way the government initiates, manages and organises particular services which are given by the state and by local councils in such areas as education, health, housing, and so on. Since it is concerned with the administration of welfare, social policy in the past has always been designed to remedy particular social problems or to examine how to achieve certain social objectives. This narrow definition of social policy has been criticised by several scholars (see, for example, Townsend, 1975). For instance, the welfarist approach defined above focuses essentially on how to maintain social order through the maintenance of the *status quo*. It therefore relegates social issues and problems to be treated as problems on the margins of the societies. Some of the problems connected with this approach have arisen because sociologists in the past have considered their work to be value-free. In other words, the execution of policies and the adoption of policies were not considered to be their specific area of activity. Such policy issues were left to be taken care of by the government. The argument, however, is that such a problem as poverty results from structural inequality in the system of allocation of resources and goods in the society. More recently Townsend (1975) has defined social policy as that which offers guidelines by which the society is steered towards some goals. He said that it is the underlying and the professed rationale by which social institutions and groups are used or brought into being to ensure social preservation or development. While social policy is different from planning in the sense that social policy has a long-term nature and is broader in terms of its objectives, it is related to planning because planning is the mechanism by which many social policies are carried out. Some subjectively measured plans also can become policy if they take a long time to execute.

Social policy has important financial and political implications for societies and therefore the problems of theory in the distribution and in the allocation of resources must be clarified. We can ask the question, when can social policy be used as an instrument to reduce inequality in the society or to satisfy the needs and the earnings or the aspirations of the people? Can we say that the sheer increase in the provision of social welfare through increased economic growth will satisfy the general needs of the people to the extent that controversy will be reduced?

It can be demonstrated that where there is stagnation in growth, the problems of social distribution are heightened. For example, in Ghana where very little growth has been recorded in the last few years the conflict between the élite groups and the larger masses of the people has become intensified. Where resources are in slightly greater abundance, as in Nigeria, the issue of inequality becomes prominent. The increasing pattern of conspicuous consumption in Nigeria is exacerbating the problems of inequality in Nigeria. For example, the conspicuousness visibility of the small élite group in terms of imported products which they buy and use is tempting to the larger mass of the people who also expect to be provided for in the society. The gap which is visible has been, in part, responsible for the higher level of criminality in the society. We can immediately see, therefore, that conflict will always arise between economic development on the one hand and political choice in the distribution of welfare on the other. How best can we distribute social policy provisions effectively and equally? Thus the issue of state intervention in resource distribution and allocation in which, as we have demonstrated, the military often indulge becomes crucial.

The question arises whether the state should take over completely the provision of social policy amenities or whether it should be left to market forces. Must state take-over, if it has to take place, be purely transitory so that with greater affluence greater market provisions of these resources and services will occur? Weale (1978, p. 6) has argued that state take-over has been viewed by some scholars as capable of guaranteeing provision of resources and goods to those people with the least earning power. Others, he claimed, have argued that the state must provide the full range of the highest quality of primary goods freely for all the citizens, irrespective of their earning power. In other words, the state must cater for both the poor and the rich or at least guarantee freedom of access to provision of primary goods such as education, health and housing for all citizens. Thus, the problems of equality implied are as well as those of need. Because of the general poverty in African societies, can we argue that the society should be restructured in such a way that the institutions which provide social welfare should have or build in agencies or units which will collectively provide goods for the people, or can we say that the individual members of the society can on their own have free access to the primary goods?

In most African societies, the lack of provision of basic human amenities becomes a crucial area of governmental expenditure. Because this is so, the implication is that there are certain political choices that must be made. Contrary to the argument of Weale (1978) and Willensky (1975), in Africa political choice plays a crucial role in determining how much should be spent on social policy provision. This issue is therefore basic to the African search for ideology and explains, in part, the varying attempts by societies in Africa to try socialism, the one-party system, military government, and so on. Willensky (1975) has argued that the level of economic development is not just one but *the* crucial determinant of spending on social policy. This may be true of industrial Western nations but not of African nations. Unlike in Western nations, political decision in Africa determines the outcome of economic programmes. The desire to bridge inequality may determine the proportion that will be spent on education, as is exemplified by the amount spent on Universal Primary Education by the federal military government in Nigeria from 1976 onwards, and on the provision of free education and free health services by states controlled by the Unity Party of Nigeria (UPN) during the civilian era from 1979. The decisions were not determined by economic but by purely political considerations.

The significance of these considerations for political theory and political development in Third World societies is great. In evaluating social policy provision by military governments in the African nations, I will attempt to determine the extent of spending and also the effect that this spending has on political choice in these nations. In addition I will try to assess the relationship between demand for welfare and political control by African military governments.

Two general structural variables will be considered: equality and need. Weale (1978, p. 9) has said that the link between equality and social policy is not a gratuitous one. It has its rationale, he said, in the redistributing role of social policy expenditure itself. He argued that equality is a genuine and substantive principle of distribution. Of course, to adhere basically to the principles of equality in distribution or redistribution may have its own problems because of its relationship in the political and economic processes to other values like economic efficiency and the freedom of the individual. Where the government role is so large as in African societies there is often a conflict. Perhaps individual freedom must be limited and economic efficiency must be sacrificed in order to provide basic social amenities for the large mass of suffering Africans. Perhaps not. But it remains to be seen how these values can be related to one another in the provision of social policy goods.

General reforms undertaken by the military include attempts to provide primary goods for the majority of the people, but also involves the mass of the people who are the majority being treated as a special category distinct from the élite groups. This treatment raises issues for political and social theory. Can élite groups also be treated equally? There must be sound policy reasons for treating any group specially, otherwise certain principles will be violated. Equality implies freedom of access to available goods. The middle classes will resent the lower classes if the lower classes are seen to be enjoying some special treatment. This kind of conflict is not peculiar to developing nations. In the USA the majority of people in the middle class resent the lower classes because of the special provision of education and welfare for them. The effects or direct results of these have been reflected in the racial conflicts which are evidenced by riots involving the bussing of black students to white schools. In other words, the notion of equality may sometimes violate the principle of justice. I make this point because the military always claim to want to establish a just and egalitarian society. To achieve this aim, they have always attempted to reduce the income gap.

Weale (1978) has claimed that since economic welfare must in all justice be equally distributed, equality is linked with the principle of justice. Justice, he claims, is an end in itself, and therefore any distribution or redistribution which is declared just requires no other ethical consideration in its favour. That is, once a distribution is seen to be just, it is perfect. However, as he himself pointed out, since justice does not regulate the result of free economic exchange but merely the condition under which it may operate, problems arise between justice and equality. Therefore, I am arguing that the dilemma of creating a just society in Third World countries is a function of the conflict between equality of provision and redistribution of social welfare products on the one hand, and the ability of the principle of justice to regulate outcomes of exchange situations on the other. In other words, can we encourage a free-market economy where exchange, however unjust, cannot be considered as robbery, or a socialist one where the conflict can be politically induced?

As I have argued in Chapter 5 under national economy, the lack of provision of roles for the middle strata is responsible for the sabotage of the effort to build national consensus in these societies. It is also probably because the middle strata are themselves not restructured in a way to make for cohesion nationally, or adequate provision is not made for them in the distribution of social welfare to afford equal access to opportunities. Therefore, a peculiar problem is raised for political theory in Third World societies. What is the balance to be maintained between state development and the encouragement of private investment which may encourage the emerging middle classes and afford them a place in national development? The Third World nations thus cannot avoid a political choice.

The second principle to be considered was that of need. Need has been defined as the necessary condition for the attainment of a specified goal or end state (Weale, 1978). It is claimed that the distribution of resources ought to be such as to correct any deficiencies in the provision of primary goods such as education, health and housing. However, it is also claimed that need has a way of increasing exponentially and therefore infinitely. It may, because of this, become incapable of being satisfied and indeed may violate the principle of inequality. For example, the provision of primary education may make it necessary to build secondary schools for the output of the primary schools and may also demand that more universities be built to absorb secondary school output. More money would then be spent to maximise the results of educational provision but other sectors and other geographical areas might begin to suffer. Weale concluded that need is not a good distributive principle because the satisfying of needs is itself a benefit to be distributed according to certain principles. In Nigeria prior to the military coup, the principle of need was used to make provision to adjust the regional imbalances in the nation. For example, special provisions were made for the northern areas of the country. Because such need feeds upon itself, it has become impossible to satisfy the increasing needs and demands of the north, while other areas in the south are being neglected.

We shall now turn attention to three specific areas of social policy distribution in the three nations under consideration. These areas are: education, health care and housing.

Education

With respect to education, equality can be viewed as the attempt to provide equal opportunity for every child of the society to grow, and for the development of his intellectual, physical and social skills as well as other talents that he may possess.

The definition of equal opportunity has been problematic for scholars of education as well as for social scientists. Can we measure equality of education by such factors as staff–pupil ratios, or the amount spent per pupil? It has been shown in the experience of the USA that the equality of expenditure on children will not guarantee equality of educational resources. This is simply because resources vary from one area to another. For example, in Nigeria, if 30 naira were spent on a child in the south and on one in the north, the longer experience of formal education in Southern Nigeria and therefore the social and educational milieu in which this child is trained may enable the southern child to produce better results than the northern child. Similarly, an attempt to measure equality of educational provision by output techniques raises several issues. There are problems of compensating for variations in costs as well as problems of compensating for disadvantaged children. We can compensate for costs when children of the same ability and background do not achieve similar results. And we can begin to see the problems of disadvantage when the children of different abilities and social milieu achieve different levels of educational performance. There are studies in the United States, however, that show that any compensatory education that may be instituted does not have great impact upon the cognitive development of children or upon their future occupational mobility (Jencks, 1973). The efforts of the military governments in Africa have been in the direction of providing state-run schools. The issue, of course, is whether state-provided education can necessarily reduce the gaps that exist currently between rural and urban areas and between larger geographical areas such as the north and the south in Nigeria, Ethiopia and Ghana.

In the Nigerian case, two factors have plagued the distribution of educational opportunities. The first is regional variation which is based upon historical factors of colonialism, contact with European nations, and religion, for example, Islam. The second set of factors are class-based variations which have limited resources for certain groups of people and have afforded the small élite access to richer educational resources than the other groups. To reduce inequality in regional provision of education in Nigeria, a situation which has had a long colonial history, successive national governments in Nigeria have embarked on attempts to make special provision for the northern part of Nigeria by instituting crash educational programmes in the effort to catch up with the south. Northern Nigeria has lagged far behind the south in the provision of formal Western education and has not in fact been seen to make equal effort with the south even in modern times. The consequence is that the gap between the two has widened.

The Nigerian pre-coup civilian government embarked upon a social policy called 'regional balancing'. This policy has had the unfortunate effect of obscuring the real problems of educational provision in the Nigerian societies. Progress in the southern states was stagnating while concrete change was not being made in the north. The Gowon regime in Nigeria initiated the policy of Universal Primary Education (UPE). This meant that there was equality of educational opportunity for all members of the society irrespective of what part of the country they originated from. The succeeding Obasanjo regime increased the provision by making primary education free throughout the federation. Such a policy has wiped away the requirement of regional need but has emphasised the criterion of equality. In other words, every child in the federation now has an equal opportunity to go to school up until the age of 11. Successive military budgets in Nigeria have demonstrated the policy of the government to increase spending on education over the last ten years. As Table 5.14 demonstrates (p.133 above), expenditure on education was about half the expenditure on general administration and internal security. In the 1979 military budget, more than 548 million naira was voted for Universal Primary Education and another 40 million was voted in grants to the states for secondary education under recurrent expenditure. At the same time, about 520 million naira was voted for defence. Apart from the amount voted for Universal Primary Education, another 326 million naira was voted for education in general. Therefore, altogether in the 1979 budget close to 1,000 million naira was voted for education and, as described above, about half of that amount was voted for defence. Therefore, in the last military rule in Nigeria, the amount voted for education increased and superseded the amount voted for defence. A similar trend can be noted under provision for capital expenditure.

The military government saw that it could no longer continue the policy of instituting crash programmes for specific areas of the country but that if equal opportunity were provided for all, then the issue of regional imbalance would be dealt with. The military government particularly between 1976 and 1979 made other far-reaching changes in the educational provisions. In the 1979/80 budget General Obasanjo said that his government had decided to encourage private voluntary organisations and local communities to build pre-primary educational institutions to take care of nursery-age children. He also enjoined employers of labour to provide opportunities for their workers to take advantage of this new provision by building nursery schools for their children. But in order to achieve the aims of these provisions the government itself should have entered into the provision of pre-primary education in a bigger way. The result of these provisions has been that the élite groups, who are the people who already had access to pre-primary schools for their children, took immediate advantage. This cannot but increase the gap between the elite and the masses in the society, and between rural and urban groups. It is interesting to observe that immediately the civilian politicians came to power in 1979, some states controlled by the Unity Party of Nigeria decided to abolish pre-primary education on the grounds that it does not encourage equality of access to such educational opportunity. However, it must be pointed out that for this provision the state had enlisted the support of private business.

In 1977 the military government also announced the abolition of tuition fees in the universities and technical colleges and extended this opportunity to secondary schools in 1979. Thus the military government in Nigeria made education free from the primary to the university level.

Education has had a fairly long colonial history in Nigeria. The colonial pattern of education has been to educate a small number of people on whom the development of the society was expected to rest. The élite nature of educational provision is reflected not only in the number of people educated but also in the varying character of provision to that small élite. This is noticeable in the establishment of special secondary schools like government colleges and special training colleges. The products of such élite institutions have been in the forefront of national decision-making in the various sectors of development in this country. This élite approach has further raised the special premium put on education as an avenue of social mobility in Nigeria.

It can be seen, therefore, that the policy of the federal military government, particularly of the Muhammed–Obasanjo regime, has tended to reduce the inequality in the élite–mass and the rural–urban sectors by making free provision for education from primary to university level. It must be argued that the above analysis showed a massive state intervention in the provision of education in Nigeria. In Ethiopia the long neglect of educational provisions, because of the attitude of the emperor to the training of the élite, and the new socialist orientation of the military government also made state intervention inevitable in educational provision. The trend in Ghana is similar too. Perhaps we can conclude, then, that military government believes in state intervention in social policy provision and in the distribution of these provisions. And in contrast to civilian government, the military has not taken account of special groups for treatment.

Health Care

The basic issue raised in the provision of health care is whether prevention would provide more efficient means of spreading health provision in the society than the curative means, and also whether the distribution of this health care system is egalitarian. It has been argued that an egalitarian system must have the following features: (1) it must be free of charge for all people, except possibly for the treatment of minor ailments; (2) there must be no obvious regional or other social variations where the quantity and quality of service are concerned (Weale, 1978). In many Western societies, for example in the United States, the status of a patient influences the availability of health care. Therefore, we can begin by arguing that some nations are egalitarian in the provision of health care services while others are not. Studies have demonstrated that in the United States lower-income families tend to spend a higher proportion of their income on medical care; and the lower-income group in that society have not received a fair share of the available health services. Therefore, this category of people are at a disadvantage in the provision of health services because of smaller financial support. We will try to see, therefore, how social policy through government expenditure on health care influences the delivery of health care services. In the 1975–80 development plan in Nigeria, the Gowon administration emphasised the need to develop preventive health services in Nigeria. However, the amount voted to be spent on prevention was so small that it achieved very little. What the government proceeded to do in reality was to encourage the building of several treatment hospitals, particularly in the main cities. The development plan also aimed at providing rural centres for the mass of the peasants. However, less than half of the projects planned for rural health care were actually executed. The amount of money spent on the health care exemplified by the building of teaching hospitals and large specialist hospitals in the cities did not justify the policy statement. Thus, the health care policy lacked direction and the implementation was a very confused one. The great majority of the people have had to migrate to the urban centres in search of medical treatment.

If we take a look at these two principles of equality and need we will discover that neither of them is satisfied in the provision of health care by the military. For example, it has been demonstrated in some recent works that greater attention is given to people of higher status than those of lower status in the delivery of health care. Thus we have not only regional discrimination but also social discrimination in these areas. One further piece of evidence of the lack of priority attention given to health care delivery by the Nigerian military government in particular is that in the three budget speeches made by General

Obasanjo between 1976 and 1979, at no time was any special heading or attention given to health care or health care delivery. Whereas on one or two occasions housing and education received priority treatment, at no time was health given such consideration. This is to emphasise the rather desultory manner in which military governments have treated health care delivery. It should be noted, however, that in most parts of Africa the great majority of the people are treated by local herbalists rather than by formal hospitals.[1]

Housing

Housing is a primary good in that it provides for the average person the opportunity to do what he wants to do. In African countries state intervention in housing is a new phenomenon. Most Africans live in their own self-built homes in the more or less traditional pattern of the extended family living together. Recently, however, great increases in population and the changing structure of that population from the elderly to the younger have necessitated the movement of the ever-increasing numbers of people to the cities and thus made the provision of houses, particularly in urban centres, imperative. Secondly, the unequal distribution of incomes in these societies makes it necessary that provisions be made for workers in the factories. In addition, due to inflationary trends in the rest of the world the cost of construction of houses has gone up. The kind of materials that are used to build houses in Africa today, such as cement, corrugated iron sheets, asbestos, pipes and toilet materials, are imported, thus adding to the cost, and so governments have had to control the price of these materials. Another area in which government intervention may become necessary is in the control of rent. This is because the better houses in urban centres are built by landlords who may wish to exploit the workers who rent these houses. The government can also intervene by providing allowances for housing.

In general, rent control has a few advantages: it may help to prevent inflation; it may also help to create popular political support for a government. This is because it may reduce the fluidity of the housing market. Where rents are controlled, families tend to remain in these rent-controlled homes for a long time even when their salaries have increased. For example, in the Nigerian situation those who live in government or institution-provided houses pay very little rent. Even when salaries have tripled and they have had the opportunity to build their own homes, they often refuse to leave the government-rented houses. Examples of this can be seen in the Nigerian public service, the civil service and the universities. This situation tends to reduce the ability of the market forces to redistribute available housing by means of the mechanism of the trickle-down theory. This theory states that when the income of a group goes up they will move to better housing, and the lower-income groups will move into the houses the former group have moved out of. But in reality this is not the case.

The government has provided housing allowances in Nigeria and Ghana as a matter of policy. In the Nigerian situation, the federal military government not only provided houses but also encouraged state housing corporations to build homes for its citizens. In September 1977 the federal government declared that to accelerate its 1975–80 plan for housing it had given each state government the right henceforth to be fully responsible for implementing federal housing programmes earmarked for its territory (*Daily Times*, 15 September 1977, p. 1). Its aim was to provide low- and middle-income groups in the public sector of the economy with housing. In his 1979/80 budget speech General Obasanjo took an additional policy decision. He asked every firm or organisation with 500 employees or more to introduce a housing scheme and/or housing loan scheme for its employees. He stated that for its part as a major employer, the federal military government had decided to sell the 1,000 units recently built for other purposes to public officers on an owner-occupier basis. Similarly to the effort of the military, the contemporary civilian government in Nigeria have also embarked on massive housing building projects, particularly for the lower-income category. It must be noted, however, that public housing for the lower-income category has met some problems.

In Nigeria the public housing projects established by the military government and continued by the present civilian government have not succeeded, for a number of reasons. First, due to inflation and the price of land, the prices of the houses that were built were too high and therefore were not competitive. In the Kwara state of Nigeria, a building corporation erected a number of houses whose cost in the end rose beyond the means of most Nigerians to buy. The houses which were originally expected to cost below 20,000 naira and were intended for the middle-income group were completed at a cost of over 40,000 naira each. In the end, none of the people for whom they were designed came to buy. In fact, this sort of thing had occurred in other states throughout Nigeria. In the Oyo State the military government abandoned the building of houses for the low-income group after putting up prototypes because it was discovered that the low-income group would not be able to afford them.

Public housing in general has other problems. Housing for the low-income group, usually houses with one or two bedrooms, carries a stigma and sometimes, because a large number are built at the same time, conjures up grim images of concrete-ware housing without any personal touch to it.

Rent control in Nigeria has also failed. The reasons are many and varied. First, rent restrictions for the low-income urban worker could not be enforced because landlords sidetracked the implementation of the policy. They ejected tenants who were not able to pay their rents, and because of the shortage of housing generally tenants had to abide by whatever price the landlord quoted. In an attempt to solve these problems, the military government established a Rent Control Tribunal, but its adjudication powers were limited, and because of manpower shortages only a few of these courts were established, resulting in cases of litigation remaining in the courts for several years. The rent control laws have, however, succeeded in another direction. Because it was the bureaucrats who fixed the rent of each house and because it was they who owned the vast majority of good houses, prices were raised very high. Most organisations and individuals who wished to rent these houses had virtually no alternative because so few houses were available the number of groups competing to rent them was very high.

The loan scheme too had limited success. The loans were available after an applicant had shown strong evidence of colateral support, but low- and middle-income categories were unable to do so. Consequently, most of the loans went to businessmen and other middle- to high-income élite groups in the society. Thus, the rent control policy, public housing policy and loan schemes have all either failed or had limited success.

It will be observed that under military as well as civilian governments, housing policies are directed towards urban dwellers, either the low-income worker or the middle- to high-income categories. The vast majority of Africans who live in traditional areas are completely neglected in this policy. Most of them live in mud-built houses that were erected a long time ago. A good housing policy would have attempted to improve the housing conditions of the traditional people by giving them small loans to plaster or reconstruct by putting in more windows, or make other minor repairs which would improve these traditional houses. In fact, the vast majority of Africans in the traditional areas fall completely outside the consideration of both military and civilian governments. This has maintained the traditional dichotomies that have been talked about so widely in the literature. Such dichotomies are the urban–rural and élite–mass gaps.

The situation is far different in Ethiopia where the military government instituted the policy guidelines for the Urban Dwellers' Associations. The associations controlled the majority of houses in the urban centres and had wide-ranging powers over rent control and other functions. The policy was, however, circumvented by the middle-income workers who avoided the category of houses controlled by the associations. While in Nigeria the independent tribunals that were set up were capable of being influenced and controlled by the middle- and higher-income groups, and were also capable of being manipulated by the landlords, the Urban Dwellers' Associations were completely free of this kind of influence because they adjudicated all the housing litigation. However, there is one similarity with the Nigerian situation in that the policy is also limited to the urban centres, and the vast majority of peasants in the traditional housing areas in the rural areas are completely neglected.

Perhaps the conclusion this leads us to is that the provision of housing for the vast majority of Africans in the traditional and rural areas has defied state intervention. It will probably be left to the more traditional structures such as the traditional building associations which have existed over the centuries to find out ways in which the mass of the people can improve their own housing. The gap between the decision-making of the government and the needs of the large mass of the people is reflected in the failures of the housing policies described in this chapter.

Notes: Chapter 7

1 A recent piece of research supports this position: see Edington and Odebiyi, 1976.

8
Conclusions

The comparative approach used in this study has afforded the opportunity to move beyond the simple characterisation of the military as either a conservative, anti-revolutionary, or progressive organisation. The problems of development in Africa such as those posed by the level of competition among the various élite groups as well as the cleavages among the many tribal groups, and the poor resources together with the low level of mobilisation, make the situation vary from one society to another in Africa. These make it necessary to look closely at each nation in an effort to make reasonable conclusions. The need to mobilise resources rapidly has brought the military with its organisational characteristics of coercion into the forefront of development. The military in Africa has had to act as an arbiter among the various competing groups and to build state power in the effort to lay the foundations for national cohesion and integration. However, the military itself in the performance of these activities has been affected as an organisation just as it has influenced the rest of the society. These are some of the conclusions that I will now proceed to examine.

The findings in this study reveal that there is a low level of professionalism in the armies of many African nations, and therefore I cannot support the position that soldiers are any more puritanical and that they possess rational norms far above the level that is operative in the rest of the society. Indigenisation, wars and deployment into the administration of civil societies have decreased the period and intensity of training of soldiers so necessary to the development of real professionalism. Another factor that has militated against the development of a real professional outlook is the civilianisation of the society which occurs on several fronts. For example, the very close physical proximity of many African armies to the rest of the civil societies has not completely insulated the army men from the rest of society. At another level, the issues of tribalism and other social factors have crept into the army and diffused the professional ethos of the military. The assumed puritanical orientation of the military is called into question by evidence of corruption and indiscipline found in the military organisation itself.

Other factors have been found which militate against the development of assumed modernising values in the military. The strength and character of leadership of the army, the clarity of the definition of goals, the level of resources available in the society, the nature of civil–military relations and the corporate interests of the military all directly influence the ability of the African military to display their organisational values. It has been concluded that military men are as guilty of corruption as the rest of the society. The attitude and orientations of several military men, and indeed certain decisions that have been taken by military rulers (for example, the Udoji salary awards in Nigeria), brought an unprecedented purchasing power into the rest of the society in a way that has harmed development. Military men have lived at a high level and consumed conspicuously. They are spurred on by the orientation and mobility values which they share with the rest of the society. By encouraging a conspicuous consumption, they have influenced the rest of the society to develop new tastes and aspirations never seen before in African societies. A recent comment on the Ghanaian situation has said that the level of corruption now obtaining in that society has been unprecedented (*West Africa*, December 1980).

Evidence has also revealed that new military men often make an effort to correct the image of the military which has been tarnished by a previous regime due to corruption and indiscipline. For example, the Muhammed–Obasanjo regime came to emphasise discipline in an effort to correct the ills of the Gowon era and improve the military image. Similarly Akuffo attempted to change the image of the Ghanaian army left by Acheampong, and in succession Rawlings attempted to do the same to Akuffo's regime. This is in agreement with the findings of Huntington that each successive military regime attempts to carry reform one or two steps forward. However, no sooner had they come into power and made great enthusiastic display than they began to decline. In other words, the military organisation in Africa has not in general been able to sustain the initial enthusiasm with which it came to power. One reason for this is that the problems of ruling a civil society as well as internal organisational problems rarely allow the initial spurt of enthusiasm to continue.

Evidence reveals that the military organisation itself was so troubled by the activities of the Gowon regime in Nigeria, the Acheampong regime in Ghana and the Andom regime in Ethiopia that stresses and internal rifts developed as a result. The feeling that their own men are corrupt and inept in governing a civilian society exists within the military organisation. This is paralleled by a similar feeling within the civilian society that the military cannot govern well. Military corruption often assumes the central focus over which many civilian and military men agree. Corruption and indiscipline among the military officers and in the military organisation in general make these offences doubly culpable. This is because the military's role is far more conspicuous. The expectations that they raise by rhetoric when they newly come to govern are never matched by the practical actions they carry out.

In general, however, military corruption is a characteristic of individual soldiers and is very different from the corporate stealing done by political parties in the effort to finance election campaigns. It has been observed, however, that the military organisation has internal mechanisms for taking care of poor behaviour by its members. In any case, it has also been observed that these internal mechanisms are not able to carry the military through when the corruption and misbehaviour concerns the general population in the society. When corruption and misbehaviour become very evident some strong military leaders immediately attempt to discipline their men and sometimes award the ultimate punishment. Several officers have been killed in Ghana, Nigeria and Ethiopia and quite a large proportion of the properties that were stolen were seized back from those guilty officers and returned to the public coffers.

Individual corruption among military men is related to upward mobility desires present among soldiers as well as among civilians. To become a military ruler sometimes may result in becoming a rich man; and, therefore, involvement in military rulership becomes an avenue of upward mobility. Consequently, many civilians have rushed to join the military, and members of the national bourgeoisie have allied with the military men over the purchase of equipment and other things. This again results in continued civilianisation of the military organisation. In fact, military coups may be not unconnected with upward mobility desires among ambitious military officers.

As an instrument of coercion the military organisation should not only enforce norms of discipline but also perform norm-generating functions. This is their professional duty. However, the African military has often failed or succeeded only minimally in performing these functions. The differences in the level of success achieved in the bringing of the values of discipline and puritanism into the society by the military rulers arise from the varying degrees of coercion employed in ruling. The slightly greater level of success in reducing corruption and inculcating discipline into the society in Ethiopia is due largely to the higher level of coercion employed. Of course, this is not to say that the nearer totalitarianism is approached the greater the level of success achieved in disciplining the society. The issue is that the military in Ethiopia through coercive efforts have built institutions which have become self-sustaining in generating norms of discipline.

Indiscipline arises from the struggle to obtain similar products by different elements in the society. The argument is that the military and civilians struggle in the same markets to obtain scarce products. In this process, identification with a particular status becomes important in the effort to obtain these scarce resources. Therefore, the military constantly attempt to identify themselves as occupying a higher status than the rest of the civil society in an effort to gain an advantage over the civilians. The theoretical point here is that in a period of rapid social change, situations become so fluid in the society that each person attempts to claim a particular superior status in the effort to gain an advantage over other people.

It is observed that while the military has taken some drastic steps to correct the ills of the society in Africa, such steps are highly moralistic and fragmented and do not add up to a real effort to discipline the society.

It was also found that while in many African societies the military possesses skills which are in short supply such as engineering, the impact of the use of these skills on the society is minimal. First, the number of skilled professional men in some African societies is often greater than the number in the military organisation. Therefore, the literature which has emphasised the civic role of the military has been exaggerated. Indeed, the efforts of the military are in the direction of welfare rather than building infrastructure, and these efforts are often fragmented and are limited. One other reason that performance in this area has been limited is that many African armies are career armies and therefore the feedback from the military organisation into the rest of the society and vice versa is very slow.

In the third chapter, it has been demonstrated that education is a very significant factor in the internal upward mobility of the soldiers in the military organisation, and this contradicts Mazrui's position that the emergence of the modern army in Africa has broken the correlations between political power and Western education. I have found that there is an observable tendency for the educational level of the military and the civilian élites to converge. It has also been demonstrated that the relationship between social origins and the efforts to raise the mobility level of other members of the society by soldiers is at best tenuous. Experiences of marginality which men from lowly origins have had do not give them a broader concern for the unfortunate ones. Indeed, the experiences gained in professional socialisation often completely erase their pre-training and socialisation experiences. Secondly, social origins are not important determinants or predictors of political behaviour. In the face of increasing pressures, the range of options that the military men have and the values which are attached to each alternative are more useful determinants of behaviour than social origins. It was also found that there are many variables between social origins and the supposed progressive attitude of the military. One such variable is occupational experience. It is not possible to say that the military allies with any particular group because it is progressive or conservative; rather, the military arbitrate among several groups and ally with any particular group which helps it to achieve its objective of strengthening state power as a precondition for development. The military rulers also limit the power of groups that contradict or antagonise their efforts to achieve this objective.

In Chapter 4 a consideration of the dependency model advanced by Latin American social scientists was examined in so far as it helps to explain development on the African scene. The dependency model says that it is the external factors of capitalism and so on that make internal development impossible. But I have argued that this position does not make it possible to examine the internal processes which are themselves highly contributive to the problems of development and thus makes comparisons impossible. Issues such as class relationships and ethnic demands as they relate to the need to enhance state power in the effort to mobilise resources were examined. The conclusion was drawn that in the three African societies compared, and even in most African societies, the state is not autonomous. This is because the national bourgeoisie is weak. Therefore the state has had the task of building capital resources for investment. In the process of doing this in Ethiopia the state has moved in the direction of eliminating the national bourgeoisie, but in Nigeria a large element of this group has been incorporated into the process of development, and the situation in Ghana is similar. The problem of eliminating a large section of the bourgeois class raises the issue of how to deal with the problems of accumulated skills and experience in the society.

To limit the power of the national bourgeoisie is to expand the power of the national bureaucracy. In the military rule of African nations there has been a more or less universal dependence on the bureaucracy who have a great interest themselves in controlling the means of distribution. Indeed, they have also demonstrated an interest in the means of production. Therefore, the effort of military governments is in the direction of liberating the state apparatus from divisive class and ethnic interests in the effort to promote development. The problems that are connected with achieving this vary from nation to nation. For example, there are the problems of feudalism and tribalism in Ethiopia, and those of a fast-rising bourgeois class and of deep ethnic cleavages in Nigeria and Ghana. Other differences are the greater experiences of colonialism in Nigeria and Ghana as compared with Ethiopia and some other African societies. Therefore, the mechanism by which the military relates to the varying strengths of ethnic and class forces are important variables with which to measure variation in development among African societies. It is important to say, therefore, that a simple characterisation of the military as either efficient or ineffective is weak. It is important to take account of regional variations from state to state depending on the ability of the military to limit the countervailing role of the national bourgeoisie. From the comparative analysis in this book we have arrived at two models of development in Africa. The first is the state-directed socialist development as practised in Ethiopia, the Congo Republic and some other African states. The second model is the state-directed capitalist development such as is found in Ghana and Nigeria. These have varying characteristics which have been dealt with in the body of the book. The state has assumed an increasing role in development in all the three nations compared although the role of the state is greater in Ethiopia than in the other societies. With the increasing power of the élite groups in the state-directed capitalist model, inequality has been exacerbated. In such societies the national bourgeoisie have eventually aligned with external capital. This situation may lead to increased military coups and instability in general. In Ghana between 1966 and 1980 there were four military coups, while there were three successful ones in Nigeria. The ability of the present civilian governments in Nigeria and Ghana to prevent a return of the military to politics will be a function of the degree to which they strengthen state power. Hence, the idea of state development is a useful one when the comparative development of African nations is considered. Rather than declining in value, the concept of the state is becoming increasingly important. Nationalism, particularly military nationalism, has enabled the idea of the state to take precedence. While in Europe the state developed because the land area was shrinking and containing increasingly ethnically homogeneous groups, the military has been trying to wield ethnically disparate groups, into homogeneous units in the developing societies through the mechanism of state power. In other words, because of military rule in Africa the idea of the state is becoming manifest both in external and in internal relations.

Where in the state-directed socialist development natural resources are meagre and the market incapable of supporting autonomous state development, crisis has ensued. These crises have been manifested in the flight of the members of the élite groups to other nations near and far. It has also been demonstrated that the longer it takes for development to come into a nation, the more powerful is the apparatus of state bureaucracy. The ability of developing nations to build state power is not defined by the power of the bourgeoisie under a capitalist system or the proletariat under a socialist system but by the distance which has been established between political power on the one hand and economic or ethnic structures on the other hand. That is, the ability of any African military to lay the foundations or the preconditions for development is a function of this distance. We have seen therefore that the military attempts to limit ethnic and class power which threatens to destroy the state. In its role as mediator and arbitrator the military assumes the obligation of building state power. Hence, any perception by the military when they have returned to the barracks that any social or political group is attempting to reduce state power may induce the military to come back to the political process.

The body of the literature which has focused on whether the military are poor or excellent managers of the national economy has employed the use of aggregate cross-national data which has often obscured the realities in those societies. Building national consensus implies certain political choices such as employing coercion in the spirit of nationalism to mobilise resources. By analysing the role of coercion and nationalism in building state power as a prerequisite for national development it has been demonstrated that various élite groups become antagonistic. A condition under which the ability to apply coercion to build national consensus fails is when the military itself cannot enforce its own organisational norms internally. Another condition is when the bourgeoisie subverts the military effort. This situation is quite common.

Military corporate interest does harm economic development because military interests assume paramountcy when the military comes to power. Defence budgets have more than tripled even in some societies where no war is being prosecuted.

It was also found that military nationalism cannot be divorced from military corporate interest. Interest in building heavy industries derives both from giving national industrial growth a solid foundation and from preparing an industrial base for producing military hardware. The economic performance of the military has varied from country to country due to the varying manner in which the national bourgeoisie has been brought into the process of development. Where the effort to destroy them has been great, the available pool of skills to run the economy has become correspondingly small, as in Ethiopia. Secondly, where resources have been small, and the national bourgeoisie is encouraged less than they were under the civilians, crises ensue. Such crises are reflected in the flight of the national élite to other nations, as is the case in Ghana. Similarly, such malpractices as hoarding and corruption increase in the society. It is, however, evident that in spite of their failures in running the economy, the military regimes in Africa have been performing well in their efforts to build national consensus–a precondition for total societal development. Where the civilian or military politicians have given the national bourgeoisie an unfettered role in national development, the tendency has been for such bourgeoisie to ally with external capital and produce long-run stultification of national development. The visible failures of the military and the emphasis put on them by scholars are in part due to the lack of perception of the need to limit, in some degree at least, the countervailing role of the national bourgeoisie in the joint national effort to generate the spirit of nationalism and to build consensus. My position does not, of course, justify the plundering of the national treasury by men of the armed forces, particularly in Nigeria and Ghana. A relatively clearer definition of the national goals in Ethiopia has prevented such plundering on the scale in which it has occurred in Ghana and Nigeria. Indeed, this plundering has visibly harmed the national economies of these nations.

The military has probably recorded greater success in their performance in the political sector than in the economic sector. They have built political institutions where the goals and strength of military leadership permit. The strength of military leadership in combination with clear goal definition encourages military politicians to go ahead and create supportive political institutions such as the Peasant and Urban Dwellers' Associations in Ethiopia.

In Nigeria it was the military that created first twelve and later nineteen states which once and for all laid a sound foundation for the participation of minority groups, and hence by extension incorporated greater proportions of the society into the political processes.

In Ethiopia the political institutions which the military built recorded little success, in large part because the military itself had not defined for them a national scope of goals and operations so that they have not developed into meaningful political structures. But even then, the scope so defined for these new institutions did not please large sections of the élite class who proceeded to sabotage such goals.

The military in Ethiopia has succeeded in destroying the feudal base of that society and has redistributed political power. The inability of the ruling military in Africa to restructure the role of the national bourgeoisie and other élite classes has not allowed for the successful establishment of radically new institutions aimed at achieving national consensus.

Because open political processes were not generally present, the military has devised its own channels of political communication. Military men have claimed that they have therefore not found the lack of open political processes a handicap to their governments. In some instances they have co-opted men of relatively expert knowledge into their Cabinets making such Cabinets highly elitist and rather removed from the grass-roots level.

It is also concluded that the military has been as benevolent in specific instances as have the civilian politicians. However, variations in benevolent orientations are due to the strength of élite opposition or what the military perceives to be such, and the character of coercive measures taken to achieve national consensus. Indeed, the same level of ambivalence which characterised relationships with the press during the days of civilian politicians was found to characterise relationships during military periods in Nigeria and Ghana, although these tend to be less friendly in Ethiopia. The Ethiopian situation might be due to the perception by the military of the press as members of the national élite who have to be destroyed. Several social and structural groups have proved to be antagonistic to these developments. The varying strength of their antagonism has influenced the ability of the military to develop national consensus.

In theory, I have posited a relationship between the structure of coercion and economic development. The nature of development in Third World societies encourages the building of a large public sector and the manner and degree of achieving this help us to understand the variations in development among nations. Mobilising of all sectors for development implies limiting consumption and derives from the military values of centralisation and discipline. Where this has not been done or seen to be done, for example during the Gowon era in Nigeria, economic development begins to show signs of decline. There has been some support for the position that coercion is positively correlated with economic development. The ability of the military to enforce organisational norms internally influences the degree to which it can apply coercion to rule the society in general. Internal organisational weaknesses and failures are reflected in poor performance on the national economic scene.

The necessity for building and strengthening state power, and the problem of inequality and poverty in African societies, together make the matter of state intervention in the provision of primary goods real and problematic. This is complicated by the gap between the rhetoric of the military to create a just and egalitarian society and their ability to do so. Two issues are raised for social and political theory. The question is, can we say that the provision of welfare should be made a priority matter? That is, can the society progress to deal with the development of the economy in the hope that increased wealth will make the provision of welfare easier; or otherwise can we plan the national economy in such a way that social policy provision is immediately guaranteed? That choice along with how much must be earmarked for social policy provision is a political one. The choice of the manner of providing the funds is also a political one, that is, can it be provided collectively or individually? The most important principle of distribution that we have focused upon is inequality. Inequality is a substantive principle of distribution and redistribution. Other criteria such as need and justice create problems in their use. Need as a criterion develops exponentially while justice cannot regulate the outcomes of free exchange. Justice merely stipulates the conditions under which free exchange can take place. Hence, it becomes a political choice whether to abandon free exchange in order to build a just society. The provision of education for all citizens by the military in Nigeria has given equal access to education and hence to social mobility in a large measure. This has been achieved only by a massive state intervention and occurred as a result of political choice. Although national wealth has increased somewhat in Nigeria, it is not sufficient justification for the educational provisions that have been made.

Provision in the area of housing has had several dimensions. There were provisions for loans to build individual homes, and also provisions establishing housing schemes by the government or to control rent or finally to give housing allowances. In Ghana and Nigeria the state has intervened in these provisions, and these policy measures have had only limited success. Provision for health has been desultory and largely unprogrammed. It therefore lacks direction. It is only recently in Nigeria that some state governments are providing large housing estates for low-salaried workers following or in competition with the federal government. Indeed, the issue of political choice and state building increases competition among the several political units in African societies.

Appendix I

Ghana under Flight Lieutenant Rawlings:
Military Officers Found Guilty of Corruption by Name, Rank
and Awarded Punishment

Name	Rank	Punishment (jail terms)
Squadron Leader G. Tagoe	Deputy Chief of Executive Cattle Development Board	95 years
Col. K. A. Takeyi	Head of Cocoa Marketing Board	80 years
Col. Kwame Baah	Foreign Affairs Commissioner under Acheampong's regime	50 years
Squadron Leader Abebress	Squadron Leader	Life
Group Captain A. Jackson	Housing Commissioner	Life
Lt Col. G. K. Ameuor	Volta Region Commissioner	Life
Lt Col. B. K. Afilijah	Industries Commissioner	Life
Col. P. K. Nkebe	Education Commissioner	20 years
Major K. Asante	Transport and Communications Commissioner	25 years
Naval Captain Joe Kyerewon	Commissioner for Cocoa Affairs	Life imprisonment and forfeiture of all assets
Col. Zcemmadi	Regional Commissioner for Ashanti	25 years with hard labour

Source: Africa Research Bulletin, 1–31 August 1979.

Appendix II

Nigeria: Forfeiture of Assets of Military Governors Found Guilty of Corruption

Name	*Assets forfeited*
Gov. Usman Farouk	3 residential houses
Gov. Audu Bako	Shares in company, farms and houses
Gov. Musa Usman	2 houses and undeveloped property
Gov. Esuene	To refund ₦25.672 in cash
Administrator U. Asika	To forfeit house worth ₦120,000
Gov. D. Spiff	To surrender 33 plots of undeveloped land
Gov. J. Gomwalk	Undeveloped land and 50 per cent of his total salary from 1967 to 1975
Gov. S. Ogbemudia	A motel and houses
Gov. A. Bamgboye	7 residential homes

Sources: Nigerian Herald, vol. III, no. 709, 7 February 1976; *Daily Times of Nigeria,* 4 February 1976.

Bibliography

Abrahamsson, Bengt, *Military Professionalisation and Political Power* (Beverly Hills, Calif.: Sage, 1972).

Adelman, Irma and C. Morris, *Society, Politics and Economic Development* (Baltimore, Md: Johns Hopkins University Press, 1967).

Afrifa, A. A., *The Ghana Coup* (London: Cass, 1966).

Alba, Victor, 'The stages of militarism in Latin America', in J. J. Johnson (ed.), *The Role of the Military in the Underdeveloped Countries* (Princeton, NJ: Princeton University Press, 1962).

Andreski, S., *Military Organisation and Society* (London: Routledge & Kegan Paul, 1954).

Austin, D., 'The Ghana case', in *The Politics of Delimitarisation,* Institute of Commonwealth Papers (London: Royal Commonwealth Institute, 1966), pp. 44–54.

Azikiwe, N., 'Zik warns on nationalisation', *West Africa,* 14 April, 1972, p. 466,

Azikiwe, N., 'Nigeria: economic review', *Africa Research Bulletin,* February 1973.

Bailey, G., *An Analysis of the Ethiopian Revolution,* unpublished MA thesis, Carleton University, Ottawa, Canada, 1979.

Barber, W. and C. Ronning, *Internal Security and Military Power* (Columbus, Ohio: Ohio State University Press, 1966).

Barnett, C., 'The education of military elites', *Journal of Contemporary History,* vol. 2 (July 1961), pp. 15–35.

Bell, M. J. V., *Army and Nation in Sub-Saharan Africa* (London: Institute of Strategic Studies, 1965).

Bienen, H., 'Public order and military in Africa: mutinies in Kenya, Uganda and Tanganyika' in H Bienen (ed.), *The Military Intervenes: Case Studies in Political Development* (New York: Russell Sage, 1968).

Bienen, H., *The Military and Modernisations* (Chicago: Aldine, 1971).

Blankstein, G., 'The politics of Latin America', in Gabriel Almond and James Coleman (eds), *The Politics of the Developing Areas* (Princeton, NJ: Princeton University Press, 1960).

Blau, P., *Bureaucracy* (New York: Random House, 1962).

Campbell, Ian, 'The Nigerian census: an essay in civil-military relations', *Journal of Commonwealth and Comparative Studies,* vol. 14 (November 1976), pp. 244–54.

Cardoso, F. H., 'The industrial elite', in S. M. Lipset and A. Solari (eds), *Elites in Latin America* (New York: Oxford University Press, 1967).

Clapham, C., *Haile Selassie's Government* (London: Longman, 1969).

Cockcroft, James, A. Gunder-Frank and Dale Johnson, *Dependence and Underdevelopment* (New York: Anchor Books, 1972).

Coleman, J. and B. Price, 'The role of the military in sub-Saharan Africa', in J. J. Johnson (ed.), *The Role of the Military in the Underdeveloped Countries* (Princeton, NJ: Princeton University Press, 1962).

Coleman, J. and C. Rosberg (eds), *Political Parties and National Integration in Tropical Africa* (Berkeley, Calif.: University of California Press, 1964).

Craig, G., *The Politics of the Prussian Army* (Oxford: Clarendon Press, 1955).

Daalder, H., *The Role of the Military in Emerging Societies* (South Gravenhage, Holland: Mouton, 1962).

de Tocqueville, A., *Democracy in America* (New York: Knopf, 1959).

Edington, G. M. and A. I. Odebiyi, 'Cancer and ageing in Ibadan: a sociological analysis', *Social Science and Medicine*, vol. 10 (1976), pp. 477–81.

Encel, S., 'The study of militarism in Australia', in J. van Doorn (ed.), *Armed Forces and Society* (The Hague: Mouton, 1968), pp. 127–47.

Enloe, Cynthia, *Multi-Ethnic Politics* (Berkeley, Calif.: Centre for South and East Asia Studies, University of California, 1970).

Feldman, A. S., 'Violence and volatility: the likelihood of revolution', in Harry Eckstein (ed.), *Internal War* (Glencoe, Ill.: The Free Press, 1964), pp. 114–29.

Festinger, Leon and J. Thebaut, 'Interpersonal communication in small groups', *Journal of Abnormal and Social Psychology*, vol. XLVI (January 1951), pp. 91–9.

Finer, S. E., *The Man on Horse Back: The Role of the Military in Politics* (New York: Praeger, 1962).

Fitzgibbon, R. H., 'Revolutions: Western hemisphere', *South Atlantic Quarterly*, vol. 55 (1960), pp. 263–79.

Frank, A. G., *Sociology of Development and the Underdevelopment of Sociology* (London: Plato Press, 1971).

Furtado, C., *Development and Underdevelopment* (Berkeley, Calif.: University of California Press, 1964).

Geertz, C., 'The integrative revolution: primordial sentiments and civil politics in the new states', in C. Geertz (ed.), *Old Societies and New States* (New York: The Free Press, 1963), pp. 105–57.

Glick, E. B., *Peaceful Conflict* (Hamburg, Pa: Stackpole Books, 1967).

Grundy, M., 'On Machiavelli and mercenaries', *Journal of Modern African Studies*, vol. VI, no. 3 (October 1968), pp. 295–310.

Gutteridge, W. F., *Armed Forces in the New States* (London: Oxford University Press, 1962).

Gutteridge, W. F., *Military Institutions and Power in the New States* (New York: Praeger, 1965).

Gutteridge, W. F., *The Military in African Politics* (London: Methuen, 1968).

Halpern, Manfred, 'Middle-Eastern armies and the new middle-class', in J. J. Johnson (ed.), *The Role of the Military in the Underdeveloped Countries*, (Princeton, NJ: Princeton Universtiy Press, 1962).

Halpern, Manfred, *The Politics of Social Change in the Middle-East and North-Africa* (Princeton, NJ: Princeton University Press, 1963).

Hempel, Carl G., 'The logic of functional analysis', in M. Brodbeck (ed.), *Reader in the Philosophy of the Social Sciences* (New York: Macmillan, 1968).

Hobben, A., *Land Tenure among the Amhara of Ethiopia* (Chicago: University of Chicago Press, 1973).

Holmberg, J., *Grain Marketing and Land Reform in Ethiopia* (Uppsala: Scandinavian Institute of African Studies, 1977).

Hoovey, H., *United States Military Assistance* (London: Institute for Strategic Studies, 1966).

Hopkins, K., 'Civil-military relations in developing countries', *British Journal of Sociology*, vol. 17 (1966), pp. 165–82.

Horowitz, Irving Louis, *Three Worlds of Development* (New York: Oxford University Press, 1966).

Horowitz, Irving Louis, *Latin American Radicalism* (New York: Random House, 1969).

Horowitz, Irving Louis and K. Trimberger, 'State power and military nationalism in Latin America', *Comparative Politics*, vol. 8 (1976), pp. 223–44.

Huntington, S. P., *Changing Patterns of Military Politics* (New York: Free Press, 1962).

Huntington, S. P., 'Political development and political decay', *World Politics*, vol. XVII (1967), pp. 386–430.

Huntington, S. P., 'Political modernisation: America versus Europe', *World Politics*, vol. XVIII (1968), pp. 378–412.

Huntington, S. P., *Soldier and State: Political Order in Changing Societies* (New Haven, Conn.: Yale University Press, 1969).

Janowitz, Morris, 'Changing patterns of organisational authority: the military establishment', *Administrative Science Quarterly*, vol. 3 (1959), pp. 473–93.

Janowitz, Morris, *The Professional Soldier: A Social and Political Portrait* (Glencoe, Ill.: Free Press, 1960).

Janowitz, Morris, *The Military in the Political Development of New Nations: An Essay in Comparative Analyses* (Chicago: University of Chicago Press, 1964).

Jemibewon, D. M., *A Combatant in Government* (Ibadan: Heinemann, 1978).

Jencks, C., *Inequality* (New York: Basic Books, 1973).

Johnson, J. J. (ed.), *The Role of the Military in Undeveloped Countries,* preface by Hans Speier (Princeton, NJ: Princeton University Press, 1962).

Johnson, J. J. (ed.), *Continuity and Change in Latin America* (Stanford, Calif.: Stanford University Press, 1964a).

Johnson, J. J., *Military and Society in Latin America* (Stanford, Calif.: Stanford University Press, 1964b).

Jordan, A., *Foreign Aid and the Defence of South-East Asia* (New York: Praeger, 1962).

Kuper, Leo, *Race, Class and Power: Ideology and Revolutionary Change in Plural Societies* (London: Duckworth, 1974).

Lee, J. M., *African Armies and Civil Order* (New York: Praeger, 1969).

Levine, D., 'The military in Ethiopian politics: capabilities and constraints', in H. Bienen (ed.), *The Military Intervenes: Case Studies in Political Development* (New York: Russell Sage, 1968).

Levy, Marion, *Modernisation and the Structure of Societies: A Setting for International Affairs* (Princeton, NJ: Princeton University Press, 1966).

Lewin, K. and P. Grabbe, 'Conduct, knowledge and acceptance of new values', *Journal of Social Issues,* vol. 1 (1945), pp. 53–64.

Lieuwen, E., *Arms and Politics in Latin America* (New York: Praeger, 1960).

Lieuwen, E., 'Militarism and politics in Latin America', in J. J. Johnson (ed.), *The Role of the Military in the Underdeveloped Countries* (Princeton, NJ: Princeton University Press, 1962).

Lieuwen, E., *General versus Presidents: The New Military in Latin America* (New York: Praeger, 1964a).

Lieuwen, E., 'The military: a force for continuity or changes?', in John Te Paske and Sydney Ficher (eds), *Explosive Forces in Latin America* (Columbus, Ohio: Ohio State University Press, 1964b).

Lovell, J. P., 'Military dominated regimes and political development: critique of some revisionist views', in Palmer and Stern (eds), *Political Development in Changing Societies* (London: Heath Lexington, 1971).

Lyons, Gene, 'The new civil–military relations', *American Political Science Review,* vol. LV, no. 1 (1961), pp. 53–80.

McAlister, L., 'Recent researches and writings on the role of the military in Latin America', *Latin American Research Review,* vol. II, no. 1 (1966), pp. 5–36.

McKinlay, R. D. and A. S. Cohan, 'Performance and instability in military and non-military regimes', *American Political Science Review,* vol. LXX, no. 3 (September 1976). pp. 850–64.

McKinley, S., *Democracy and Military Power* (New York: Vanguard Press. 1934).

McWilliams, A., *Garrisons and Governments: Politics and the Military in the New States* (San Francisco, Calif.: Chandler, 1967).

Mazrui Ali, A., 'The lumpen-proletariat and the lumpen-militariat: African soldiers as a new political class' *Political Studies,* vol. XXI, no. 1 (1973), pp. 1–12.

Merton, R., *Social Theory and Social Structure* (Glencoe, Ill.: Free Press, 1963).

Miliband, R., *The State in Capitalist Society* (London: Weidenfeld & Nicolson, 1969).

Moore, W., *The Professions, Roles and Rules* (New York: Russell Sage, 1970).

Mosca, G., *The Ruling Class* (New York: McGraw-Hill, 1939).

Murray, Roger, 'Militarism in Africa', *New Left Review* (July–August 1966), pp. 33–57.

Needler, Martin, 'Political development and military intervention in Latin America', *American Political Science Review,* vol. LX (September 1966), pp. 616–26.

Needler, Martin, 'Political development and socio-economic development: the case of Latin America', *American Political Science Review,* vol. LXII (September 1968), pp. 889–97.

Nordlinger, Eric, 'Soldiers in mufti: the impact of military rule upon economic and social change in the non-Western societies', *American Political Science Review,* vol. LXIV, no. 4 (December 1970), pp. 1131–42.

Nun, José, 'The middle class military coup', in Claudio Veliz (ed.), *The Politics of Conformity* (New York: Oxford University Press, 1967), pp. 323–56.

Obasanjo, O., 'The military as an instrument of modernisation', *Ubiquitous-A Magazine of the Nigerian Army,* vol. 2, no. 6 (1975), pp. 14–18.

Obasanjo, O., 'The Nigerian army engineers in national reconstruction'. *Ubiquitous,* vol. 1, no. 4 (August 1973), pp. 17–22.

Obasanjo, O., *New Highlights,* Nigerian Navy Magazine, no. 1 (1977), Ministry of Defence, Lagos, Nigeria.

Obasanjo, O., *The March of Progress: Collected Speeches of General Obasanjo* (New York: Third Press International, 1980).

Ocran, A. K., *A Myth is Broken: An Account of the Ghana Coup d'Etat* (London: Longman, 1968).

Ocran, A. K., *Politics of the Sword* (Rex Collins: London, 1977).

Odetola, T. O., *Military Politics in Nigeria: Economic Development and Political Stability* (New Brunswick, NJ: Transaction Books, 1978).

Odetola, T. O., 'Political behaviour of the military in crisis situation', paper presented at the 20th Anniversary of the Inter-University Seminar on the Armed Forces, Chicago, October 1980.

Ogbebor, P., 'Training the Nigerian army', *Ubiquitous–A Magazine of the Nigerian Army,* vol. 3, no. 7 (1976).

Otley, C. B., 'Militarism and the social affiliations of the British Army élite', in J. Van Doorn (ed.), *Armed Forces and Society* (The Hague: Mouton, 1968), pp. 84–108.

Pauker, G., 'South-East Asia as a problem area in the next decade', *World Politics,* vol. XI, no. 3 (1959), pp. 325–45.

Perlmutter, A., 'The praetorian state and the praetorian army: toward a taxonomy of civil–military relations in developing countries', *World Politics,* vol. I, no. 3 (April 1969), pp. 382–405.

Petras, James, *Politics and Social Structure in Latin America* (New York: Monthly Review Press, 1970).

Possony, S. A., *Forward Strategy for America* (New York: Harper, 1961).

Poulatzas, N., 'The problem of the capitalist state', *New Left Review,* no. 58 (1970), pp. 67–78.

Price, Robert, 'A theoretical approach to military rule in the new states: reference group theory and the Ghanaian case', *World Politics,* vol. XXIII, no. 3 (April 1971a), pp. 399–429.

Price, Robert, 'Military officers and political leadership: the Ghanaian case', *Comparative Politics,* vol. III, no. 3 (1971b), pp. 361–79.

Pye, Lucian, 'Armies in the process of political modernisation', in J. J. Johnson (ed.), *The Role of the Military in the Underdeveloped Countries* (Princeton; NJ: Princeton University Press, 1962).

Rathbone, R., *Education and Politics in Ghana* (London: Institute of Commonwealth Studies, 1968).

Rawlings, J., *West Africa,* 21 June 1980.

Rosberg, C. and J. Nottingham, *The Myth of Mau Mau: Nationalism in Kenya* (New York: Praeger, 1966).

Russett, Bruce *et al., World Handbook of Political and Social Indicators* (New Haven, Conn.: Yale University Press, 1964).

Schmitter, Philippe, *Military Rule in Latin America: Function, Consequences and Perspectives* (Beverly Hills, Calif.: Sage, 1973).

Shils, Edward, 'The military in the political development of the new states', in J. J. Johnson (ed.), *The Role of the Military in the Underdeveloped Countries* (Princeton, NJ: Princeton University Press, 1962).

Shlomo, A., 'The Palestinians and Israel', *Commentary* vol. 49, no. 6 (1970), pp. 31–44.

Siegel, S., 'Reference groups, membership groups and attitude change', *Journal of Abnormal and Social Psychology*, vol. LV (November 1957), pp. 360–4.

Silvert, Kilt, *Reaction and Revolution in Latin America* (New Orleans, La: Hauser, 1961).

Slover, R., 'This is military civic action', *Army* (July 1963), pp. 46–52.

Stokes, S., 'Violence as a power factor in Latin American politics', *Western Political Quarterly*, vol. 5 (1952), pp. 445–68.

Tiger, Lionel, 'Bureaucracy in Ghana', unpublished Ph.D. thesis, London, 1963.

Townsend, Peter, *Sociology and Social Policy* (London: Allen Lane, 1975).

Vagt, A., *A History of Militarism* (New York: Meridian, 1959).

Von der Mehden, F., and C. B. Anderson, 'Political action by the military in developing areas', *Sociological Research*, vol. 28 (Winter 1961), pp. 459–79.

Walterhouse, H., *A Time to Build: Military–Civic Action–Medium for Economic Development and Social Reform* (Columbia, S.C. Institute of International Studies, 1964).

Weale, R., *Equality and Social Policy* (London: Routledge & Kegan Paul, 1978).

Welch, Claude (ed.), *Soldier and State in Africa* (Evanston, Ill.: Northwestern University Press, 1970).

Wey, S., 'The military under a civilian regime 1960–1966', paper presented at the Seminar on the Military in a Presidential System of Government for Senior Armed Forces, Lagos, Nigeria, 1979.

Willensky, H., *The Welfare State and Equality* (Berkeley, Calif.: University of California Press, 1975).

Wood, D., *The Armed Forces of African States* (London: Institute of Strategic Studies, 1966).

Zolberg, Aristide, 'Military intervention in the new states of tropical Africa', in H. Bienen (ed.), *The Military Intervenes: Case Studies in Political Development* (New York: Russell Sage, 1968).

List of Documents, Journals and Newspapers

1 US Senate Committee on Foreign Relations: Compilation Studies, 87th Congress, 1st Session, Document No. 24, 15 March 1961.
2 *The Rockefeller Report,* 91st Congress, 20 November 1969.
3 *Congressional Weekly Report,* XXVIII, 6 February 1970.
4 *Department of State Bulletin,* LXI, 22 December 1969.
5 Nigeria's *Sunday Punch,* vol. 7, 8 June 1980.
6 *Africa Research Bulletin (ARB),* 1974–9.
7 *West Africa,* 1972–80.
8 *Daily Times of Nigeria.*
9 *Nigerian Herald.*
10 *Africa Report,* 1976.
11 Federal Government of Nigeria, Guidelines on Local Government Reforms, 1976.
12 National Bank of Ethiopia Reports, 1978.
13 Federal Government of Nigeria, Nigerian National Development Plan, 1970.
14 Food and Agricultural Organisation (FAO), *World Report,* 1968.

Index